The
Call of the Wise

G. Steve Kinnard

The
Call of the Wise

An Introduction and
Topical Index to
the Book of Proverbs

DISCIPLESHIP
PUBLICATIONS
INTERNATIONAL

One Merrill Street
Woburn, MA 01801
1-888-DPI-BOOK Fax: (617) 937-3889

The Call of the Wise
©1997 by Discipleship Publications International
One Merrill Street, Woburn, MA 01801

Printed in the United States of America

Cover design: Chris Costello
Interior design: Chris Costello and Laura Root

This book includes material originally published under the title *The
Beginning of Wisdom* © 1988 by G. Steve Kinnard and published by the
New York City Church of Christ.

ISBN 1-57782-003-7

To Steve and Lisa Johnson

Our friends, advisors and partners.
You have breathed life into us on more than one occasion.
Leigh and I will never be able to fully express
our love for you.
If every debt we owed you
were a grain of sand, we could build a sand castle
the size of the Taj Mahal.

Wisdom calls aloud in the street,
   she raises her voice in the public squares;
at the head of the noisy streets she cries out,
   in the gateways of the city she makes her speech:

"How long will you simple ones love your simple ways?
   How long will mockers delight in mockery
   and fools hate knowledge?
If you had responded to my rebuke,
   I would have poured out my heart to you
   and made my thoughts known to you."

PROVERBS 1:20-23

CONTENTS

Acknowledgments

Declan Joyce, for his help editing.
Tom Jones and DPI, for bringing it all together.
The staff of the New York City Church of Christ,
for years of encouragement and support.
Leigh, Chelsea and Daniel, for your love,
patience and understanding.

A Reader's Guide

A Book That Brings Blessings

The proverbs of Solomon son of David, king of Israel:

for attaining wisdom and discipline;
    for understanding words of insight;
for acquiring a disciplined and prudent life,
    doing what is right and just and fair;
for giving prudence to the simple,
    knowledge and discretion to the young—
let the wise listen and add to their learning,
    and let the discerning get guidance—
for understanding proverbs and parables,
    the sayings and riddles of the wise.

The fear of the LORD is the beginning of knowledge,
    but fools despise wisdom and discipline.

PROVERBS 1:1-7

I knew a farmer in Tennessee who had only completed the first six grades of school. He did not read well, and he never really studied any book except the Bible. Division and multiplication proved too difficult for his understanding. He never read poetry for enjoyment or wrote to pass the time. He was an uneducated man, yet I have rarely met anyone as wise as this Southern farmer. People were his books. When it came to people, he was a speed reader. Human nature and the character of the heart were poetry to this man. He always seemed to know the difference between someone who was genuine and someone who was a liar. His advice was right on the money. His wisdom was the gift of God. A gift which sprang from the depths of a heart that deeply loved God and that longed to think as God thinks.

This type of wisdom does not come from books. God gives it as a gift to those who seek to know his mind. There are those who possess an unbelievable amount of information, yet are not wise. There are also those who are uneducated in any formal sense, yet are extremely wise. Wisdom is not the grasping of facts and figures. Wisdom goes deeper. It goes to the heart of what it means to be human and a creation of God. Wisdom shows her face to the person who understands humanity, knows what is important in life, and struggles to grasp the nature of the Divine.

Anyone can become wise. Our genetic makeup does not determine how wise we are. James 1:5 reads, "If any of you lacks wisdom, he should ask God, who gives generously to all without finding fault, and it will be given to him." Every disciple should be thrilled at the prospect of gaining God's wisdom. We are not able to change our IQ, but we can change our "WQ" (wisdom quotient). Granted, wisdom does not grow on trees, but neither is it the product of genetic engineering. Wisdom is God's gift offered to anyone who dares ask for it in prayer.

Solomon is certainly a man who was not afraid to ask God for wisdom (2 Chronicles 1:7-10). Nowhere has God so clearly demonstrated his willingness to give us wisdom as through the book of Proverbs. This book was written to give us insight, understanding, discernment, learning and knowledge. God's wisdom is poured out in the proverbs, and that wisdom becomes more and more apparent as we apply it to our everyday lives. When we study the proverbs, we are studying the mind of God. What does God think about poverty, advice, zeal, compassion, blessings, sacrifice or generosity? Proverbs has the answers. Proverbs offers an invitation to inherit the wisdom of God. A greater invitation could not be received.

The Penning of Proverbs

"A bird in the hand is worth two in the bush."

"A penny saved is a penny earned."

"Takes one to know one."

"Never trust a man with two first names."

"God have mercy on the man who doubts what he is sure of."

Proverbs can be ingeniously simple or profoundly complex. Every culture of every civilization has had its proverbs. Humanity's passion for philosophical conviction has prompted sages throughout time to record thoughts in the form of proverbs. Ancient Israel was no different from any other ancient society in which certain people became the collectors of wise sayings and instruction. Out of Israel's collection came the proverbs that we find in the Bible today. These proverbs have survived for all of us to learn from and to enjoy.

How were the proverbs collected through the centuries? Just envision a dusty room full of scrolls and yellowed bits of parchment lying in every corner. Gray-haired scribes and sages sit on benches cut out of cedar, sifting through rolls and rolls of scrolls with Hebrew lettering adorning the pages. Sweat drips from the nose of one overweight scribe in a remote, dimly lit corner of the room as he patiently reads through a first-edition, autographed copy of *Solomon's Greatest Proverbs*. He sips honey-sweetened tea from a pottery cup as he ponders one of Solomon's loftier bits of wisdom.

As he sets down his cup and turns the scroll, his eyes shift to the next line of the text. Laughter resounds through the room. Not a little "ha-ha," but a deep belly laugh. The other scribes shuffle over to the dark corner to see what is so funny. The scribe says, "Listen to this one, guys. You've got to hear this." He waits for the shuffling to die down and then delivers the line: "'Like a gold ring in a pig's snout is a beautiful woman who shows no discretion.'" The whole room begins to shake with laughter. The manager slaps his knee and adds, "Old Solomon was quite a card. It's bad enough to compare a foolish woman with a lion or bear wearing a nose ring. But a nose ring in a pig's snout—that's too much. Solomon, what a hoot." Everyone begins to drift back to their work with the same thought running through their minds: Solomon, what a hoot.

This same scene has happened to us, too, if we have spent any time in the proverbs. We know the impact a proverb can make. A feeling of joy might fill us, or a realization of conviction. The proverbs are life-changing statements. They are full of beauty, and they state the most profound truths in a simple and even entertaining form. These bits of wisdom were penned for our edification. Wisdom from the past to help us with today. Thank God for Proverbs!

The Power of Proverbs

The Israelites believed that God had placed a fundamental order in his created cosmos. It was this order that allowed the world to operate in a systematic and logical way. Proverbs speaks of wisdom as existing before the creation of the world. Wisdom was viewed as being the first of God's created works (Proverbs 8:22-31). Proverbs 8:30 speaks of wisdom as "the craftsman at his [God's] side."

Since this fundamental order exists in creation, discerning this order will help us live our lives with security. James L. Crenshaw, a scholar of Old Testament wisdom, writes, "Discovery of this 'rational rule' enabled the wise to secure their existence by acting in harmony with the universal order that sustained the cosmos."[1] The search for knowledge became the means by which a person could escape the turmoil of life. Wisdom, personified as a woman, speaks of this in Proverbs 8:35-36:

> "For whoever finds me finds life,
>   and receives favor from the LORD.
> But whoever fails to find me harms himself;
>   all who hate me love death."

Doesn't everyone want this type of security in their lives? Even the most confident of people notice the inconsistencies of life, and they look for answers.

New York presents itself as the most wealthy and powerful city in the world. Sinatra sings, "If I can make it there, I'll make it anywhere." Some of the most self-assured people in the world live in New York. Dynamic actors, beautiful models, sharp business executives and brilliant financial experts flock to the city year after year pursuing fame and fortune. All of this "worldly wisdom" in one place, yet New York is still a place of questions and confusion. Senseless beatings over meaningless issues occur every single day. Family quarrels result in destroyed homes. Sexual laxity leads to guilt, depression and worse. New York demonstrates the futility of worldly wisdom. God himself has placed order in the universe, and he can order our individual worlds as well. Proverbs guides us in his wisdom, the only wisdom that can deeply enrich our lives.

If wisdom represents understanding the deeper secrets of humanity and divinity, then foolishness is the inability to grasp these ideas. Foolishness is not the lack of education or the deficiency of facts about the universe. Gerhard von Rad, an Old Testament theologian, says that "foolishness is a disorder in a person's deepest being; that is why Proverbs says, 'the heart of a fool is not right.'"[2] Being wise or being foolish becomes a matter of faith. Wisdom and foolishness are not characteristics received at birth. We choose to be wise or foolish when we decide to faithfully accept or reject the order that God has placed in the universe. It is a decision of faith. Proverbs 1:7 states, "The fear of the Lord is the beginning of knowledge." We are on the road to knowledge when we make a decision to fear God. The proverbs must not be separated into ideas about the secular and the holy. All the proverbs, in one way or another, prepare us for godly living. Faithfully following God and his precepts as stated in the different proverbs enables us to grasp deep spiritual truths.

The proverbs also benefit the disciple in his life within the world, particularly in regard to relationships and work. As we strive to follow the righteous path, God gives us guidance to prosper us along the way. Observing how the ancient Israelites viewed the proverbs, Theodore Robinson, a scholar of Hebrew poetry states,

> By following the lines laid down, any man may reasonably expect to live "a quiet and inoffensive" life, achieving a certain measure of worldly success, and that was an ideal not to be despised in an age in which personal security was far less easily attainable than it is in the more highly organized society of our own day."[3]

When we apply ourselves to faithfully learning and applying the principles in Proverbs, we will gain prosperity within the secular world. Certainly this wisdom should be a valued commodity in our world today.

The Purpose of Proverbs

What are the practical ways of using Proverbs today? By viewing the purpose for which the proverbs were written, one can discover the best use of the book. Proverbs 1:1-7 states its purposes, as listed below:

Knowledge

Proverbs gives us wisdom as we read it. Proverbs 1:4 states that proverbs are "for giving prudence to the simple, knowledge and discretion to the young." This knowledge can only be gained from God because it is only his to give. As we read and study the proverbs, we are given an inside look at how life really works. God's knowledge is free to all who decide to investigate it.

Insight

The proverbs of Solomon are given "for attaining wisdom and discipline; for understanding words of insight" (Proverbs 1:2). Knowledge is helpful in being able to grasp and understand the facts about life, but wisdom goes beyond the facts to the discernment of good from evil. Wisdom affects judgment and gives us what is generally thought of as common sense. Insight is the ability to make correct judgments concerning situations and people. A person of godly insight rarely makes wrong decisions because his discernment comes from God. How can a leader know exactly what to say at just the right time? God gives him insight. This same insight is available to every disciple regardless of his position or his spiritual age.

Discipline

Many passages in Proverbs relate to laziness and hard work. Proverbs 1:2-3 speaks of the importance of "attaining wisdom and discipline; for understanding words of insight; for acquiring a disciplined and prudent life." A disciplined life can be acquired by studying Proverbs since it teaches the principles by which one lives day to day. We do not have to guess the pitfalls of life; they are all marked out clearly. Wisdom and discipline go hand-in-hand.

Righteousness

Proverbs 1:3 shows that Proverbs was written so that we can learn to do "what is right and just and fair." This ability is gained through God who fills Proverbs with messages of righteousness. Proverbs can change the heart and thereby shape our character. The wicked can become righteous, the scoundrel can become just, and the swindler can become fair. Proverbs are not just pithy wise sayings, but life-changing nuggets of power.

When I was in elementary school, every Sunday morning I would wake up and eat a bowl of Coco-Puffs while watching *The Three Stooges* on TV. My two brothers and I would then spend the next couple of hours acting like Moe, Larry and Curly (of course, I usually was stuck with being Curly). We were not that good at remembering the lines, but we were excellent at throwing punches and poking eyes. One sequence went like this:

Slap!

Punch!

Smack!

Moe yells angrily at Curly, "Think you're a wise guy, huh?"
Smack!

No one likes a wise guy. The Three Stooges were right. No
one likes a wise guy, but most people like a man of wisdom.
God gives us the power to become wise through the proverbs. Power of this magnitude could be auctioned off for millions of dollars to the highest bidder. Yet no auction will be
held. This power is available to any faithful person who de-
cides to study and apply this book of wisdom that God has
given freely to humanity. He has ordered the world with his
Word, and he has ordered the wisdom of the proverbs to
reveal his secrets to his people. Within these words is a life-
changing power based on centuries of wise counsel. The proverbs are the beginning of wisdom. Anyone who wants wisdom should begin with the proverbs.

Authorship and Date

The authorship of Proverbs must be considered in sections,
since different parts of Proverbs were penned by different men.

Solomon

The majority of the proverbs are attributed to the genius of
Solomon, the son of David. Proverbs 1:1 reads, "The proverbs
of Solomon son of David, king of Israel." This statement seems
to entitle Solomon as the author of the book of Proverbs. It is
certain that Proverbs 10:1 through 22:16 and 25:1 through 29:27
are from Solomon. 1 Kings 4:32 states that Solomon "spoke
three thousand proverbs and his songs numbered a thousand
and five." Since Proverbs contain only 800 verses, it is obvious
that Solomon's original sayings provided ample material to fill
the entire book. Proverbs 25:1 demonstrates that through the
centuries Solomon's proverbs went through editorial review:
King Hezekiah (716-687 B.C.) appointed a committee to select

and publish Solomon's proverbs and the edited product ended up in the book of Proverbs. The proverbs of Solomon are the nucleus of Proverbs.

Solomon was the son of the great King David. Solomon might have inherited his love of words and his desire to write from his father, the psalmist. Is it only incidental that a large portion of the book of Proverbs deals with sexual sins and adultery? Solomon could easily have seen these lessons in David's life. Teaching always occurs between father and son, sometimes on purpose and sometimes not. If we read the proverbs and David's hand is seen, it should come as no surprise. David influenced his son in many ways, some obvious and some subtle. The proverbs of Solomon are a testimony to the intrinsic power of discipling. These passages stand as a memorial that our actions do not die with us, but they live on in those we have influenced, especially our children.

Wise Men or Sages

There are two sections of Proverbs that are attributed to wise men or "sages." Proverbs 22:17 reads, "Pay attention and listen to the sayings of the wise." Proverbs 22:17 through 24:34 are attributed to a group of men who specialized in wisdom writings. These men probably served on the royal court of King Solomon as mentioned in 1 Kings 4:31. These men must have antedated Solomon, and he could be responsible for editing these sections. These sages, along with Solomon, were responsible for a wisdom movement in Israel that resulted in the collection of the book of Proverbs.

Agur ben Jakeh

Proverbs 30:1-33 is attributed to the pen of a man of whom little or nothing is known named Agur ben Jakeh.

King Lemuel

King Lemuel is the author of Proverbs 31:1-9. Lemuel was certainly not a King of Israel, and little information is given except what is contained within the proverbs themselves.

Unknown

Proverbs 31:10-31 is an alphabetic acrostic from an anonymous writer. This section appears to be the latest work within Proverbs.

The final form of Proverbs could not have appeared before the editorial revision during the time of King Hezekiah (716-687 B.C.). Some 250 years after the life of Solomon, the proverbs were arranged in a collection that would exist for all time. His legacy of wisdom will never die. Solomon's mark is left in Proverbs, and it is through this book that his desire to attain wisdom benefits all of God's faithful (1 Kings 3:4-15).

An Outline
of Proverbs

I. Title and Purpose (1:1-7)

The proverbs of Solomon, son of David, are written to give practical help and moral edification to the faithful (vv. 3-5). They also provide intellectual truth, but only to those who fear the LORD (vv. 6-7).

II. Fifteen lessons on wisdom (1:8 - 9:18)

This section contains various discourses attributed to Solomon, son of David.[1]

1. Training at home is necessary as a moral safeguard (1:8-19).
2. Wisdom denounces those who despise moral instruction (1:20-33).
3. The search for wisdom brings understanding of religion and morality (2:1-22).
4. Physical and spiritual well-being come from following wisdom (3:1-18).
5. Wisdom gives the faithful security on this earth (3:19-26).
6. Wisdom always gives the greatest practical advice (3:27-35).
7. The lessons of wisdom must be learned (4:1-27).
8. A "no" is given to sexual debauchery and a "yes" to marital faithfulness (5:1-23).
9. Care must be taken in giving a loan to a neighbor (6:1-5).

(6:12-19).

12. Wisdom must be followed and adultery must be avoided (6:20-35).
13. Wisdom serves as a safeguard against adultery (7:1-27).
14. Wisdom declares the treasures of her reward (8:1-36).
15. Wisdom and Folly invite men to two banquets (9:1-18).

There are three sections that may be viewed as essays with special themes.[2]

1. Many warnings are given against joining criminals who scheme to gain riches at the expense of the poor (1:10-19).
2. Sexual immorality has many heavy risks (6:20-35).
3. The woman "Folly" is skilled at smooth talk inviting the listener toward forbidden treasure (9:13-18).

III. The first collection of the proverbs of Solomon, 10:1 - 22:16
This section is a series of approximately 375 short maxims. They can be subdivided into two sections: (1) 10:1 - 15:33: These proverbs are typically written in the form of antithetical parallelisms. Many proverbs in this section deal with the theme of righteousness versus wickedness; (2) 16:1 - 22:26: These are a continuation of Solomon's proverbs that are not dependent on antithetical parallelisms. There are many proverbs in this section that center around the theme of Yahweh, the Hebraic name for God, and his king.

IV. The first collection of the sayings of the wise men, 22:17 - 24:22
1 Kings 4:31 speaks of Solomon's wisdom being greater than the other wise men of his day. It reads,

"He was wiser than any other man, including Ethan the Ezrahite—wiser than Heman, Calcol and Darda, the sons of Mahol. And his fame spread to all the surrounding nations."

the sons of Mahol. And his fame spread to all the surrounding nations."

The wise men of King Solomon's court could have been the ones to produce this collection of sayings. This section displays striking similarities to the Egyptian book of wisdom entitled, *The Instructions of Amen-em-ope.* This similarity demonstrates the wide circulation of the wisdom literature between nations. This section contains a brief essay describing the awful plight of the drunkard (Proverbs 23:29-35).

V. The second collection of the sayings of the wise men, 24:23-34

This section contains a short collection of sayings from the wise men of Solomon's court. It includes sayings on justice, integrity, deceit and a great section on the sluggard.

VI. The second collection of the proverbs of Solomon, transcribed by the committee of Hezekiah the king, 25:1 - 29:27

These proverbs were evidently collected by a scribal establishment under the royal patronage of King Hezekiah of Judah. Chapters 25-27 are written in a parabolic form often utilizing nature and agriculture as illustrations. Chapters 28-29 are stocked with antithetical parallelisms speaking on the theme of the king and the potential rulers.

VII. The sayings of Agur ben Jakeh from Massa, 30:1-33

This section opens with a discourse between a skeptic and an orthodox believer (30:1-9). Agur ben Jakeh appears to be the name of the skeptic. There follows a collection of warnings and numerical proverbs of classification (30:10-33).

VIII. The sayings of Lemuel, king of Massa, 31:1-9

A royal mother exhorts her son, the king, to conduct himself in the way expected of kings. She especially emphasizes a warning against the use of liquor and an exhortation toward integrity in judgment.

IX. A poem of praise to the ideal wife, 31:10-31

A beautifully written acrostic poem is included praising the virtues and accomplishments of the ideal wife. Each line of an acrostic poem begins with a letter of the Hebrew alphabet. (Although this passage sketches a rich portrait of the ideal wife, note that nowhere in the passage is she described physically!)

The Language of Proverbs

...for understanding proverbs and parables,
the sayings and riddles of the wise.

PROVERBS 1:6

One day during a church staff meeting in New York we were stumped by a problem. Every person in the meeting was racking his or her brain trying to think of the solution. After a few minutes had passed, Mike Taliaferro, one of the evangelists, spoke up and offered just the right idea to settle the issue. One of the brothers excitedly agreed to his idea saying, "Mike, you are exactly right. When you said that, in my brain 'the lights went out.'" In his enthusiasm, he got his tongue tangled, but we all knew what he meant. Everyone has known inspiration, that special moment when you discover a new idea, or you understand something that once eluded you. The reading of Proverbs can bring such moments.

Most of the proverbs are so direct that they hit like a prize fighter's right to the jaw. But sometimes the meaning of a proverb can elude us. This section is written so that the student of the proverbs might better understand the language and structure of the book. Many times the meaning of a proverb will become clear when we understand the structure in which it is written. The literary background of Proverbs can help us in gaining insight into individual proverbs within the book. You may feel ready to skip this introductory information and just plunge into Proverbs, but you would be wise to consider some of this background information. It will help you gain much more from your reading and study.

Proverbs is unique in the canon of Scripture. Although wisdom literature abounds throughout the Old Testament, the genre of proverbs is not widely used in the Scriptures. Except in Proverbs and a few scattered places in the Bible, the proverb is not found as a literary device. We must go to the literature of the ancient Semitic world and to a literary critic to learn of the proverb.

The Masal

Masal is the Hebrew word for proverb. The origin of the word is unclear. James L. Crenshaw, a scholar of Old Testament wisdom literature, believes there are two different options to consider in defining *masal*. One option is that it is the Hebrew word meaning "to be like" much like a simile or an analogy. In this case, a proverb would be a literary device that uses comparisons to make a point.[1] The second possibility is that *masal* is derived from the Hebrew *msl* meaning "to rule." This definition involves the paradigmatic and exemplary character of the proverb. The proverb when spoken itself would be powerful and authoritative. The proverb becomes "a winged word, outliving the fleeting moment."[2] By its declaration, the proverb releases power to convict hearts and change lives. A proverb is much more than a nice literary form. The proverb is the carrier of hidden truth waiting to be revealed.

A collector of precious stones may sift through thousands of stones until he finds one that is worth keeping. In the same way, the wise sage mulls over thousands of words, images, descriptions until he chooses the one that will be remembered and repeated for centuries in a proverb. R.B.Y. Scott, an Old Testament wisdom scholar, writes,

A proverb is a short, pregnant sentence whose meaning is applicable in many situations, with imagery or striking verbal form to assist the memory.[3]

The proverb is a gem of truth. It leaves us with an idea that can easily be recalled.

Anyone who has spent time counseling people through their problems can understand the usefulness of a proverb. I am always trying to encapsulate ideas so that they are memorable and clear. I often want to sum up a two-hour appointment with a single sentence that carries the weight of everything that was said. What an extremely difficult task, but not if I rely on God's wisdom so readily available in Proverbs. Here are a few examples of how a proverb says it all.

Adultery

"This is the way of an adulteress:
    She eats and wipes her mouth
    and says, 'I've done nothing wrong'" (30:20).

Independence

For lack of guidance a nation falls,
    but many advisers make victory sure (11:14).

Plans fail for lack of counsel,
    but with many advisers they succeed (15:22).

Alcohol

Wine is a mocker and beer a brawler;
    whoever is led astray by them is not wise (20:1).

Temper

A hot-tempered man must pay the penalty;
    if you rescue him, you will have to do it again (19:19).

A Divisive Person

A scoundrel and villain,
    who goes about with a corrupt mouth,
    who winks with his eye,
    signals with his feet
    and motions with his fingers,

who plots evil with deceit in his heart—
he always stirs up dissension (6:12-14).

Drive out the mocker, and out goes strife;
quarrels and insults are ended (22:10).

Lying

A false witness will not go unpunished,
and he who pours out lies will not go free (19:5).

Laziness

One who is slack in his work
is brother to one who destroys (18:9).

Do not love sleep or you will grow poor;
stay awake and you will have food to spare (20:13).

Selfishness

Do not eat the food of a stingy man,
do not crave his delicacies;
for he is the kind of man
who is always thinking about the cost.
"Eat and drink," he says to you,
but his heart is not with you.
You will vomit up the little you have eaten
and will have wasted your compliments (23:6-8).

I have had numerous counseling situations where one of
these proverbs would have been the perfect summation. The
counsel of the proverbs is great for others and for ourselves.

Characteristics of Proverbs

Not every wise saying is a proverb. The proverb has certain characteristics that distinguish it from other types of literature. James L. Crenshaw lists five literary characteristics
of a proverb.[4]

1. The proverb must be grounded in real experience. Proverbs
come from everyday life experiences that teach truth about life.

2. Brevity characterizes a proverb. For the sake of memorization brevity is an essential ingredient.

3. Observation is a key ingredient in creating a proverb. The proverb announces an important discovery.

4. A proverb grows out of experience. There are no proverbs that spring up overnight. The wisdom inherent in a proverb is passed from one generation to the next.

5. The proverb must embody truth. Truth is an essential ingredient in a proverb. If wisdom is to be gained from the proverb, then it must clearly be based on the truth.

A good proverb is known for its shortness, sense and salt. Over the centuries the Hebrew term *masal* grew and changed in meaning. Early on a *masal* simply identified any pithy statement that was a declaration of wisdom. Later, the term could be applied to a whole collection of sayings, such as the book of Proverbs. Proverbs 1:1 states, "The proverbs [*masal*] of Solomon son of David, king of Israel." Here *masal* applies to the whole collection of Solomonic proverbs. Many of the proverbs of Solomon have taken the basic characteristics of the proverb and expanded and enriched this standard literary device. When reading the proverbs the power of the proverbial saying should be recognized. The truth of the proverb should pierce the heart deeply and be considered and applied. This use enables the proverb to be much more than a literary type; it becomes the powerful word of God!

Types of Proverbs

Just as there are different types of psalms, there are also different types of proverbs. R.B.Y. Scott lists eight discernible patterns in the anonymous folk sayings of different cultures.[5] These patterns also apply to the proverbs.

Words that appear to be distinct but are used as synonyms

> A fool's lips bring him strife,
>   and his mouth invites a beating (Proverbs 18:6).

Although mouth and lips are not the quite the same, they are used identically here for the word "speech."

Concepts that appear to be the same but directly contrast each other

> Wounds from a friend can be trusted,
>   but an enemy multiplies kisses (Proverbs 27:6).

At first glance, wounds from a friend and kisses from an enemy both seem undesirable. Yet the writer states that wounds from a friend can actually be trusted. These similar concepts are set in contrast to each other.

Use of analogy, simile or metaphor

> Like a club or a sword or a sharp arrow
>   is the man who gives false testimony against his neighbor
>   (Proverbs 25:18).

The proverb writers were adroit at making comparisons. Many of the most memorable proverbs fall in this category because analogies help paint images in our mind. We can picture an ant laboring along with a piece of cracker in its mouth or a lion stalking through the jungle afraid of nothing. These pictures reinforce the truth of the proverb in the reader's mind.

Use of a futile or an absurd image

This type of imagery appears in the proverb to draw attention to some distinct truth. These are also some of the most lively proverbs. Proverbs 26:17-18 states:

> Like one who seizes a dog by the ears
>   is a passerby who meddles in a quarrel not his own.
> Like a madman shooting
>   firebrands or deadly arrows
> is a man who deceives his neighbor
>   and says, "I was only joking!"

Displaying characteristic behavior of people

The fool, the sluggard, the wise man and the righteous person are all characterized in Proverbs. Proverbs 12:27 reads:

> The lazy man does not roast his game,
>   but the diligent man prizes his possessions.
>
> The poor are shunned even by their neighbors,
>   but the rich have many friends
>   (Proverbs 14:20).

This type of proverb abounds in the Bible. These are descriptive pictures of people so clearly drawn they are cartoonish. We can picture the man who is so lazy he just bites into his chicken raw. Much can be learned about people and their hearts by studying this type of proverb.

Use of relative values

These proverbs compare one thought with another thought to show the difference between the two. These comparisons are based on amount or degree. Proverbs 15:16 states,

> Better a little with the fear of the LORD
>   than great wealth with turmoil.
>
> To do what is right and just
>   is more acceptable to the LORD than sacrifice
>   (Proverbs 15:32).

A contrast is made between one concept and another to show the qualitative difference between the two. This enables us to choose one item over the other. When teaching people the Bible, it is helpful for them to see the error of their negative responses by demonstrating to them what the positive response should be. I once studied the Bible with a person who never knew how negative he was until he saw the positive attitudes of disciples. Stating relative values can help people see what is really important.

Demonstration of consequences for unwise choices

There are always repercussions to the choices that we make in life. A fool does not learn from wrong choices and is destined to repeat his actions. Many valuable lessons may be learned from the errors that other people make. This type of proverb shows pitfalls that can be avoided. Proverbs 15:22 states,

> Plans fail for lack of counsel,
>   but with many advisers they succeed.

> He who ignores discipline despises himself,
>   but whoever heeds correction gains understanding
>   (Proverbs 15:32).

Lessons can be learned from these proverbs without having to experience the consequence of a wrong choice. Once again, this type of proverb is a great teaching tool. How wonderful to be able to learn from another person's mistakes, even if they lived centuries ago.

Appropriate retribution for corrupt action

The last pattern evidenced in folk proverbs is a special type of the proverb of consequence. The proverb of appropriate retribution expresses the joy of the casual spectator as he views a person experiencing a disaster which that person had planned for someone else. Proverbs 26:27 reads:

> If a man digs a pit, he will fall into it;
>   if a man rolls a stone, it will roll back on him.

This proverb is just like the scenario played out every Saturday morning between the coyote and the roadrunner. Behind these proverbs lies the truth that divine justice is at work in the world to protect the way of the innocent. These proverbs demonstrate the justice that God has ordered in his creation. God not only created justice, but he continues to guard and protect this order. These proverbs should prompt us to turn to God, and shout a loud "Amen!"

These eight types of proverbs have been identified throughout literature as typical ways of stating a hidden truth. The proverbs of the Bible follow these same patterns.

Parallelism

I enjoy poetry. I especially like music and the rhythm and rhyme of modern songs. Writing poetry is an art that I have attempted—usually not very successfully. Songs come easier for me. When I write a song, I transform an idea into words. After a time, the words take over the idea. Believe it or not, this process simulates the structure of a proverb. The writer stacks ideas together to form a proverb. Who knows, maybe Solomon tried his hand at poetry.

Proverbs are a form of Hebrew poetry. The poetry of the ancient Hebrews differs greatly from the English poetry of the twentieth century commonly studied in our schools. English poetry is largely based upon sound. Rhythm and rhyme are used to give the literature a cadence and sound that are different from narrative works. Hebrew poetry is not based on sound but on thought. Ideas are built and then placed into verses. Every verse must consist of at least two ideas. The second idea must complement the first in some way. The complement might be restating the first idea, adding to it or even contrasting it completely. This structure is known as parallelism. Three types of parallelisms exist in the proverbs.

Synonymous Parallelism

This type of parallelism is a theme stated in the first part of the verse and restated in the second part with some variation. The entire verse makes one point and the variation drives the point home. Proverbs 20:2 states,

> A king's wrath is like the roar of a lion;
> he who angers him forfeits his life.

The theme of this verse is stated in a simile. Picture a hot-tempered king in the midst of a tantrum who roars like a lion.

His face contorts, his eyes narrow and his teeth clench. The smoke starts pouring from his nostrils and the sweat drips from his forehead. He gets hotter and hotter until he cuts loose a roar that wakes up every sleeping baby and makes every head turn. The only thing worse than an angry king is if he happens to be angry at you. This idea is underscored by the second phrase, which demonstrates what happens when the king loses his temper. When similar ideas are reinforced in a proverb, it is known as synonymous parallelism.

Antithetical Parallelism

This type of parallelism is the opposite of synonymous parallelism. The idea stated in the first part of the verse is restated in the second idea in an opposing or contrasting manner. Proverbs 13:16 says,

> Every prudent man acts out of knowledge,
> but a fool exposes his folly.

The foolish man is contrasted with the prudent man. One runs after knowledge and the other after folly. These opposing ideas, when shown side by side, make a point which cannot be mistaken. Proverbs 21:8 states,

> The way of the guilty is devious,
> but the conduct of the innocent is upright.

When used as a teaching tool, antithetical parallelism can help us to see truth we might otherwise overlook.

Synthetic Parallelism

Synthetic or formal parallelism is sometimes harder to spot than synonymous or antithetical parallelism. In this form the second part of the verse does not restate or contrast the first, rather, it carries on the idea of the first part. This thread can be continued further into many sections of a verse, or it can break off abruptly. See an example in Proverbs 23:31-32:

> Do not gaze at wine when it is red,
>   when it sparkles in the cup,
>   when it goes down smoothly!
> In the end it bites like a snake
>   and poisons like a viper.

The idea of the tantalizing sight of wine is carried on through the verse only to be picked up by the destructive conclusion when one succumbs to the temptation.

Proverbs 24:13-14 states,

> Eat honey, my son, for it is good;
>   honey from the comb is sweet to your taste.
> Know also that wisdom is sweet to your soul;
>   if you find it, there is a future hope for you,
>   and your hope will not be cut off.

The idea of this verse begins with "honey being sweet to the taste," then continues with the idea of "wisdom being sweet to the soul." The progression is made from wisdom to a future hope that will never he cut off. The synthetic parallelism builds one idea on top of another until the complete idea has been communicated.

Hebrew poetry is expressed in parallelisms. Synonymous, antithetical, and synthetic parallelisms all express ideas and then build on those ideas either by restating the same idea, stating the opposite idea, or running the idea toward a conclusion. Knowing the specific parallelism employed in a proverb can help us understand its meaning. Parallelisms are effective ways of painting pictures that can be easily memorized and incorporated into our lives.

Understanding the language of proverbs will enrich and enlighten your study of the book. But much more important than determining the language is seeing its truth. Never get so technical with the language that you overlook the message. That would be like missing the inspirational thoughts of Handel's *Messiah* because you were concentrating on the violins. The message is of first importance.

How to Read Proverbs

My son, preserve sound judgment and discernment,
    do not let them out of your sight;
they will be life for you,
    an ornament to grace your neck.

PROVERBS 3:21-22

Proverbs is one of the most interesting books of the entire Bible. It contains both deeply spiritual insights and extremely practical guidance. It can lift us to new heights in devotional thought or come down on us like a two-by-four with its simplicity and directness. To gain the most by reading Proverbs consider the following ideas.

First, there is little to be learned by reading the book all the way through without breaks. Proverbs is not written like *David Copperfield* or *The Sound and the Fury*. It cannot be approached like a novel and still be understood. Each section, sometimes even subsection, should be considered as an entity and studied as such. Likewise, each proverb should be looked at individually. Each proverb should be read, meditated upon, and finally lived out. Great insight can be gained from Proverbs by following a slow, careful method of study.

Second, a topical approach to Proverbs will greatly benefit the reader. Since many proverbs share the same theme, a

41

topical study will provide a lesson of specific instruction on a specific issue. Poverty and wealth, the tongue, advice and correction, boldness, parents and children, and discipline, for examples, can all be studied topically through Proverbs.

Third, exercise your imagination and sense of humor while reading through Proverbs. The book stands as one of the most creative works in the history of writing. A study of proverbs should not be stale, but lively. Vivid illustrations are used in Proverbs to drive home the points. Consider the dramatic imagery of Proverbs 30:17:

> "The eye that mocks a father,
>   that scorns obedience to a mother;
> will be pecked out by the ravens of the valley,
>   will be eaten by the vultures."

The heart may laugh and be convicted by the picture painted in Proverbs 23:6-8:

> Do not eat the food of a stingy man,
>   do not crave his delicacies;
> for he is the kind of man
>   who is always thinking about the cost.
> "Eat and drink," he says to you,
>   but his heart is not with you.
> You will vomit up the little you have eaten
>   and will have wasted your compliments.

These proverbs should entertain and delight us, but also move and motivate us. Most importantly, through the images conjured by the proverbs, we should gain wisdom and learn to fear the Lord.

Fourth, the great spiritual insights presented in Proverbs should never be neglected. Proverbs is packed with practical insight, but it is also full of spiritual wisdom. Proverbs can teach us some great lessons about the nature of God and his dealings with man. We learn what God likes and dislikes. Maps are drawn detailing the route of righteousness and the way of wisdom. Proverbs 15:3 states, "The eyes of the LORD are everywhere, keeping watch on the wicked and the good." Proverbs 20:12 reads, "Ears that hear and eyes that see—the LORD has made them both." Proverbs 16:17 says, "The highway of the upright avoids evil; he who guards his way guards his life." Do not overlook the great insight that Proverbs can give to the spiritual life. The purpose is not to make you more clever, but more spiritual.

Proverbs teaches us how to react and live in this material world, while reaching up to take hold of heaven. The modern believer will find ample direction about how to live life here and into eternity. Reading Proverbs is essential for every disciple. In fact, eternity should be the main purpose behind any study of Proverbs.

Let the reading begin!

Great Themes

History teaches us that men and nations behave wisely once they have exhausted all other alternatives.

ABBA EBAN

1

Wisdom

By wisdom a house is built,
    and through understanding it is established;
through knowledge its rooms are filled
    with rare and beautiful treasures.

PROVERBS 24:3-4

He who gets wisdom loves his own soul;
    he who cherishes understanding prospers.

PROVERBS 19:8

O ver the years people have asked me how they could gain more wisdom. Some ask it in reference to their children. Others ask it in reference to their ministry and working with people. Others ask it in reference to their own personal lives.

Have you noticed that some people seem to have wisdom innately? Others learn wisdom from experience—the school of hard knocks. Some study others and gain wisdom from seeing their mistakes. Yet, some of the wisest people I've even known were not the most educated people. They had gained wisdom from a source other than books—they had gained it from God.

James 1:5-8 reads:

> If any of you lacks wisdom, he should ask God, who
> gives generously to all without finding fault, and it
> will be given to him. But when he asks, he must be-
> lieve and not doubt, because he who doubts is like a
> wave of the sea, blown and tossed by the wind. That
> man should not think he will receive anything from
> the Lord; he is a double-minded man, unstable in all
> he does.

This verse teaches us that wisdom is a gift from God. Just as Solomon received wisdom by asking the Lord, we too can receive wisdom from God. It is his gift to give.

This is not to say that God will give wisdom *miraculously* to all who ask. God may work through normal, everyday events to teach us wisdom. He will work on us through our experiences. He will put people in our lives to teach us and help us grow. He will let us face tough times and then pull us through them. Through these collective experiences we can learn wisdom.

My wife, Leigh, has a great intuition when it comes to people. She is almost always right in her first impression of people. (You might ask—if she is such a great judge of character, then why did she marry you? Well, I guess there is no rhyme or reason when it comes to Cupid's arrow!)

When you first meet Leigh, however, you might wonder how such an unassuming, humble person could have acquired such perception about people. I believe it is a gift of God, but God taught her through some very tough experiences. At an early age she faced the trauma of her mom and dad going through a divorce. In her late teens she almost died due to a misdiagnosed illness. During our marriage we suffered through trials together: first a tubal pregnancy and later a life-threaten-ing situation with our son when he was just seven months old. Tough situations can teach you about life. Leigh gained much wisdom through difficult experiences.

In the Bible wisdom is practical. It has to do with every-day living. God-given wisdom is the ability to make the right decision in each and every situation. It is the ability to help others make right decisions as well. It is not a quest for intellectual knowledge. There is a vast difference between wisdom and knowledge. Wisdom is practical and life-centered. Wisdom is not found at the end of a mystical search for a unifying principle that explains the universe—like in Eastern religions. The Bible makes clear the unifying principle of the universe: God. Wisdom is therefore found by respecting God, listening to God, and by paying attention to what God is doing through the circumstances of our lives.

If You Would Become Wise

The fear of the Lord is the beginning of wisdom.

"The fear of the Lord is the beginning of wisdom,
     and knowledge of the Holy One is understanding"
     (Proverbs 9:10).

Where do we pursue wisdom? Do we go to the philosophers or the poets? Can we trust the politicians or journalists? Should we shave our heads and make a trip to the monasteries of Tibet? Can we gain wisdom from the lyrics of rock musicians and pop artists? No! Searching for wisdom from these sources is like a dog chasing its tail. Even if he catches it, what has he gained?

If you want to gain true wisdom, then go to the source. God created wisdom. Jesus is wisdom incarnate. If you want to fix your car, you get out the car manual. You don't take a TV repair course to learn how to fix cars. To learn about how to live life, don't go to people who have no idea of what righteous living is about. Go to the source of righteousness— God and Jesus. Go to those who themselves have gone to God. This is where wisdom is gained.

Wisdom training should begin early.

Listen to your father, who gave you life,
     and do not despise your mother when she is old.
Buy the truth and do not sell it;
     get wisdom, discipline and understanding.

> The father of a righteous man has great joy;
>   he who has a wise son delights in him.
> May your father and mother be glad;
>   may she who gave you birth rejoice!
>   (Proverbs 23:22-25).

It is my personal conviction that we should begin to teach our children the proverbs at an early age because they are practical and easy to remember. I strongly suspect that the proverbs played a central part in the education of Hebrew children. Some scholars suggest that in the Hebrew schools part of the core curriculum was the study of the proverbs. If one can embrace the proverbs, then he can avoid many of life's painful pitfalls.

Here are some examples of themes we can teach our children today from Proverbs:

Being encouraging: 15:4	Learning patience: 14:29
Being generous: 3:27-28	Learning self-control: 25:28
Being happy: 15:13	Listening to your parents: 23:22
Being humble: 22:4	Loving, not hating: 10:12
Being teachable: 22:17-18	Lying is wrong: 19:5
Controlling your temper: 15:18	Not acting foolishly: 17:21
Desiring a good name: 22:1	Not being a glutton: 23:19-21
Goodness of discipline: 13:24	Not gossiping: 16:28
Not being selfish: 28:22	Not trusting your feelings: 14:12
Not mocking people: 21:24	Obeying your parents: 13:1
Not procrastinating: 3:28	Purity: 5:30-20
Drunkenness: 20:1	Respecting God: 1:7
Evangelism: 11:30	Taking care of your things: 27:23-27
Forgiving others: 17:9	Listening to advice: 15:22
Guarding your heart: 4:23	Value of friendship: 17:17
Hating bribes: 6:35	Watching out for bad companions: 24:1-2
Having integrity: 10:9	Watching what you say: 12:18
Being kind to the poor: 19:17	Working hard: 10:4
Learning from the ant: 6:6-8	

Let God's two-by-fours make an impact.

I believe that the book of Proverbs is the most practical book in the Bible (along with the book of James in the New

Testament). I call the proverbs "God's two-by-fours" because they hit you right between the eyes. They warn clearly and directly about laziness, the destructiveness of impurity, and the folly of the fool. If we want a pathway to wisdom, then we should follow the direction given in the book of Proverbs—it points to the everlasting way.

Some of us are destined to learn from life the hard way. If we continue blindly walking down the path we are on now, we will trip over every pebble, twig or banana peel in our way. It hurts to fall on one's face. I propose a better alternative in learning life's lessons. Let's learn from those who have gone before. Let's gain wisdom and insight from the creator of the universe. Let's learn life from the giver of life. God is the great giver of wisdom. He will give it to you if you ask without doubting. Are you ready to ask?

And the Devil did grin, for his darling sin
Is pride that apes humility.

SAMUEL TAYLOR COLERIDGE

Proud people breed sad sorrows for themselves.

EMILY BRONTË

Man, proud man,
Drest in a little brief authority,
Most ignorant of what he's most assur'd,
His glassy essence, like an angry ape,
Plays such fantastic tricks before high heaven,
As make the angels weep.

WILLIAM SHAKESPEARE

If you bow at all, bow low.

CHINESE PROVERB

The greatest fault is to be conscious of none.

THOMAS CARLYLE

2

Pride and Humility

~~~~~

Pride goes before destruction,
a haughty spirit before a fall.

PROVERBS 16:18

" Speed kills." This is a popular axiom that has developed not only on the highways but in American college football. After the Nebraska Cornhuskers trounced the Florida Gators for the National Championship in the 1996 Fiesta Bowl, a Florida fan humbly shared what he had learned from the game: "I learned small and fast is no match for big and fast." Nebraska had had great teams in the past, built around massive offensive and defensive lines, huge running backs and a conservative game plan. Then coach Tom Osborne learned that "speed kills." He kept the massive size in his line and supplemented it with blazing speed in the backfield and swift receivers, thus forming one of the greatest college teams to ever play the game. His team had an undefeated season and won the national championship. Speed kills.

"Pride kills." This is a spiritual axiom that has returned to prominence in the church over the last few years. The idea itself is as old as humanity: Cain's pride incited him to kill his brother Abel. King Saul's pride led to numerous attempts on David's life. David himself lost his son Absalom to pride as his son attempted to wrest the throne from him in a coup. Pride has led to the physical death of multitudes of people, but more importantly, it has led to the spiritual death of millions. Pride kills.

The New Testament Greek word for pride is *hyperephania*. It means to be "puffed up with pride." This is a very descriptive word. Like a peacock spreading its feathers and strutting its grandeur, the proud person puts on airs in the mistaken belief that he is greater than he is. Pride or arrogance, according to the Scriptures, begins in the heart of man (Mark 7:21-22). But God scatters the proud and exalts the meek (Luke 1:51ff). In both James 4:6 and 1 Peter 5:5, Proverbs 3:34 is quoted to emphasize the contrast between the meek (*tapeinois*), whom God favors, and the proud (*hyperephanois*), whom God resists. The proud man does not submit to God, and thus becomes God's enemy. Proverbs is very direct concerning how deadly pride can be.

Pride Kills

Pride kills our relationship with God.

> The Lord detests all the proud of heart.
> Be sure of this: They will not go unpunished
> (Proverbs 16:5).

Perhaps one reason that the Bible is so adamant about pride is its effect on our view of God. When we puff ourselves up with pride, we begin to act as if we are God, and we attempt to take God's place. Instead of man being made in the image of God, we try to make God into our image.

This happens in many ways. It happens when we make God into a national god who prospers our country and our country only. It happens when we begin to tamper with the doctrine of the Bible, watering it down to suit our sensibilities. It happens when we believe we are a special case and that God will overlook our pet sin.

The ultimate example of pride is Satan. He was cast from heaven because of his desire to be like God (Revelation 12:5-9, 13:4-9).

Pride kills our relationships with others.

Pride only breeds quarrels,
    but wisdom is found in those who take advice
    (Proverbs 13:10).

An unfriendly man pursues selfish ends;
    he defies all sound judgment (Proverbs 18:1).

I once read an illustration of how pride destroys relationships: when the caterpillar exists in its lowly state it can get as close as it wants to other caterpillars. They climb all over each other and share their grounds selflessly. But as soon as the caterpillar spreads its wings and takes flight, it can never again get as close as it once did to other creatures. The beauty of its wings is the very thing that prevents it from getting close. Likewise, when we puff ourselves up with pride, we cannot get close to people around us. We beat our wings against theirs, and we are both destroyed.

The most deadly attribute of pride in relationships is selfishness. It takes humility to have truly great relationships. When we are selfish, we refuse to share what we have with others. This is true of our possessions, our time, our selves. If we fail to share ourselves, then no one will really know us. It is impossible to be really close to people and be selfish.

Pride kills our self-esteem.

Do you see a man wise in his own eyes?
    There is more hope for a fool than for him
    (Proverbs 26:12).

Pride blinds us to who we really are. We get a false image of ourselves and cling to that image instead of the truth. Underneath our arrogance and pride are feelings of self-loathing and extreme neediness. In order to overcome a low opinion of ourselves, we puff up with pride, acting as if we have no failures, weaknesses, or shortcomings. Unfortunately, we only fool and hurt ourselves, because others can easily see through our veneer of pride to the lost, hurting person inside. This shell of pride can also keep others away as we duck our heads back inside like a tortoise retreating from danger. As long as we stay in the shell we are prisoners of our own pride, destined to live a lonely life.

Humility Heals

God honors humility.

> He mocks proud mockers
> but gives grace to the humble (Proverbs 3:34).

When we become humble we become more like God himself. We take on the character and heart of Jesus who "humbled himself and became obedient to death—even death on a cross" (Philippians 2:8). God honors humility, and the first step toward having a great relationship with God is to humble yourself and see your need for him. God promises he will then draw near to you (James 4:8). Humility, however, does not come from a onetime decision. We must continue to humble ourselves before God for him to continue to honor us.

Humility heals relationships with others.

> ...then do this, my son, to free yourself,
> since you have fallen into your neighbor's hands:
> Go and humble yourself;
> press your plea with your neighbor! (Proverbs 6:3).

To heal relationships, someone must take the first step. Nowhere is this so clearly seen as in marriage. To settle a marital tiff, one partner must be willing to say "I'm sorry." When both partners are so adamant about winning the argument that neither one can admit a mistake, they are in a dangerous situation. Jesus said "blessed are the peacemakers," not "blessed is the one who wins the argument" or "blessed is the one who is right." Someone has to be willing to say, "I'm sorry," and it must be us!

The purpose of Christian relationships is to remove pride from each other's lives so that we can get to heaven. In Colossians 1:28-29 Paul states,

> We proclaim him, admonishing and teaching ev-
> eryone with all wisdom, so that we may present ev-
> eryone perfect in Christ. To this end I labor, strug-
> gling with all his energy, which so powerfully works
> in me.

We must work to help each other be humble and in this way glorify God.

Humility heals our view of self.

> The fear of the LORD teaches a man wisdom,
>   and humility comes before honor
>   (Proverbs 15:33).

> Humility and the fear of the LORD
>   bring wealth and honor and life (Proverbs 22:4).

There is a world of difference between godly confidence and pride. The person who walks with godly confidence walks tall because he knows he is the child of the king. He does not have a haughty, arrogant spirit that declares, "I am better than you." But he does walk with an attitude that proclaims, "I know someone you need to know" or "I have something you need to have." This was the meekness that people noticed in Jesus. Meekness means "power under control," or more colloquially, confidence. We need to be confident of who we are, the valuable life we have found, and the righteous lives we are living. People will be attracted to this type of confidence. As pride repels people, godly confidence attracts them.

Symptoms of Pride

Unwillingness to Admit Mistakes

How difficult is it for you to say "I'm sorry"? Are your apologies wholehearted, halfhearted, or without a heart? The proud man has difficulty seeing his mistakes and an even harder time admitting them. Soren Kierkegaard, the Danish philosopher, uses this parable:

It is related of a peasant who came (barefooted) to the Capital, and had made so much money that he could buy himself a pair of shoes and stockings and still had enough left over to get drunk on—it is related that as he was trying in his drunken state to find his way home he lay down in the middle of the highway and fell asleep. Then along came a wagon, and the driver shouted to him to move or he would run over his legs. Then the drunken peasant awoke, looked at his legs, and since by reason of the shoes and stockings didn't recognize them, he said to the driver, "Drive on, they are not my legs."[1]

Hating to Look Bad

Can you laugh at yourself? If you drop ice cream on your lap in a restaurant, do you laugh it off by calling yourself a "klutz," or burn inside, hoping no one saw it? The humble person knows his weaknesses and can laugh at his shortcomings.

Attitude of Haughtiness

Are you used to privilege? Do you feel you deserve certain perks? Do you find yourself getting upset if you don't get the respect you feel is your due? When we develop the attitude that God owes us rather than realizing how much we owe him, we are in a terrible place.

Aversion to Accountability

Do you have someone in your life who helps you be more like Jesus? Are they willing to ask you tough questions and confront your sin? How do you respond to these questions—change the topic, give them the brush-off, turn the shoulder of coldness? Pride keeps us from getting close to people. The proud man refuses to let others into his life.

My wife found this list comparing prideful attitudes to humble attitudes. I'm not sure who first worked it up, but we want to share it here with due thanks to whoever first developed it.

Prideful Attitude

Humble Attitude

Prideful Attitude	Humble Attitude
"I know enough already"–satisfied	Has a desire to learn–wants wisdom (Proverbs 1:2)
"I know what is best in this situation."	Seeks counsel and guidance (Proverbs 1:3)
Must always be right and have the last word	Willing to back down when wrong (Proverbs 6:2-3)
Holds grudges when corrected or rebuked	Responds positively to rebukes (Proverbs 1:23-24)
Will not accept rebuke	Listens to wisdom and changes (Proverbs 1:25-33)
"God's my buddy. He won't judge me."	Realizes sin and fears God (Luke 18:10-14)
Hears and agrees with mouth, but not with heart	Listens to instruction–changes life (Proverbs 1:8)
Minimizes sin, and argues nit-picky points	Agreeable when shown a better way (Proverbs 1:5)
No respect for leaders	Willing to weigh out leader's advice (Hebrews 13:17)
Ignores advice–is rebellious	Responds to advice, follows through (Matthew 21:28-31)
Rejects people who want to help	Welcomes and appreciates the help (Proverbs 2:1-4)
Leans on own understanding	Leans on the word of God (Psalm 119:105)
Wise in own eyes–praises self	Knows God's wisdom (Proverbs 3:5-7, 27:2)
Angry when God disciplines him/her	Welcomes God's discipline (Proverbs 3:11-12)
Wants to be served	Will serve others (Mark 9:35)
Mocks or insults the truth in heart	Treasures God's word (Proverbs 3:34, 9:8, 30:5-6)
Sees no need to learn more about God	Hungers and thirsts for Bible study (Proverbs 9:9)
Sees no practical need for Jesus	Realizes total need for Jesus (John 15:5)
Slow to apologize and repent when wrong	Quick to make restitution for wrongs (Luke 19:8)
Scorns God's commands	Respects God's commands (Proverbs 5:7-14, 13:13)
Thinks life is his/her own	Realizes life is God's (Galatians 2:20)
Quarrels in relationships	Peace in relationships (1 Corinthians 1:10)
Loner–keeps to own activities	Wants fellowship with the body (Proverbs 24:5-6)
Stubborn in "my way of doing things"	Yielding–waits for God's way (Ecclesiastes 5:2)
Puts others down in speech and actions	Builds others up in word and deed (Ephesians 4:29)
Rash–jumps into things	Thinks before acts (Proverbs 14:8)
Consults those who say what he/she wants to hear	Consults the wise (Proverbs 15:12)
Delights when others fail	Rejoices in victories of others (1 Corinthians 13:6)
Keeps records of wrongs	Forgiving heart and spirit (1 Corinthians 13:5)
Thinking and talking about self	Thinking and talking about others (Philippians 2:4)
Wants to be loved	Loves from the heart–affectionate (1 Thessalonians 2:8)
Won't do menial jobs–feels above them	Will gladly do lowly jobs (John 13:5)
Is selfish and rebellious	Is sacrificial and submissive (Philippians 2:1-11)

I am not a very good skier. I tend to get going so fast that I get out of control. Once I headed down a steep slope, got going very fast, and realized I was out of control. I saw myself heading for the edge of the ski run and was faced with a decision of where to land. My choices were a huge, six-foot boulder on my left or a trunk of an evergreen three feet wide on my right, or a soft bank of new snow five feet deep. I quickly chose the snow over the boulder or the tree.

In life we can choose to be humble or to be puffed-up with pride. Pride is like heading full speed into a huge boulder or a giant evergreen. Humility is the five feet of fresh snow. Choose humility!

3

Advice and Instruction

Plans fail for lack of counsel,
but with may advisers they succeed.

PROVERBS 15:22

Two major events occurred in the American Civil War on the 3rd of July 1862. The two previous 4th of July celebrations had been tainted for President Abraham Lincoln. The war was not progressing as he wished. But on July 3, 1862, he received word that the Union forces had won major battles in the eastern and western theaters of battle—the battle of Gettysburg and the battle of Vicksburg.

Gettysburg was the turning point of the war. It was the Union's first decisive victory over the Army of Virginia led by General Robert E. Lee. He had led his forces into the northern states taking an offensive posture in the war. When the Union army followed him into Pennsylvania, he found a spot on the map where several roads joined at an intersection called Gettysburg. Here he would stand and fight. But Lee was not prepared to fight the battle of Gettysburg.

General Lee did not know the number of Union soldiers he was facing. These numbers should have been discovered and reported by his cavalry leader Jeb Stuart, but he was nowhere to be found. Stuart, without orders from General Lee, had decided to go on a raiding expedition. The cavalry was the eyes of the army. Without the counsel of his cavalry leader, Lee was blind.

Unprepared, Lee went on to lose the battle at Gettysburg. It was just the victory Lincoln had been looking for.

> For lack of guidance a nation falls,
>   but many advisers make victory sure.
>   (Proverbs 11:14)

In the life of a disciple, we need eyes all around us. We need our cavalry—our brothers and sisters—giving us advice and instruction. They tell us where the enemy is and how strong his forces are. They equip us to do battle with the enemy. They fortify us when we are lacking in zeal. We need these people in our lives. We need advisers. We cannot win the battles alone.

The giving and taking of advice was important to the disciples of the early church. David W. Berçot in his excellent book, *Will the Real Heretics Please Stand Up,* gives an example of how one new Christian took the advice of his leaders in the church. This new disciple was a trained actor, but he realized that the acting profession put him in positions that required compromise. The plays of Rome were perverse, steeped in immorality, pagan religion and homosexuality. Since it went against his conscience to act in these plays, the new Christian decided to start an acting school and train young actors.

Before he proceeded in his plan to begin a school, he submitted his idea to the elders of his church for their input. The leaders decided that if it was wrong for him to engage in acting, then it would be just as wrong for him to train others to participate in this occupation. Wanting to be sure of their decision, the leaders wrote to Cyprian of Carthage to get his opinion on this matter. Cyprian agreed with their decision adding that if the brother lost his means of support due to his godly decision, then the church should help support him financially.

The young disciple and the church followed the advice given by Cyprian. Berçot notes, "How many of us would be so concerned about righteousness that we would submit our employment decisions to our body of elders or board of deacons? How many church leaders today would be so concerned about offending God that they would take such an uncompromising position?"[1]

Five Lessons to Learn

Proverbs has much to say about advice and instruction. Various passages encourage us to develop an eager attitude with respect to advice. What do we learn from Proverbs?

1. Seek help.

There is a way that seems right to a man,
    but in the end it leads to death" (Proverbs 14:12).

The heart of the discerning acquires knowledge;
    the ears of the wise seek it out" (Proverbs 18:15).

If we were going to buy a house for the first time, most of us would seek much advice. We would ask others what kind of interest rates we might get, what condition the house was in, what the value was. Before we purchase cars, compact disc players or cameras, we consult *Consumer Reports* and get specifications and prices. We shop in bookstores where the self-help sections are expanding year by year. We go to career counselors, family counselors, and therapists pursuing the help we admittedly need in so many areas of our lives. Yet, why do we so often spurn help with our spiritual lives?

If we need help in other areas, then our spiritual life should be the place where we get the most help. After all, there is no other aspect to our lives more important than our spiritual state. We need to seek out help. We need to find people who are spiritually mature, who have been tested in the spiritual fires and are proven disciples. These men and women can give us godly advice that will help us to mature spiritually.

2. Advisors bring victory.

> For lack of guidance a nation falls,
>   but many advisers make victory sure
>   (Proverbs 11:14).

> Like an earring of gold or an ornament of fine gold
>   is a wise man's rebuke to a listening ear
>   (Proverbs 25:12).

Do we want to succeed? Do we want to be winners? The Bible gives us the formula for success—*seek advice*. Why do we think we can do it on our own when the Bible says we need others in our lives? Do we believe the Bible is flawless or that we are? The best athletes in the world need coaches and trainers. In baseball, a pitching coach can look at a pitcher and discern mistakes the pitcher could never detect himself. In the 1996 season the New York Yankees picked up an ex–New York Met pitcher, Dwight Gooden. A pitching coach for the Yankees began to instruct Gooden on his pitching style. He shortened his delivery and worked on his pitches. Gooden was a seasoned veteran who had to make major changes in his pitching style, but he followed the coach's advice and was soon rewarded by pitching his first major league "no-hitter." His victory came as a result of taking his coach's advice.

3. Without instruction, bad things happen.

> Stop listening to instruction, my son,
>   and you will stray from the words of knowledge
>   (Proverbs 19:27).

> A man who strays from the path of understanding
>   comes to rest in the company of the dead
>   (Proverbs 21:16).

Sometimes we are just thick-headed. We have to learn things the hard way. Others can go out of their way to try to warn us that we are headed down the wrong path, but we still take that path.

This is how I was the first time I tried to bunt a baseball. I was just a kid entering Little League. I had a great coach who spent hours demonstrating the fundamentals of baseball, drilling the basics into our heads. As a kid, I did not appreciate all the time spent on instruction. I wanted to hit, pitch and run. I certainly did not come to the field to listen.

As Coach Tidwell was instructing us on the proper form in bunting, I was searching the sky looking at the clouds. The coach went over the stance, when to turn and commit yourself, and most importantly—never to hold the bat with your fingers facing the pitcher. If you did this, you were inviting the ball to hit your fingers. You were to make a fist and place the bat above your fist securing it with your thumb.

Unfortunately, while this great point was delivered, I was flying from one cloud to the next like Peter Pan. When my turn came to bunt, I turned to face the pitcher with my hand fully extended around the body of the bat. The ball hit me squarely in the knuckles. I had to learn the hard way. Eventually, I became very proficient in bunting the baseball, but I could have learned a lot faster by being attentive to instruction.

4. Without instruction, you hurts others.

> He who heeds discipline shows the way to life,
> but whoever ignores correction leads others
> astray (Proverbs 10:17).

How often have we said or heard, "I'm only hurting myself." If we were all living on individual islands with no contact with anyone else, this might be true. But as the metaphysical poet John Donne wrote,

> No man is an island entire of itself; every man is a piece of
> the Continent, a part of the main.... Any man's death diminishes me because I am involved in Mankind; and therefore
> never send to know for whom the bell tolls; it tolls for thee.[2]

When in our independence we disregard godly advice, we hurt others as well as ourselves. We set an example which by action and attitude say that we do not need others in our lives.

5. Without instruction, we are stupid.

> Whoever loves discipline loves knowledge,
> but he who hates correction is stupid
> (Proverbs 12:1).

The Bible uses the word "stupid" sparingly. It is found only four times in the New International Version (Job 18:3, Proverbs 12:1, Ecclesiastes 10:3, 2 Timothy 2:23). In Proverbs it refers to the person who hates correction. Pride makes us stupid. When we are unwilling to receive godly correction, we are trusting our own way over that of our advisors. This type of pride makes us stupid.

This is easily understood in other areas of our lives. If we had a specific disease that was troubling us, we would seek out the most experienced doctor we could find in treating that disease, one with a track record of success. If after giving us a thorough examination he concluded that we needed a particular therapy, we would be stupid to ignore his advice and come up with our own plan.

When faced with spiritual problems that trouble us, we should seek out help from godly men and women who have faced similar problems, people who have proven their spiritual maturity by victoriously overcoming struggles. They will be happy to give us advice. Their advice might be as simple as encouragement to study out the situation in the Bible and develop a conviction about it. Or it may be as radical as quitting one's job and changing professions. But the test is how we react to godly advice. To reject it hands down is stupid. We should pray, fast, study the Scriptures and develop our own convictions about the advice. Then we can embrace a decision with faith. Victory comes from this approach to solving our spiritual problems.

Welcome a Rebuke?

How do you react when someone really challenges you? Are you the type that listens attentively on the outside while on the inside all systems are shut down? Are you the type that has a calm, serene exterior while internally your gut is an overheated boiler ready to explode? Do you stomp away from the rebuke cursing under your breath, "Who does that person think he is?" Or do you listen with a heart ready to change?

There are times when we need wake-up calls. We often fail to see our own weaknesses. We can even fail to see them after someone has pointed them out time and time again. Sometimes we need to be challenged in a way that gets our attention. This is when the rebuke comes in. In 2 Timothy 3:16-17 Paul told Timothy,

> All Scripture is God-breathed and is useful for teaching, rebuking, correcting and training in righteousness, so that the man of God may be thoroughly equipped for every good work.

God has given us his Word to rebuke us. It is spiritual dynamite which can blast sin out of our lives. If we heed the rebukes of God's word, then we will not stray from God's path. Sometimes rebukes are needed to keep us on the path.

What does the book of Proverbs say about rebukes?

- Rebukes show love. Proverbs 27:5 reads, "Better is open rebuke than hidden love."
- Rebukes give life. Proverbs 15:31 reads, "He who listens to a life-giving rebuke will be at home among the wise."
- Don't let rebukes harden your heart. Proverbs 29:1 states, "A man who remains stiff-necked after many rebukes will suddenly be destroyed—without remedy."

Few men have the virtue to withstand the highest bidder.
GEORGE WASHINGTON

It is necessary to the happiness of man that he be mentally faithful to himself. Infidelity does not consist in believing, or in disbelieving; it consists in professing to believe what he does not believe.
THOMAS PAINE

4

Integrity

What a man desires is unfailing love;
better to be poor than a liar.

PROVERBS 19:22

Food gained by fraud tastes sweet to a man,
but he ends up with a mouth full of gravel.

PROVERBS 20:17

The March 20, 1996, edition of *The New York Times* carried an interesting article in the sports section entitled, "More Than a Drop of Integrity." It was about a golfer named Jeff Sluman. On the Friday round of the Bay Hill Invitational, Sluman hit his ball into the water and then took a drop from the water. (For you non-golfers, he dropped the ball near the point it went in). During the night he began to question whether his drop was legal or illegal. He found it difficult to sleep that night. The next morning he approached the PGA officials and told them of his dilemma. Before the tournament official had a chance to make a difficult decision on the matter, Sluman disqualified himself. "'I'm not sure,' Sluman said later. 'And if I'm not sure, I couldn't live with myself and keep playing. What if I won? It would be a curse.'"[1]

Not many people today have the attitude of Jeff Sluman. How many weekend golfers fudge on their scores? In most sports today the rule is to see what you can get by with. As long as you don't get caught, cheating is okay. Yet, for the man of integrity cheating is never okay. It is never even an option.

We live in an age in which integrity is lost. We no longer trust our politicians. Campaign promises are expected to be broken. Parents laugh at "little Johnny" cheating at pin-the-tail-on-the-donkey. They shrug and say, "Isn't he so competitive?" In business you are expected to lie—anything to sell a product or make the corporation look good.

Stephen Carter, a law professor at Yale University, has written a book entitled *Integrity*. At the opening of his book he tells of a commencement address which he was asked to deliver. He began his address by stating his theme of integrity. Upon the mere mention of the word, the crowd broke into applause. Carter comments,

> Applause! Just because they had heard the word integrity—that's how starved they were. They had no idea how I was using the word, or what I was going to say about it, or indeed, whether I was for it or against it. But they knew they liked the idea of simply talking about it.[2]

The *American Heritage Dictionary* defines integrity as a "steadfast adherence to a strict moral or ethical code." It also mentions "soundness, the quality or condition of being whole or undivided; completeness."[3] When someone is a person of integrity, there is a wholeness about them. Too many people are not like what they present to the world. Their "life" does not match their "doctrine." The are two-faced, fake.

We occasionally hear of people who live up to the standard of integrity. In Buena Park, California, Tom and Pauline Nichter are such examples. During the past year they lost their jobs, house and most of their possessions. But through it all they kept their integrity.

The Nichters and their son, Jason, 11, were living on toast

and milk when they found a wallet stuffed with hundred-dollar bills lying in a toy shop at the Buena Park Mall. Upon finding the wallet, Pauline Nichter admitted, "I did think about how I could use the money to keep from losing my car. But it wasn't our money and we didn't want to set a bad example for our son." The Nichters handed the wallet in to the police. The cash belonged to Theas Yann, a tourist from the South Pacific island of New Caledonia who thanked the Nichters but offered no reward. Their reward was that they did the right thing. They chose integrity.

In the Bible, Pilate was a man who lacked integrity. His decision to crucify Jesus was based on what the crowds thought and not on the truth. Judas was a follower of Jesus, yet he betrayed his Rabbi for thirty pieces of silver. The Jews who crucified Jesus were thankful that Pilot and Judas lacked integrity.

In the Old Testament, Pharaoh lacked integrity. He made promises to Israel and reneged on them as quickly as they had been made. Pharaoh's lack of integrity led to the death of his firstborn son. King Saul, the first king of Israel, also lacked integrity. Early in his reign he listened to God's voice and obeyed his command. Later in his life, he stopped listening to God. He died a man full of fear, a man without integrity.

Joseph and Daniel are great Old Testament examples of integrity. Nothing negative is said about either of these men in the Bible. In the face of extreme adversity, they were men of integrity.

Many men and women in the Bible were known for their integrity. Jesus, of course, tops the list. He was the most complete person to ever walk the earth. As you can see at the trial of Jesus, people had problems even inventing bad things to say about him.

Today we need those same kinds of examples: men and women who follow God and who follow the Bible with all integrity. Proverbs gives us many of the lessons on integrity we need to be those men and women.

Integrity lasts forever.

> Truthful lips endure forever,
>> but a lying tongue lasts only a moment
>> (Proverbs 12:19).

Integrity lasts forever. People lie to escape something. They might be trying to escape the truth. Perhaps they are trying to keep from being discovered. They might be lying in an attempt to appear greater than they are. Whatever the reason, escape is on their minds.

When we lie, we feel like we are clever. We act as if we will never be discovered. We believe our escape is secure. (But we may also live in fear—fear of being caught, fear of someone discovering who we really are.)

Not every lie will be discovered in this life. Many people live out lies for decades and are never discovered. They fool others. They escape detection. But no matter how many people they fool, they never escape from God or from themselves.

Whenever we lie, we ruin a part of our character. One lie leads to another. The more we lie the easier it becomes to lie and eventually lying becomes our nature. In this way we can never escape the contamination of a lie. We might never get caught. We might avoid the consequences of the act we are desperately trying to conceal. But we cannot escape the harmful effects on our character. You cannot be in a mud fight without getting dirty. Deceit, like all sin, always has consequences. Proverbs 28:13 reads:

> He who conceals his sins does not prosper,
>> but whoever confesses and renounces them finds
>> mercy.

By turning away from deceit we are making a decision to be real—to be whole. This wholeness of character cannot be taken from us. Men can take many things away from us, but they cannot steal our integrity, our good name. Integrity must be thrown away; it cannot be taken.

Integrity pleases God.

> The Lord detests lying lips,
>> but he delights in men who are truthful
>> (Proverbs 12:22).

God hates lies and loves the truth. God has never lied. Lying is against his nature. His enemy, Satan, is the father of lies. In John's Gospel, Jesus tells the Jews,

> "You belong to your father, the devil, and you want to carry out your father's desire. He was a murderer from the beginning, not holding to the truth, for there is no truth in him. When he lies, he speaks his native language, for his is a liar and the father of lies" (John 8:44).

Lies are a part of Satan's arsenal. When we lie, we are using the weapons of Satan. We are embracing one of his most potent tricks to contaminate humanity.

If Satan is the father of lies, then God is the father of truth. Whenever we decide to tell the truth over telling a lie, we are choosing God over Satan. This delights God!

When you lose integrity, you hurt yourself.

> The wisdom of the prudent is to give thought to their
>> ways,
>> but the folly of fools is deception (Proverbs 14:8).

"The folly of fools is deception." I learned this when I was in the second grade. I've had to be reminded of it many times over the years, but I first learned it in Mrs. Anderson's class. She caught me talking during one of her lessons and as punishment she asked me to write the sentence, "I will never talk in Mrs. Anderson's class again," one-hundred times. But to make it a little longer she added, "never ever again." I worked hard trying to finish my punishment before the day ended.

As I left her class and headed for the bus, I placed the finished product on her desk. She looked over her horned-rimmed glasses and said, "That's fine, Steve. Now get your mother to sign this." Oops! What was I going to do now? I picked up the bundle of papers and headed to the bus.

I decided on my way home that these papers would never be seen by my mother. I would forge her signature. Surely Mrs. Anderson would never notice the difference. In my best second grade penmanship, I forged my mother's signature.

The next day in class came the moment of truth. Would I escape discovery or not? I handed the paper to Mrs. Anderson. She looked over all the sentences and saw that I had completed the assignment. Then she looked at the signature. Once again her eyes popped above her horned-rimmed glasses and she stared down at me. "Steve, did your mother really sign this?" she asked. I replied, "Yes, Mrs. Anderson. She did." She looked back at the signature and then one more time at me. "Let me give her a call," she said.

Busted! I was busted. And soon my bottom would be busted as well. Mrs. Anderson spanked me for lying. Then when I got home my mom gave me two spankings—one for talking in class and one for lying.

"The folly of fools is deception." Whom did I think I was going to fool by forging my mother's signature? I ended up fooling myself.

Deception ends in destruction.

> A man of perverse heart does not prosper,
>   he whose tongue is deceitful falls into trouble
>   (Proverbs 17:20).

> A false witness will not go unpunished,
>   and he who pours out lies will not go free
>   (Proverbs 19:5).

At some point our lies will find us out. It might not happen here in this life. But in the next world they will find us out. If you sow the wind, you will reap the whirlwind.

When I was a little boy, I loved to watch *Looney Tunes*. I

find it interesting that these cartoons are still around, and now my children love to watch them. I especially loved to watch the Roadrunner and Wile E. Coyote. The coyote would dream up elaborate schemes to catch the roadrunner. Many of the schemes involved chain reactions—a cannon would fire, knocking over a pail of water, filling a bucket, tipping a scale, lighting a match, igniting a rocket designed to hit the roadrunner. These schemes would always backfire and the coyote would end up being hurt by his own invention.

Such is the way of lies and deception. In Acts 5 Ananias and Sapphira sold a field to raise money to give to the church. When it came time to actually give the money, they held back part for themselves and lied about what they had done. They both died for their sin. Their sin found them out. We might escape discovery for a season, but in time we will be found out. Lies destroy our integrity. They cripple our character. They hurt God and keep us from being like him. We must decide to give up deception and be people of integrity. When we decide to live lives of integrity, interesting things begin to happen to us.

A close sister of mine in the church related a story of her decision to be a woman of integrity. This is her story:

One of the bigger lies I told and lived out was a scheme to get financial aid for college. I needed to prove that I was "independent" to qualify. My mother and I concocted a story that my stepfather kicked me out and wouldn't support me. We got friends to join in the lie supporting us with signed letters. I then related the story to my high school guidance counselor in order to get a letter from her, sealing my fate and assuring me the $4,000 a year.

It worked! For two years I received a grant as an independent student. I can't imagine what the story did to my stepfather's self-esteem and to my parents' marriage. The lie tainted my own respect for my stepfather.

Then, while on an internship, I became a Christian. As I was applying to local schools to finish my degree, a sermon was preached on Mark 9:42-48—the message was to "cut off sin radically." I realized that I needed to stop this lie and stop receiving the money falsely. It was going to be renewed each year automatically. I told the financial aid department of my new college that I didn't qualify. Now I had to pay tuition on my own. My mother didn't support my decision to change schools and then I really was cut off from her help.

But God encouraged me. I found out I would receive financial aid (more than the grant) living on campus. I gained credits by transferring so I had to pay for less credits to receive my degree. Then when I joined the college literary magazine, I received tuition credit for being on staff. But most importantly, while working on the college magazine the editor-in-chief became a Christian! God truly blessed my decision to hold on to his standard of integrity.

And he always will.

An Integrity Test

1. When you sign your name at the bottom of tax forms, have you made every effort to see that all numbers are correct?

2. Do the speed laws and seat belt laws of your state apply to you? One couple I am close to noted, "Once we 'fasted' from speeding for a harvest month at church. It was challenging, but we gave ourselves the out of ending the fast." Is this like fasting from immorality? Now that's preposterous! Fasting from sin!

3. Do you ever use the company expense account to buy personal items?

4. In sticky situations would you lie to save face?

5. If you asked your spouse, your best friend, your co-workers, your parents, or even someone who doesn't like you very much, would they say you are a person of great integrity?

6. Do you constantly have to promise, swear, make guarantees for people to believe you?

7. When you say you will be at a particular place at a particular time, are you there? Does this apply to church equally as it applies to work?

8. Do you do anything that you would not want your spouse knowing that you are doing? Is there anything you would not want Jesus to know you are doing? (If so, stop it because he knows.)

9. When the cashier at the store hands you back ten dollars more than you were supposed to get in change, do you alert him to the mistake and hand him back the ten or pocket it?

10. Do you find yourself adding details to stories about your day to make them a bit more interesting or exciting?

Generosity lies less in giving much than in giving at the right moment.

JEAN DE LE BRUYÈRE

Selfish persons are incapable of loving others, but they are not capable of loving themselves either.

ERICH FROMM

5

Generosity and Selfishness

Do not eat the food of a stingy man,
do not crave his delicacies;
for he is the kind of man
who is always thinking about the cost.
"Eat and drink," he says to you,
but his heart is not with you.

PROVERBS 23:6-7

Charles Dickens' *A Christmas Carol*, the beloved story of Ebenezer Scrooge, is told every Christmas season. It is a classic tale of a man confronted by his own selfishness, so familiar to all of us that there is no need to retell it here. The sad thing about the story is that it is only thought of around the holiday. The victory of generosity over selfishness should have no seasonal boundaries.

My wife and I have lived in New York City for over a decade. For two people from the rural south, our move to New York was shocking. We were not prepared for the bold, aggressive pace of the city. People generally think of New Yorkers as rude. I discovered after living here for several months that they're not rude—they're just in a hurry. The typical store clerk in New York has to deal with more people in a day than many clerks in a Southern store deal with in a week. There is no time for the pleasantries that are so much a part of the Southern life-style, such as: "How are you doing?" or "Nice weather, isn't it?" or "How about them Knicks?" You are much more likely to be greeted by a stern and aggressive "next!"

The one time of year that the atmosphere changes is the Christmas season. From late November through December people seem to change. They are just as hurried as the rest of the year (even more so), but they take that extra moment to exchange a pleasantry with the passing stranger. For a few fleeting weeks, the attitude of the city takes a profound turn for the better. I've heard many New Yorkers mutter, "Why can't it be like this all year round?" Why indeed?

Giving should not be relegated to a season of the year. We must develop lives where giving characterizes our nature. What if Ebenezer Scrooge had woken up on the 26th of December and returned to his old, stingy, selfish self? Not quite a tale of Christmas cheer anymore, is it? But he did not wake up the same. He was transformed—selfishness had given way to generosity. As Dickens wrote:

> Scrooge was better than his word. He did it all, and infinitely more; and to Tiny Tim, who did NOT die, he was a second father. He became as good a friend, as good a master, and as good a man, as the good old city knew, or any other good old city, town, or borough, in the good old world.

For Scrooge to change he needed help. Three spirits compelled him to confront his hideous nature, thereby giving him the power to change. Just like old Ebenezer, we need help to change. God will give us a spirit of generosity if we strive to have one, but we need his help. To revise the words of Tiny Tim just a bit, "God *help* us, every one!"

Three Lessons to Learn

1. Be impulsive with generosity.

> Do not withhold good from those who deserve it,
> when it is in your power to act.

Do not say to your neighbor
"Come back later; I'll give it tomorrow"—
when you now have it with you (Proverbs 3:27-28).

Thoughts of generosity often enter our minds during the day. We think: I should send her a card. I should buy her a flower. I should give him a phone call. Wouldn't it be nice if I dropped her a letter? Yet if we do not act on these urges, they pass as quickly as they came. When urges of generosity hit, we should act upon them.

Two points will help us. First, never forget that "little" giving-impulses are as important as "big" ones—more important in a way, because they help us to form the habit of giving. Generosity must become second nature for it to pay its fullest dividends. In fact, until it becomes second nature, we have not become a truly generous people. Don't quash the "little" impulses. They feed our generous nature.

Second, start responding to the impulses of generosity as early in the morning as possible. Like a car engine on a cold winter morning, our motor of generosity can be hard to start. The earlier we begin to crank it up, the sooner it will turn over and begin to run smoothly. Let's start the day with a warm, generous greeting to the first person we meet, whether it's our employer or our two-year-old girl pouncing on our stomach screaming, "Good morning, Daddy." Regardless of the situation, let us continue to meet it with generosity throughout our day.

2. Generosity blesses the giver as much as the receiver.

One man gives freely, yet gains even more;
another withholds unduly, but comes to poverty
(Proverbs 11:24).

A generous man will prosper,
he who refreshes others will himself be refreshed
(Proverbs 11:25).

It is an irony of life that the person who initiates a true act of generosity receives as much as he gives. But this is only true if the giving is done without any expectation of return. Seneca, the Roman philosopher, wrote, "There is no grace in a benefit that sticks to the fingers."

Often the returns of giving come in wholly unexpected ways, perhaps long after we have performed our acts of kindness. A creative lady in Alexandria, Virginia, wrote a letter to a little girl she knew who had the measles. She created a whimsical piece with clever drawings and signed it "Susie Cucumber." The girl told her friends about the Susie Cucumber letter, and naturally they all wanted letters from "Susie" too. Parents, grandparent, uncles, and aunts caught on to the idea, and soon this woman was doing a profitable business sending out as many as 100,000 letters a year to children all over the world. A small act of kindness grew into something much larger than ever expected.

One area where giving is returned to the giver is evangelism. The disciples who are active in sharing their faith are the happiest, most generous, most grace-filled and appreciative. Vice versa, when we lose our gratitude, we lose our evangelistic zeal. Gratitude for one's own salvation and urgency to see other people saved go hand in hand. Reaching out to others who do not have a relationship with God helps us see and appreciate our own salvation.

3. Develop a heart for the poor.

> He who is kind to the poor lends to the LORD
>   and he will reward him for what he has done
>   (Proverbs 19:17).

> He who gives to the poor will lack nothing,
>   but he who closes his eyes to them receives many
>   curses (Proverbs 28:27).

> If a man shuts his ears to the cry of the poor,
>   he too will cry out and not be answered
>   (Proverbs 21:13).

> He who mocks the poor shows contempt for their
>   Maker;

whoever gloats over disaster will not go unpunished (Proverbs 17:5).

Have you heard some of the following comments? "If those people would get off their duffs and do some work, they wouldn't be so bad off." "Haven't they ever heard of birth control? Why don't they just stop having babies?" "When you give to the poor all you are doing is supporting their drug and alcohol problems."

The Bible warns us not to mock the poor. People are poor for many different reasons. Certainly the comments above could not apply to the children of the poor. Many people suffer for no other reason than being born into families with few resources.

How can we help the poor? We can begin by developing a heart of generosity. What do you have to give?

- time
- experience
- special abilities/talents
- influence
- understanding and tolerance
- good will
- courage and faith
- attention
- prayer
- insight

Who is the most generous person you have ever known? That person is probably also one of the most liked people that you have known. Who is the most selfish person you have ever known? That person is probably one of the least liked people you have known. How do you want to be known? Would you rather be Ebenezer Scrooge *before* the visitation of the ghosts or after their visits? This is an easy question for us to answer. But the real answer will be found in the way you live your life doing little acts of kindness for others every day.

Work is life, you know, and without it, there's nothing but fear and insecurity.

JOHN LENNON

Far and away the best prize that life offers is the chance to work hard at work worth doing.

THEODORE ROOSEVELT

Work! Labor the aspergas me of life; the one great sacrament of humanity from which all other things flow— security, leisure, joy, art, literature, even divinity itself.

SEAN O'CASEY

If you lose yourself in your work, you find who you are.

FREDERICK BUECHNER

6

Hard Work and Laziness

One who is slack in his work
is brother to one who destroys.

PROVERBS 18:9

Have you ever seen a picture of a three-toed sloth? It is one ugly creature. When kindergarten children are asked to select their favorite animals, the three-toed sloth never ranks high on the list. The sloth spends most of its time hanging from a tree with its back to the ground. It is slow as molasses in winter, the very picture of laziness.

The sluggard is the spiritual three-toed sloth. The Bible has nothing good to say of him, but condemnation can be found in abundance:

> I went past the field of the sluggard,
>   past the vineyard of the man who lacks judgment;
> thorns had come up everywhere,
>   the ground was covered with weeds,
>   and the stone wall was in ruins.
> I applied my heart to what I observed
>   and learned a lesson from what I saw:
> A little sleep, a little slumber,
>   a little folding of the hands to rest—
> and poverty will come on you like a bandit
>   and scarcity like an armed man
>   (Proverbs 24:30-34).

I think of this proverb often. It doesn't say *much* sleep or *much* folding of the hands, but just *a little*. Laziness comes in little spurts. Little amounts of unproductive, lost time add up to much lost time. Time that can never be regained. We must value every second.

> As a door turns on its hinges,
>   so a sluggard turns on his bed (Proverbs 26:14).

The sluggard has a difficult time getting out of bed, and loves that device made for the truly lazy at heart: the snooze button. It caters to us who can't begin our day on time. With one push of a button we can delay our day's start for five minutes. Another push and it's ten minutes. Thus we turn on our hinges. Turn once to hit the snooze button, turn back to catch five more minutes of sleep, turn back again to hit the button. If our bed squeaks, we even sound like a squeaky hinge turning. Thus is the life of a sluggard—the spiritual three-toed sloth.

> The sluggard buries his hand in the dish;
>   he is too lazy to bring it back to his mouth
>   (Proverbs 26:15).

Here is another picturesque description of the sluggard. He is so lazy that he needs someone to spoon him his meal. This description should warn us of how disgusting laziness is to God.

> The sluggard is wiser in his own eyes
>   than seven men who answer discreetly
>   (Proverbs 26:16).

The saddest aspect of the life of the sluggard is that many times he does not even realize how lazy he is. He looks at his unproductive day and actually believes he had no control over his lack of productivity. He blames it on other things—the children, the weather, bad health or lack of knowledge—failing to see that the problem is within, lurking in his own heart.

The Disciplined Life

How do we develop a disciplined mind and a disciplined life? Here are some pearls of the disciplined life:

Carpe diem—seize the day.
I love the movie *Dead Poets Society.* In this movie, Robin Williams plays a high school English professor in a New England preparatory school. His goal is to teach a class of unmotivated students the value and beauty of literature, and he uses a Latin term to motivate them: *carpe diem* or "seize the day."

We are only given a certain amount of time in a day and in our lives. The challenge of life is not that we have too little time, but in how we are going to spend the time we do have. I am reminded of a meditation by Michael Quoist in a little devotional book entitled *Prayers:*

I went out, Lord.
Men were coming and going,
Walking and running.

Everything was rushing: cars, trucks, the street, the whole town.
Men were rushing not to waste time.
They were rushing after time,
To catch up with time,
To gain time.

Good-bye, Sir, excuse me, I haven't time.
I'll come back, I can't wait, I haven't time.
I must end this letter—I haven't time.
I'd love to help you, but I haven't time.
I can't accept, having no time.
I can't think, I can't read, I'm swamped, I haven't time.
I'd like to pray, but I haven't time.
You understand, Lord, they simply haven't the time.
The child is playing, he hasn't time right now....Later on....
The schoolboy has his homework to do, he hasn't time....
    Later on....
The student has his courses, and so much work....Later on....

The young man is at his sports, he hasn't time....Later on...
The young married man has his new house; he has to fix it up.
    He hasn't time....Later on....
The grandparents have their grandchildren. They haven't time....
    Later on....
They are ill, they have their treatments, they haven't time....
    Later on....
They are dying, they have not....
Too late!...They have not more time!...

You who are beyond time, Lord, you smile to see us fighting it.
And you know what you are doing.
You make no mistakes in your distribution of time to men.
You give each one time to do what you want him to do.
But we must not lose time
    waste time
    kill time,
For time is a gift that you give us,
But a perishable gift,
A gift that does not keep....[1]

Beware of the "little things."

The disciplined life is not demonstrated in the big things that must be done, but in the little things that we have an option to do or not. We must go to work, but while we are there, do we do all the little things that make us a great employee? Anyone can have a child, but do we do the little things that make us a great parent?

Some little things we must watch out for:
- punctuality
- paying bills on time
- sending birthday cards
- keeping the desk clean
- picking up after yourself
- returning phone calls
- looking presentable

Don't overcommit.

One thing that can cripple the disciplined life is trying to do too much. A frazzled, frayed life is not the mark of discipline. Discipline is deciding what can be done and doing it well. It is better to do three things well than ten things badly.

An important part of this is scheduling. How much time do we spend thinking about what must be done and how to do it? Five concentrated minutes of planning can save us hours. Many people find it helpful to spend ten minutes every morning writing down a "to-do" list, then sitting down at night with the list to actually see what did and did not get accomplished. These twenty minutes can be the most valuable of the day.

Worry won't help.

The Bible teaches us to "not be anxious about anything" (Philippians 4:6). Worry is an unproductive emotion—it will not change anything. We should, instead, cast our anxiety on God, because he cares for us (1 Peter 5:7). Yet, if it is within our power to fix or remedy the problem, we must take appropriate action.

Simplify.

Life in the '90s has become very complex. When I was growing up, there were three brands of sneakers for sale. For me the choice was usually between Adidas or Converse. Now when you go into a store, there are literally hundreds of types and brands of sneakers to choose from. There are running shoes, basketball shoes, cross-trainers, hiking shoes, aerobic shoes and even good old tennis shoes. This typifies the attitude in the '90s—that more is always better.

The disciplined person will not get caught up in this quest for more. The disciplined life is the simple life. Richard Foster has written a classic book about the spiritual disciplines entitled *Celebration of Discipline*. Foster writes,

Simplicity is freedom. Duplicity is bondage. Simplicity brings joy and balance. Duplicity brings anxiety and fear. The preacher of Ecclesiastes observes that "God made man simple; man's complex problems are of his own devising" (Ecclesiastes 7:30, Jerusalem Bible).

Foster gives these hints on how to simplify life:
- Buy things that are useful rather than buying things for status.
- Do not buy anything that is producing an addiction in you.
- Develop the characteristic of giving things away.
- Refuse to be seduced by modern gadgetry.
- Learn how to enjoy things without owning them.
- Develop a deeper appreciation for God's creation.
- Look skeptically on all "buy now, pay later" schemes.
- Shun anything that keeps you from seeking first God's kingdom or his righteousness.[2]

Ask for help.

If you have a problem with discipline in any area of your life, then find someone who can help you to make changes in that area. Many people have problems keeping up with their finances. Some have never learned how to balance a checkbook or figure out a budget. One of the great advantages of being in the church is that we are family. We have many brothers and sisters around us who have expertise and want to help us. If you will ask for help, someone will be willing to give it.

Start today.

The sluggard would read this chapter, be convicted of what changes they needed to make, then procrastinate or never make any changes at all. Do not put off what you can do now. Start making changes today!

The child is father of the man.

WILLIAM WORDSWORTH

Nothing you do for children is ever wasted. They seem not to notice us, hovering, averting our eyes, and they seldom offer thanks, but what we do for them is never wasted.

GARRISON

7

Children

Fix these words of mine in your hearts and minds; tie them as symbols on your hands and bind them on your foreheads. Teach them to your children, talking about them when you sit at home and when you walk along the road, when you lie down and when you get up.

DEUTERONOMY 11:18-19

Train a child in the way he should go,
   and when he is old he will not turn from it.

PROVERBS 22:6

Jesus told his disciples to allow the children to come to him. They seemed to think that Jesus was too busy to be with kids. Jesus was busy, sure enough, but he also knew what was important in life, and one of the most important activities in life is to spend time with our kids. Francis Thompson, the poet, wrote, "Look for me in the nurseries of Heaven." I believe Jesus will be found there, too.

As a parent of two small children (ages 7 and 4), I do not feel experienced enough to write about the whole process of parenting. But I can point us to the Scriptures for guidance. Give careful attention to Proverbs and you will learn many powerful lessons about raising children.

Lessons for Parents
(and Other Concerned Adults)

Teach your children to fear the Lord.

> He who fears the LORD has a secure fortress,
> and for his children it will be a refuge
> (Proverbs 14:26).

The proverbs are very clear that the starting point of raising kids is to teach them to fear the Lord. Without this foundation a child's life will be based on shifting sand. Instruction of children must begin with a proper respect and understanding of God. This can be taught by focusing on the Scriptures or creation, or through examples of parental love. But it must be taught.

I recently sat in my back yard around 10:00 P.M. with my four-year-old son, Daniel, and stared up at the moon. We talked about the beauty of the moon, how bright it was, the shapes on its face. Then we talked about God. We talked about how great God was to make the moon. Then we prayed together. We stared up at the sky and thanked God for making the moon. Isn't it sad that many parents share the wonders of the world with their children without sharing the greatest wonder of all—that Yahweh God made these wonders from nothing? Everything begins and ends with a proper fear of God.

Teach them to listen and obey.

> A wise son heeds his father's instruction,
> but a mocker does not listen to rebuke
> (Proverbs 13:1).

> "The eye that mocks a father,
> that scorns obedience to a mother,
> will be pecked out by the ravens of the valley,
> will be eaten by the vultures" (Proverbs 30:17).

> Listen, my son, to your father's instruction
> and do not forsake your mother's teaching.
> They will be a garland to grace your head
> and a chain to adorn your neck (Proverbs 1:8-9).

Children need to be taught to listen and obey. As every parent knows, this does not come naturally for most children! And, sadly, the expectation of it does not come naturally for most parents. What does it take to get our child's attention? Do we have to shout, wave our hands, hit on pots and pans? Much of a child's behavior is based on what we expect of him. If we expect her to listen and obey the first time, then that becomes normal for her. If we expect him to disobey the first three times he is told something, then that is what we will get. Remember Proverbs 30:17 (above).

Let's have high expectations when it comes to our children listening and obeying what we say. Here are some specific expectations we can have for our children.

- Expect them to respect what you say.
- Expect them to listen when you talk.
- Expect them to look you in the eye when you correct them.
- Expect them to obey the first time.

Teach children to respect authority.

> Fear the LORD and the king, my son,
> and do not join with the rebellious,
> for those two will send sudden destruction upon them,
> and who knows what calamities they can bring?
> (Proverbs 24:21-22).

> He who keeps the law is a discerning son,
> but a companion of gluttons disgraces his father
> (Proverbs 28:7).

Children must be taught respect. Respect can be seen in warm greetings, gracious thank-yous, and genuine apologies. Here is a list of some things children must learn to respect:
- God
- God's word (the Bible)
- Prayer
- Others' feelings

- Others' wishes
- Others' property
- The government
- Police
- Parents
- Teachers
- Siblings
- Baby-sitters

Notice a child's actions.
> Even a child is known by his actions,
>> by whether his conduct is pure and right
>> (Proverbs 20:11).

I am amazed at how many parents are oblivious to the actions of their children. I'm not talking about parents who don't know what their teens are doing away from home. I'm talking about parents whose four-year-olds are right under their noses showing disrespectful, rebellious attitudes. It is almost like these parents don't want to know what their children are doing. But it is by our children's actions that we know their character. Rebellious actions must not go unpunished. Disrespectful attitudes must be addressed. If we sow indifference to these behaviors when our children are small, then we will reap a whirlwind during their teenage years.

Study your children. Watch how they play with older kids and with younger kids. See if they are respectful with their grandparents. While they are small, watch their every move. It will not be long before their movements will be concealed under a cloak of teenage subterfuge. Watch and correct their bad actions. Watch and encourage their good actions. Be aware of who they are and what they are doing.

Train the hearts of children.
> My son, if your heart is wise,
>> then my heart will be glad;
> my inmost being will rejoice
>> when your lips speak what is right
>> (Proverbs 23:15-16).

Listen, my son, and be wise,
   and keep your heart on the right path
   (Proverbs 23:19).

Make no mistake about it—the battle is for the hearts of our children. My wife and I want our kids to be great in sports, talented in the arts, and smart in school, but above all we want them to have the heart of Jesus. This is why it is so important to watch their attitude. What type of attitude do they have when corrected? Are they whiners, moaners or silently rebellious? Do they obey with a good attitude, or with words or hands only and not the heart? Our job is not done until the attitude is discipled. Children can apologize with an attitude or with genuine contrition. We cannot rest until their heart is right.

Give children the discipline they need.

The Bible teaches that we are to discipline our children when needed. My children hate spankings: They would rather have anything happen other than a spanking. I don't enjoy giving them, but when the need arises, I know it is my God-given responsibility not to "spare the rod" (Proverbs 13:24, below). In our home, the rod is actually a wooden spoon. It is saved for the most dire situations (open rebelliousness, lying, hitting other children), but when it is needed, I reach for it. We can't be afraid to spank.

With the spanking should come much instruction. Before the spanking we should sit down and carefully explain to our child why he or she is being punished. The spanking should never be done in anger. It you are still hot, then wait until you've cooled down. After the spanking, time should be spent holding and loving the child. Once again we need to explain why we punished them and make sure they understand the reason. Also, let them know that you still love them in spite of their actions or the consequences of them. Discipline is a way of showing love. When we fail to discipline our children, we fail to love them. Here is what Proverbs has to say about discipline:

Don't spare the rod.

> He who spares the rod hates his son,
>> but he who loves him is careful to discipline him
>> (Proverbs 13:24).

Discipline will save your kids.

> Discipline your son, for in that there is hope;
>> do not be a willing party to his death
>> (Proverbs 19:18).

> Do not withhold discipline from a child;
>> if you punish him with the rod, he will not die.
> Punish him with the rod
>> and save his soul from death
>> (Proverbs 23:13-14).

Disciple drives out foolishness.

> Folly is bound up in the heart of a child,
>> but the rod of discipline will drive it far from him
>> (Proverbs 22:15).

> Discipline your son, and he will give you peace;
>> he will bring delight to your soul
>> (Proverbs 29:17).

Lack of discipline will be your disgrace.

> The rod of correction imparts wisdom,
>
>> but a child left to himself disgraces his mother
>> (Proverbs 29:15).

Make lying a "capital offense."

> Truthful lips endure forever,
>> but a lying tongue lasts only a moment
>> (Proverbs 12:19).

If we want our children to last forever, then we must teach them to tell the truth. Above everything else, Leigh and I expect this from our children. We are trying to teach them that no matter what they have done, telling the truth about it will lessen its severity. On the other hand, if they did some trivial thing but lied about it, then it becomes a big deal. In our house lying is a "capital offense." It is always punished swiftly and severely. We want to be able to trust our children, and in order to do this, they must understand that lying is not acceptable in any form.

Teach generosity.

> A generous man will prosper;
> he who refreshes others will himself be refreshed
> (Proverbs 11:25).

> If a man shuts his ears to the cry of the poor,
> he too will cry out and not be answered
> (Proverbs 21:13).

At an early age children should be taught to share. They must learn to take turns, even with their favorite toy. If we want our children to prosper, then we must teach them to be generous. It is good periodically to sort through your children's toys with them and pick some out to be given away. They shouldn't just pick out worn and discarded toys, but some well-loved toys also. This is a real test of their heart and teaches generosity.

Teach friendliness and gratitude.

> An unfriendly man pursues selfish ends;
> he defies all sound judgment
> (Proverbs 18:1).

Our children should be taught to be friendly. "Thank you" should fall naturally off their lips. I don't believe our kids should run up and give hugs to strangers, but they should be expected to look people in the eyes and greet them warmly. When a thank-you is the proper response, the same applies. Children should be taught to show hospitality and appreciation.

Teach children the value of hard work.

> He who gathers crops in summer is a wise son,
> but he who sleeps during harvest is a disgraceful
> son (Proverbs 10:5).

Children should be given chores to do with the expectation that they complete them. If parents wait on them hand and foot, they will grow up expecting this treatment. Children should pick up after themselves, keep their rooms tidy, clean their dishes after a meal, and wash behind their ears (OK, that might be a stretch). But whatever jobs you give your children, the expectation must be that these are their jobs to perform, and they must be done well. Consistency here, as in all areas of life, will pay big dividends.

Make your children proud of you.

> Children's children are a crown to the aged,
> and parents are the pride of their children
> (Proverbs 17:6).

We want our children to make us proud, but are you making your child proud? Dads, can you still throw a baseball with a moderate amount of accuracy and velocity? Can you name the starting quarterback for the Green Bay Packers or the Dallas Cowboys? Have you seen the latest flick everyone is talking about? Do you think Pearl Jam is something you spread on toast? Don't get lost in the seventies: Be up on the latest fads. This will help your kids feel like you care about what they care about.

Moms, are you up on the latest styles? Does your hairstyle look the same as it did in your high school yearbook? Have you stayed in shape over the years? Does your daughter want to be like you? Neil Young said, "It's better to burn out, than fade away." I once heard Sam Laing, co-author of *Raising Awesome Kids in Troubled Times*,[1] comment,

> Cool without commitment is worldliness and will fail, but commitment without cool will also fail, and will break the hearts of more and more of our disciples who are too lazy and selfish to "become all things to all men."

Let's give our children every reason to be proud of us. Let's stay up-to-date, in shape, and looking great!

Children 101

Trust proper training.

> Train a child in the way he should go,
> and when he is old he will not turn from it
> (Proverbs 22:6).

No area of life can cause greater anxiety for us than our children. When one of them is sick, we would rather have the fever and vomiting ourselves than to watch them suffer. When they leave for school, we want to follow them around with a hidden camera and watch their every move. If we are tempted not to trust God in any area of life, it is with our kids. God has promised that if we train them in the way they should go, then when they are old, they will remember their training and follow his way. We must trust God here. Worry will not help them be faithful. It will only steal the joy of watching our kids grow up in the Lord. We must trust his promise and train our kids in his way. Train, train, train!

The book of Proverbs is a training manual for raising children. We should use it as our handbook while training our kids. We should read it to them, memorize scriptures from it and teach these to our children. It should be a constant resource book for information on raising kids. We should use it in discipling times and family devotionals. God has given us a great resource as parents—the book of Proverbs. Let's wear it out as we study it for insight into how to raise our kids.

8

Purity and Lust

The LORD detests the thoughts of the wicked,
but those of the pure are pleasing to him.

PROVERBS 15:26

The Bible has much to say on the topics of lust and purity. The reader of Proverbs does not go far before hearing about the joy of married love and the foolishness of adultery. Early in the book the reader hears of the seductive voice of the adulteress. Her tempting voice calls young men to their destruction like the mythical sirens called the sailors of Odysseus's day toward the rocky coast.

Perhaps the reason Proverbs has so much to say about issues of lust and purity is that Solomon reflected upon the destructive course David took in pursuing Bathsheba, his mother. Or perhaps, he was sharing the outcome of his own life: He amassed over 1,000 wives and concubines to be his sexual partners. For whatever reason, Proverbs contains strong warnings against lust and resonates with the call for purity.

We live in a time when we desperately need godly teaching about sex. God created sex to be enjoyed by a husband and a wife. Sex is good, very good. What we have done with it has often been shameful. Sam and Geri Laing comment on this in their excellent book on marriage entitled *Friends and Lovers:*

> God did not make sex dirty, shameful or evil—it is we who have done that. We have dragged it from its pristine glory and have stained it with selfishness and perversion. It is we who have turned its great power for good to unspeakable horrors of destruction, degradation and misery. It is we who have turned the sex act into a curse word.[1]

It is time we reclaimed the proper understanding of our sexual nature. It is not true that the impure have more fun. If we are to enjoy all of life as God intended, we must fight against lust and impurity. The proverbs give specific instruction for this fight.

The Path to Purity

Lust leads to destruction.

> With persuasive words she [the adulteress] led him
>   astray;
>   she seduced him with her smooth talk.
> All at once he followed her
>   like an ox going to the slaughter,
> like a deer stepping into a noose
>   till an arrow pierces his liver,
> like a bird darting into a snare,
>   little knowing it will cost him his life
>   (Proverbs 7:21-23).

> Can a man walk on hot coals
>   without his feet being scorched?
> So is he who sleeps with another man's wife;
>   no one who touches her will go unpunished
>   (Proverbs 6:28-29).

The proverbs are very clear that nothing good will come out of giving in to lust. The metaphors are heaped one on top of the other—an ox to slaughter, a deer in a noose, a bird in a snare, feet on hot coals. The pursuit of lustful satisfaction is a one-way street to destruction. To overcome lust in your life, you must understand this. You must believe that giving in to lust is not only sinful, but wasteful. Whether it is the lustful look or the lustful act, both are wrong before God. The momentary pleasure of the act may lie and tell us it is natural, pleasing and normal, but the Bible says it is sinful and ruinous.

You do not have to look far to see the destructive effects of giving in to lust—affairs, divorce, unwanted pregnancies, abortion, sexual abuse, pedophilia (child molestation), sexually transmitted diseases, guilt, a loss of innocence. Years ago Hugh Hefner and others advocated a playboy life-style that exploded with the "sexual revolution." Along with this revolution came a rise in sexually aggravated crime, divorce, prostitution and pornography. Lust is a sin that once fed, has a unceasing appetite for more.

Watch your companions.

> My son, if sinners entice you,
>   do not give in to them.
> If they say, "Come along with us;
>   let's lie in wait for someone's blood,
>   let's waylay some harmless soul;
> let's swallow them alive, like the grave,
>   and whole, like those who go down to the pit;
> we will get all sorts of valuable things
>   and fill our houses with plunder;
> throw in your lot with us,
>   and we will share a common purse"—
> my son, do not go along with them,
>   do not set foot on their paths;
> for their feet rush into sin,
>   they are swift to shed blood
>   (Proverbs 1:10-16).

> Wisdom will save you from the ways of wicked men,
>   from men whose words are perverse,
> who leave the straight paths
>   to walk in dark ways,
> who delight in doing wrong
>   and rejoice in the perverseness of evil,

> whose paths are crooked
> and who are devious in their ways
> (Proverbs 2:12-15).

I love Disney movies. I like both the old ones and the new ones and one of my favorites is *Pinocchio*. A wooden puppet comes to life and begins to experience life in the world. Part of his education comes at the hands of two hoodlums who teach him to skip school, smoke cigars and vandalize property. In the end the boys who live like this are turned into donkeys. Pinocchio himself narrowly escapes being turned into a donkey with the help of his conscience, Jiminy Cricket. It is a classic tale of how "bad company corrupts good character" (1 Corinthians 15:33). It is a valuable lesson to learn.

Most of us can remember some of our early school friends who took it upon themselves to educate us about sex. At the time we thought they were doing us a great favor. Looking back, we realize they were really opening Pandora's box. Imagine the scars to our self-esteem that could have been saved if we had avoided these so-called "friends." Hindsight is better than foresight. The proverbs warn us to choose our friends carefully. We must pick friends that will encourage us spiritually and not lead us down the path of destruction.

Avoid evil by clinging to the good.

> My son, keep my words
> and store up my commands within you.
> Keep my commands and you will live;
> guard my teachings as the apple of your eye.
> Bind them on your fingers;
> write them on the tablets of your heart.
> Say to wisdom, "You are my sister,"
> and call understanding your kinsman;
> they will deep you from the adulteress,
> from the wayward wife with her seductive words
> (Proverbs 7:1-5).

There is an old computer adage that says, "Garbage in, garbage out." This saying is also true spiritually. What we put into our minds is what will come out in our actions. This is why pornography is so damaging. Once the images are in our minds they can stay for weeks, months, even years. The only way to refocus our minds is by concentrating on pure ideals.

This is one reason why consistent, daily Bible study and prayer are so important to the disciple. By beginning the day with the positive message of God's word, we fight against the constant bombardment from the world around us. During the day, the world is on the attack—through advertisements, pop music, and the lives of coworkers or fellow students. To guard against this onslaught of worldliness, our minds must be prepared and armed for battle. We cannot miss our time with God any day.

Avoid the attraction.

> Do not set foot on the path of the wicked
>   or walk in the way of evil men.
> Avoid it, do not travel on it;
>   turn from it and go on your way
>   (Proverbs 4:14-15).

> Let your eyes look straight ahead,
>   fix your gaze directly before you.
> Make level paths for your feet
>   and take only ways that are firm.
> Do not swerve to the right or the left;
>   keep your foot from evil
>   (Proverbs 4:25-27).

One way not to give in to lust is to avoid it or flee from it. Avoid the places that are the most tempting—bars and dance clubs, worldly parties, seedy parts of town. I have known brothers who had to kick a drug habit when becoming a disciple. Whenever they would walk down the street where they once used drugs, they would be tempted to use again. To overcome the temptation they would have to make a conscious decision not even to walk down that street anymore. This might have meant taking the subway an extra stop or walking a few extra blocks, but for them the inconvenience was well worth it.

Our sexual appetite has to be starved the same way a drug habit would have to be starved. We must avoid the things that tempt us the most. If we are drawn to sordid programs on television late at night, then we must not watch television late at night. If there is a certain coworker who tempts us, then conversation with that coworker must stay on a strict "business only" level in "business only" situations. Certain catalogues that are sent to our houses should go straight to the garbage. To conquer lust we must avoid it.

Let's not kid ourselves that this battle will be easy. If the great King David could fall prey to lust, then all of us are susceptible to it as well. It is one of Satan's major weapons, but we must stand ready to do battle with him. We must arm ourselves with the sword of the Spirit and the shield of faith. We can have victory in this area of our lives, but it will only come with a resolute mind and a fighting spirit. We must fight for purity in our lives.

Notes

A Book That Brings Blessings

[1]James L. Crenshaw, *Old Testament Wisdom: An Introduction* (Atlanta: John Knox Press, 1981), p. 68.

[2]Gerhard von Rad, *God at Work in Israel* (Nashville: Abingdon Press, 1980), p. 178.

[3]Theodore H. Robinson, *The Poetry of the Old Testament* (London: Gerald Duckworth and Co. Ltd., 1947), p. 184.

An Outline of Proverbs

[1]Gleason L. Archer, *A Survey of the Old Testament: Introduction* (Chicago: Moody Press, 1974), p. 466.

[2]Crenshaw, p. 72.

The Language of Proverbs

[1]Crenshaw, p. 67.

[2]Crenshaw, p. 67.

[3]R.B.Y. Scott, *The Way of Wisdom: In the Old Testament* (New York: Macmillian Publishing Co., Inc., 1971), p. 58.

[4]Crenshaw, p. 67-68.

[5]R.B.Y. Scott, pp. 59-63.

CHAPTER 2 Pride and Humility

[1]*Parables of Kierkegaard,* edited by Thomas C. Oden (Princeton, N.J.: Princeton University Press, 1978), p. 19.

CHAPTER 3 Advice and Instruction

[1]David W. Berçot, *Will the Real Heretics Please Stand Up* (Tyler, Tex.: Scroll Publishing Company, 1989), p. 20.

[2]John Donne, "Meditation XVII," *Devotions.*

CHAPTER 4 Integrity

[1]Larry Dorman, "More than a Drop of Integrity," *The New York Times,* March 20, 1996.

[2]Stephen Carter, *Integrity* (New York: BasicBooks, 1996), pp. 5-6.

[3]*The American Heritage Dictionary,* Third Edition (New York: Houghton Mifflin Company, 1992), p. 938.

CHAPTER 6 Hard Work and Laziness

[1]Michael Quoist, *Prayers,* translated by Agnes M. Forsyth and Anne Marie de Commaille (New York: Sheed and Ward, 1963), pp. 96-98.

[2]Richard Foster, *Celebration of Discipline* (San Francisco: Harper and Row, Publishers, 1978), p. 79.

CHAPTER 7 Children

[1]Sam and Geri Laing, *Raising Awesome Kids in Troubled Times* (Woburn, Mass.: Discipleship Publications International, 1994).

CHAPTER 8 Purity and Lust

[1]Sam and Geri Laing, *Friends and Lovers* (Woburn, Mass.: Discipleship Publications International, 1996), p. 81.

Topical Index

ABOMINATIONS
3:31-32
Do not envy a violent man
  or choose any of his ways,
[32]for the LORD detests a perverse man
  but takes the upright into his
    confidence.

6:16-19
There are six things the LORD hates,
  seven that are detestable to him:
    [17]haughty eyes,
    a lying tongue,
    hands that shed innocent blood,
    [18]a heart that devises wicked
      schemes,
    feet that are quick to rush into evil,
    [19]a false witness who pours out lies
    and a man who stirs up dissension
      among brothers.

8:7
"My [wisdom's] mouth speaks what is
  true,
  for my lips detest wickedness."

11:20
The LORD detests men of perverse heart
  but he delights in those whose ways
    are blameless.

12:22
The LORD detests lying lips,
  but he delights in men who are
    truthful.

13:19
A longing fulfilled is sweet to the soul,
  but fools detest turning from evil.

15:8-9
The LORD detests the sacrifice of the
  wicked,
  but the prayer of the upright pleases
    him.

[9]The LORD detests the way of the
  wicked
  but he loves those who pursue
    righteousness.

16:5
The LORD detests all the proud of heart.
  Be sure of this: They will not go
    unpunished.

16:12
Kings detest wrongdoing,
  for a throne is established through
    righteousness.

17:15
Acquitting the guilty and condemning
    the innocent—
  the LORD detests them both.

20:10
Differing weights and differing
    measures—
  the LORD detests them both.

20:23
The LORD detests differing weights,
  and dishonest scales do not please
    him.

21:27
The sacrifice of the wicked is detest-
    able—
  how much more so when brought
    with evil intent!

24:9
The schemes of folly are sin,
  and men detest a mocker.

26:24-25
A malicious man disguises himself with
  his lips,
  but in his heart he harbors deceit.
[25]Though his speech is charming, do
  not believe him,
  for seven abominations fill his heart.

28:9
If anyone turns a deaf ear to the law,
  even his prayers are detestable.

29:27
The righteous detest the dishonest;
  the wicked detest the upright.

ADULTERY
2:16-19

It [wisdom] will save you also from the
adulteress,
from the wayward wife with her
seductive words,
[17]who has left the partner of her youth
and ignored the covenant she made
before God.
[18]For her house leads down to death
and her paths to the spirits of the
dead.
[19]None who go to her return
or attain the paths of life.

5:3-20

For the lips of an adulteress drip honey,
and her speech is smoother than oil;
[4]but in the end she is bitter as gall,
sharp as a double-edged sword.
[5]Her feet go down to death;
her steps lead straight to the grave.
[6]She gives no thought to the way of
life;
her paths are crooked, but she knows
it not.

[7]Now then, my sons, listen to me;
do not turn aside from what I say.
[8]Keep to a path far from her,
do not go near the door of her
house,
[9]lest you give your best strength to
others
and your years to one who is cruel,
[10]lest strangers feast on your wealth
and your toil enrich another man's
house.
[11]At the end of your life you will groan,
when your flesh and body are spent.
[12]You will say, "How I hated discipline!
How my heart spurned correction!
[13]I would not obey my teachers
or listen to my instructors.
[14]I have come to the brink of utter ruin
in the midst of the whole assembly."

[15]Drink water from your own cistern,
running water from your own well.
[16]Should your springs overflow in the
streets,

your streams of water in the public
squares?
[17]Let them be yours alone,
never to be shared with strangers.
[18]May your fountain be blessed,
and may you rejoice in the wife of
your youth.
[19]A loving doe, a graceful deer—
may her breasts satisfy you always,
may you ever be captivated by her
love.
[20]Why be captivated, my son, by an
adulteress?
Why embrace the bosom of another
man's wife?

6:20-29

My son, keep your father's commands
and do not forsake your mother's
teaching.
[21]Bind them upon your heart forever;
fasten them around your neck.
[22]When you walk, they will guide you;
when you sleep, they will watch over
you;
when you awake, they will speak to
you.
[23]For these commands are a lamp,
this teaching is a light,
and the corrections of discipline
are the way to life,
[24]keeping you from the immoral
woman,
from the smooth tongue of the
wayward wife.
[25]Do not lust in your heart after her
beauty
or let her captivate you with her
eyes,
[26]for the prostitute reduces you to a loaf
of bread,
and the adulteress preys upon your
very life.
[27]Can a man scoop fire into his lap
without his clothes being burned?
[28]Can a man walk on hot coals
without his feet being scorched?
[29]So is he who sleeps with another
man's wife;
no one who touches her will go
unpunished.

7:1-27
My son, keep my words
and store up my commands within
you.
²Keep my commands and you will live;
guard my teachings as the apple of
your eye.
³Bind them on your fingers;
write them on the tablet of your
heart.
⁴Say to wisdom, "You are my sister,"
and call understanding your kinsman;
⁵they will keep you from the adulteress,
from the wayward wife with her
seductive words.

⁶At the window of my house
I looked out through the lattice.
⁷I saw among the simple,
I noticed among the young men,
a youth who lacked judgment.
⁸He was going down the street near her
corner,
walking along in the direction of her
house
⁹at twilight, as the day was fading,
as the dark of night set in.

¹⁰Then out came a woman to meet him,
dressed like a prostitute and with
crafty intent.
¹¹(She is loud and defiant,
her feet never stay at home;
¹²now in the street, now in the squares,
at every corner she lurks.)
¹³She took hold of him and kissed him
and with a brazen face she said:

¹⁴"I have fellowship offerings at home;
today I fulfilled my vows.
¹⁵So I came out to meet you;
I looked for you and have found you!
¹⁶I have covered my bed
with colored linens from Egypt.
¹⁷I have perfumed my bed
with myrrh, aloes and cinnamon.
¹⁸Come, let's drink deep of love till
morning;
let's enjoy ourselves with love!
¹⁹My husband is not at home;
he has gone on a long journey.

²⁰He took his purse filled with money
and will not be home till full moon."

²¹With persuasive words she led him
astray;
she seduced him with her smooth
talk.
²²All at once he followed her
like an ox going to the slaughter,
like a deer stepping into a noose
²³till an arrow pierces his liver,
like a bird darting into a snare,
little knowing it will cost him his life.

²⁴Now then, my sons, listen to me;
pay attention to what I say.
²⁵Do not let your heart turn to her ways
or stray into her paths.
²⁶Many are the victims she has brought
down;
her slain are a mighty throng.
²⁷Her house is a highway to the grave,
leading down to the chambers of
death.

22:14
The mouth of an adulteress is a deep
pit;
he who is under the LORD's wrath will
fall into it.

23:26-28
My son, give me your heart
and let your eyes keep to my ways,
²⁷for a prostitute is a deep pit
and a wayward wife is a narrow well.
²⁸Like a bandit she lies in wait,
and multiplies the unfaithful among
men.

29:3
A man who loves wisdom brings joy to
his father,
but a companion of prostitutes
squanders his wealth.

30:20
"This is the way of an adulteress:
She eats and wipes her mouth
and says, 'I've done nothing wrong.'"

ADVICE

(See also Discernment, Discipline, Rebukes)

1:2
[Proverbs] for attaining wisdom and
    discipline;
for understanding words of insight...

8:14
"Counsel and sound judgment are mine
    [wisdom's];
I have understanding and power."

10:17
He who heeds discipline shows the
    way to life,
but whoever ignores correction leads
    others astray.

11:14
For lack of guidance a nation falls,
but many advisers make victory sure.

12:1
Whoever loves discipline loves
    knowledge,
but he who hates correction is stupid.

12:5
The plans of the righteous are just,
but the advice of the wicked is
    deceitful.

12:15
The way of a fool seems right to him,
but a wise man listens to advice.

13:10
Pride only breeds quarrels,
but wisdom is found in those who
    take advice.

13:13
He who scorns instruction will pay for it,
but he who respects a command is
    rewarded.

13:18
He who ignores discipline comes to
    poverty and shame,
but whoever heeds correction is
    honored.

15:5
A fool spurns his father's discipline,
but whoever heeds correction shows
    prudence.

15:10
Stern discipline awaits him who leaves
    the path;
he who hates correction will die.

15:12
A mocker resents correction;
he will not consult the wise.

15:22
Plans fail for lack of counsel,
but with many advisers they succeed.

16:20-21
Whoever gives heed to instruction
    prospers,
and blessed is he who trusts in the
    LORD.

[21]The wise in heart are called
    discerning,
and pleasant words promote
    instruction.

16:23
A wise man's heart guides his mouth,
and his lips promote instruction.

18:15
The heart of the discerning acquires
    knowledge;
the ears of the wise seek it out.

19:16
He who obeys instructions guards his
    life,
but he who is contemptuous of his
    ways will die.

19:20
Listen to advice and accept instruction,
and in the end you will be wise.

19:27
Stop listening to instruction, my son,
and you will stray from the words of
knowledge.

20:18
Make plans by seeking advice;
if you wage war, obtain guidance.

23:12
Apply your heart to instruction
and your ears to words of knowledge.

24:5-6
A wise man has great power,
and a man of knowledge increases
strength;
⁶for waging war you need guidance,
and for victory many advisers.

25:12
Like an earring of gold or an ornament
of fine gold
is a wise man's rebuke to a listening
ear.

27:9
Perfume and incense bring joy to the
heart,
and the pleasantness of one's friend
springs from his earnest
counsel.

AGE
16:31
Gray hair is a crown of splendor;
it is attained by a righteous life.

20:29
The glory of young men is their
strength,
gray hair the splendor of the old.

ALCOHOL
20:1
Wine is a mocker and beer a brawler;
whoever is led astray by them is not
wise.

21:17
He who loves pleasure will become
poor;
whoever loves wine and oil will
never be rich.

23:19-21
Listen, my son, and be wise,
and keep your heart on the right
path.
²⁰Do not join those who drink too
much wine
or gorge themselves on meat,
²¹for drunkards and gluttons become
poor,
and drowsiness clothes them in rags.

23:29-35
Who has woe? Who has sorrow?
Who has strife? Who has complaints?
Who has needless bruises? Who has
bloodshot eyes?
³⁰Those who linger over wine,
who go to sample bowls of mixed
wine.
³¹Do not gaze at wine when it is red,
when it sparkles in the cup,
when it goes down smoothly!
³²In the end it bites like a snake
and poisons like a viper.
³³Your eyes will see strange sights
and your mind imagine confusing
things.
³⁴You will be like one sleeping on the
high seas,
lying on top of the rigging.
³⁵"They hit me," you will say, "but I'm
not hurt!
They beat me, but I don't feel it!
When will I wake up
so I can find another drink?"

31:4-7
"It is not for kings, O Lemuel—
not for kings to drink wine,
not for rulers to crave beer,
⁵lest they drink and forget what the law
decrees,
and deprive all the oppressed of their
rights.

ALCOHOL

⁶Give beer to those who are perishing,
   wine to those who are in anguish;
⁷let them drink and forget their poverty
   and remember their misery no more."

ANGER
(See Temper)

ANIMALS
6:6-8
Go to the ant, you sluggard;
   consider its ways and be wise!
⁷It has no commander,
   no overseer or ruler,
⁸yet it stores its provisions in summer
   and gathers its food at harvest.

17:12
Better to meet a bear robbed of her
      cubs
   than a fool in his folly.

19:12
A king's rage is like the roar of a lion,
   but his favor is like dew on the grass.

20:2
A king's wrath is like the roar of a lion;
   he who angers him forfeits his life.

21:31
The horse is made ready for the day of
      battle,
   but victory rests with the LORD.

22:13
The sluggard says, "There is a lion
      outside!"
   or, "I will be murdered in the streets!"

23:5
Cast but a glance at riches, and they are
      gone,
   for they will surely sprout wings
   and fly off to the sky like an eagle.

23:32
In the end it [wine] bites like a snake
   and poisons like a viper.

26:2-3
Like a fluttering sparrow or a darting
      swallow,
   an undeserved curse does not come
      to rest.

³A whip for the horse, a halter for the
      donkey,
   and a rod for the backs of fools!

26:11
As a dog returns to its vomit,
   so a fool repeats his folly.

26:17
Like one who seizes a dog by the ears
   is a passer-by who meddles in a
      quarrel not his own.

28:1
The wicked man flees though no one
      pursues,
   but the righteous are as bold as a
      lion.

28:15
Like a roaring lion or a charging bear
   is a wicked man ruling over a
      helpless people.

30:24-31
"Four things on earth are small,
   yet they are extremely wise:
²⁵Ants are creatures of little strength,
   yet they store up their food in the
      summer;
²⁶coneys are creatures of little power,
   yet they make their home in the
      crags;
²⁷locusts have no king,
   yet they advance together in ranks;
²⁸a lizard can be caught with the hand,
   yet it is found in kings' palaces.

²⁹"There are three things that are stately
      in their stride,
   four that move with stately bearing:
³⁰a lion, mighty among beasts,
   who retreats before nothing;

[31]a strutting rooster, a he-goat,
  and a king with his army around
    him."

ANXIETY
12:25
An anxious heart weighs a man down,
  but a kind word cheers him up.

24:19-20
Do not fret because of evil men
  or be envious of the wicked,
[20]for the evil man has no future hope,
  and the lamp of the wicked will be
    snuffed out.

ARROGANCE
(See Pride)

BAD COMPANIONS
(See Friendship)

BARGAIN DRIVER
(See Financial Matters)

BLAMELESS
(Also see Righteousness, Upright)

2:7
He [God] holds victory in store for the
    upright,
  he is a shield to those whose walk is
    blameless...

2:21
For the upright will live in the land,
  and the blameless will remain in it...

11:5
The righteousness of the blameless
    makes a straight way for them,
  but the wicked are brought down by
    their own wickedness.

11:20
The Lord detests men of perverse heart
  but he delights in those whose ways
    are blameless.

19:1
Better a poor man whose walk is
    blameless
  than a fool whose lips are perverse.

20:7
The righteous man leads a blameless
    life;
  blessed are his children after him.

28:6
Better a poor man whose walk is
    blameless
  than a rich man whose ways are
    perverse.

28:10
He who leads the upright along an evil
    path
  will fall into his own trap,
  but the blameless will receive a good
    inheritance.

28:18
He whose walk is blameless is kept
    safe,
  but he whose ways are perverse will
    suddenly fall.

BLESSINGS
(Also see Curses)
3:3
Let love and faithfulness never leave
    you;
  bind them around your neck,
  write them on the tablet of your
    heart.

3:18
She [wisdom] is a tree of life to those
    who embrace her;
  those who lay hold of her will be
    blessed.

3:33
The Lord's curse is on the house of the
    wicked,
  but he blesses the home of the
    righteous.

5:18
May your fountain be blessed,
and may you rejoice in the wife of
your youth.

8:32
"Now then, my sons, listen to me
[wisdom];
blessed are those who keep my ways."

10:6-7
Blessings crown the head of the
righteous,
but violence overwhelms the mouth
of the wicked.

⁷The memory of the righteous will be a
blessing,
but the name of the wicked will rot.

10:22
The blessing of the LORD brings wealth,
and he adds no trouble to it.

11:11
Through the blessing of the upright a
city is exalted,
but by the mouth of the wicked it is
destroyed.

11:26
People curse the man who hoards
grain,
but blessing crowns him who is
willing to sell.

14:21
He who despises his neighbor sins,
but blessed is he who is kind to the
needy.

16:20
Whoever gives heed to instruction
prospers,
and blessed is he who trusts in the
LORD.

20:7
The righteous man leads a blameless
life;
blessed are his children after him.

20:21
An inheritance quickly gained at the
beginning
will not be blessed at the end.

22:9
A generous man will himself be
blessed,
for he shares his food with the poor.

24:25
But it will go well with those who
convict the guilty,
and rich blessing will come upon
them.

27:14
If a man loudly blesses his neighbor
early in the morning,
it will be taken as a curse.

28:14
Blessed is the man who always fears
the LORD,
but he who hardens his heart falls
into trouble.

28:20
A faithful man will be richly blessed,
but one eager to get rich will not go
unpunished.

29:18
Where there is no revelation, the
people cast off restraint;
but blessed is he who keeps the law.

BOLDNESS
(Also see Zeal)
21:29
A wicked man puts up a bold front,
but an upright man gives thought to
his ways.

28:1
The wicked man flees though no one
pursues,
but the righteous are as bold as a lion.

BRIBES
(See Financial Matters)

BROTHER
(Also see Family)
6:16, 19
There are six things the Lord hates,
seven that are detestable to him:
...a false witness who pours out
lies
and a man who stirs up dissension
among brothers.

17:2
A wise servant will rule over a
disgraceful son,
and will share the inheritance as one
of the brothers.

17:17
A friend loves at all times,
and a brother is born for adversity.

18:9
One who is slack in his work
is brother to one who destroys.

18:19
An offended brother is more unyielding
than a fortified city,
and disputes are like the barred gates
of a citadel.

18:24
A man of many companions may come
to ruin,
but there is a friend who sticks closer
than a brother.

27:10
Do not forsake your friend and the
friend of your father,
and do not go to your brother's
house when disaster strikes
you—
better a neighbor nearby than a
brother far away.

BUSINESS
*(See Financial Matters, Poverty,
Prosperity)*

CALAMITY
(See Disaster)

CHILDREN
(Also see Discipline, Family, Parents)
10:1
The proverbs of Solomon:

A wise son brings joy to his father,
but a foolish son grief to his mother.

10:5
He who gathers crops in summer is a
wise son,
but he who sleeps during harvest is a
disgraceful son.

13:1
A wise son heeds his father's instruction,
but a mocker does not listen to
rebuke.

13:22
A good man leaves an inheritance for
his children's children,
but a sinner's wealth is stored up for
the righteous.

13:24
He who spares the rod hates his son,
but he who loves him is careful to
discipline him.

14:26
He who fears the Lord has a secure
fortress,
and for his children it will be a
refuge.

15:5
A fool spurns his father's discipline,
but whoever heeds correction shows
prudence.

15:20
A wise son brings joy to his father,
but a foolish man despises his
mother.

17:2
A wise servant will rule over a
disgraceful son,

and will share the inheritance as one
of the brothers.

17:6
Children's children are a crown to the
aged,
and parents are the pride of their
children.

17:21
To have a fool for a son brings grief;
there is no joy for the father of a fool.

17:25
A foolish son brings grief to his father
and bitterness to the one who bore him.

19:13
A foolish son is his father's ruin,
and a quarrelsome wife is like a
constant dripping.

19:18
Discipline your son, for in that there is
hope;
do not be a willing party to his death.

19:26
He who robs his father and drives out
his mother
is a son who brings shame and
disgrace.

20:7
The righteous man leads a blameless
life;
blessed are his children after him.

20:11
Even a child is known by his actions,
by whether his conduct is pure and
right.

22:6
Train a child in the way he should go,
and when he is old he will not turn
from it.

22:15
Folly is bound up in the heart of a
child,

but the rod of discipline will drive it
far from him.

23:13-16
Do not withhold discipline from a
child;
if you punish him with the rod, he
will not die.
[14]Punish him with the rod
and save his soul from death.

[15]My son, if your heart is wise,
then my heart will be glad;
[16]my inmost being will rejoice
when your lips speak what is right.

23:19-25
Listen, my son, and be wise,
and keep your heart on the right
path.
[20]Do not join those who drink too
much wine
or gorge themselves on meat,
[21]for drunkards and gluttons become
poor,
and drowsiness clothes them in rags.

[22]Listen to your father, who gave you
life,
and do not despise your mother
when she is old.
[23]Buy the truth and do not sell it;
get wisdom, discipline and understanding.
[24]The father of a righteous man has
great joy;
he who has a wise son delights in
him.
[25]May your father and mother be glad;
may she who gave you birth rejoice!

24:13-14
Eat honey, my son, for it is good;
honey from the comb is sweet to
your taste.
[14]Know also that wisdom is sweet to
your soul;
if you find it, there is a future hope
for you,
and your hope will not be cut off.

24:21-22
Fear the LORD and the king, my son,
and do not join with the rebellious,
²²for those two will send sudden
destruction upon them,
and who knows what calamities they
can bring?

27:11
Be wise, my son, and bring joy to my
heart;
then I can answer anyone who treats
me with contempt.

29:7
The righteous care about justice for the
poor,
but the wicked have no such
concern.

29:15
The rod of correction imparts wisdom,
but a child left to himself disgraces
his mother.

29:17
Discipline your son, and he will give
you peace;
he will bring delight to your soul.

30:17
"The eye that mocks a father,
that scorns obedience to a mother,
will be pecked out by the ravens of the
valley,
will be eaten by the vultures."

COMMANDS
(Also see The Law, Obedience)
2:1, 5
My son, if you accept my words
and store up my commands within
you,
...then you will understand the fear
of the LORD
and find the knowledge of God.

3:1-2
My son, do not forget my teaching,
but keep my commands in your
heart,

²for they will prolong your life many
years
and bring you prosperity.

6:20-24
My son, keep your father's commands
and do not forsake your mother's
teaching.
²¹Bind them upon your heart forever;
fasten them around your neck.
²²When you walk, they will guide you;
when you sleep, they will watch over
you;
when you awake, they will speak to
you.
²³For these commands are a lamp,
this teaching is a light,
and the corrections of discipline
are the way to life,
²⁴keeping you from the immoral
woman,
from the smooth tongue of the
wayward wife.

7:1-3
My son, keep my words
and store up my commands within
you.
²Keep my commands and you will live;
guard my teachings as the apple of
your eye.
³Bind them on your fingers;
write them on the tablet of your heart.

10:8
The wise in heart accept commands,
but a chattering fool comes to ruin.

13:13
He who scorns instruction will pay for
it,
but he who respects a command is
rewarded.

19:16
He who obeys instructions guards his
life,
but he who is contemptuous of his
ways will die.

COMMITMENT
(Also see Law, Obedience)
16:3
Commit to the Lord whatever you do,
and your plans will succeed.

COMPASSION
(See Justice, Oppression, Poverty)
19:17
He who is kind to the poor lends to the
Lord,
and he will reward him for what he
has done.

22:9
A generous man will himself be blessed,
for he shares his food with the poor.

28:27
He who gives to the poor will lack
nothing,
but he who closes his eyes to them
receives many curses.

29:7
The righteous care about justice for the
poor,
but the wicked have no such concern.

CONFESSION
28:13
He who conceals his sins does not
prosper,
but whoever confesses and re-
nounces them finds mercy.

CORRECTION
(See Justice, Oppression, Poverty)

COURSE
(See Path)

CRAFTY
7:10
Then out came a woman to meet him,
dressed like a prostitute and with
crafty intent.

12:2
A good man obtains favor from the Lord,
but the Lord condemns a crafty man.

14:7
Stay away from a foolish man,
for you will not find knowledge on
his lips.

CROWN
4:9
"She will set a garland of grace on your
head
and present you with a crown of
splendor."

10:6
Blessings crown the head of the
righteous,
but violence overwhelms the mouth
of the wicked.

11:26
People curse the man who hoards
grain,
but blessing crowns him who is
willing to sell.

12:4
A wife of noble character is her
husband's crown,
but a disgraceful wife is like decay in
his bones.

14:18
The simple inherit folly,
but the prudent are crowned with
knowledge.

14:24
The wealth of the wise is their crown,
but the folly of fools yields folly.

16:31
Gray hair is a crown of splendor;
it is attained by a righteous life.

17:6
Children's children are a crown to the
aged,
and parents are the pride of their
children.

27:24
for riches do not endure forever,

and a crown is not secure for all
generations.

CURSES
(Also see Blessings)
3:33
The LORD's curse is on the house of the
wicked,
but he blesses the home of the
righteous.

20:20
If a man curses his father or mother,
his lamp will be snuffed out in pitch
darkness.

24:24
Whoever says to the guilty, "You are
innocent"—
peoples will curse him and nations
denounce him.

26:2
Like a fluttering sparrow or a darting
swallow,
an undeserved curse does not come
to rest.

28:27
He who gives to the poor will lack
nothing,
but he who closes his eyes to them
receives many curses.

30:10
"Do not slander a servant to his master,
or he will curse you, and you will
pay for it."

DEATH
(Also see Grave, Life)
8:36
"But whoever fails to find me [wisdom]
harms himself;
all who hate me love death."

10:2
Ill-gotten treasures are of no value,
but righteousness delivers from death.

11:4
Wealth is worthless in the day of wrath,
but righteousness delivers from
death.

11:19
The truly righteous man attains life,
but he who pursues evil goes to his
death.

13:14
The teaching of the wise is a fountain
of life,
turning a man from the snares of
death.

14:12
There is a way that seems right to a
man,
but in the end it leads to death.

14:27
The fear of the LORD is a fountain of
life,
turning a man from the snares of
death.

14:32
When calamity comes, the wicked are
brought down,
but even in death the righteous have
a refuge.

15:10-11
Stern discipline awaits him who leaves
the path;
he who hates correction will die.

[11]Death and Destruction lie open before
the LORD—
how much more the hearts of men!

15:24
The path of life leads upward for the
wise
to keep him from going down to the
grave.

16:25
There is a way that seems right to a man,
but in the end it leads to death.

18:21
The tongue has the power of life and
    death,
    and those who love it will eat its
        fruit.

19:18
Discipline your son, for in that there is
    hope;
    do not be a willing party to his death.

21:16
A man who strays from the path of
    understanding
    comes to rest in the company of the
        dead.

21:25
The sluggard's craving will be the death
    of him,
    because his hands refuse to work.

23:13-14
Do not withhold discipline from a
    child;
    if you punish him with the rod, he
        will not die.
[14]Punish him with the rod
    and save his soul from death.

24:11-12
Rescue those being led away to death;
    hold back those staggering toward
        slaughter.
[12]If you say, "But we knew nothing
    about this,"
    does not he who weighs the heart
        perceive it?
Does not he who guards your life
    know it?
    Will he not repay each person
        according to what he has
            done?

27:20
Death and Destruction are never
    satisfied,
    and neither are the eyes of man.

DECEPTION
(See Lying)

DESTRUCTION
(Also see Disaster, Trouble)
1:32
For the waywardness of the simple will
    kill them,
    and the complacency of fools will
        destroy them...

6:15
Therefore disaster will overtake him [a
    scoundrel and villain] in an
        instant;
    he will suddenly be destroyed—
        without remedy.

6:32
But a man who commits adultery lacks
    judgment;
    whoever does so destroys himself.

11:3
The integrity of the upright guides them,
    but the unfaithful are destroyed by
        their duplicity.

11:9
With his mouth the godless destroys his
    neighbor,
    but through knowledge the righteous
        escape.

11:11
Through the blessing of the upright a
    city is exalted,
    but by the mouth of the wicked it is
        destroyed.

14:11
The house of the wicked will be
    destroyed,
    but the tent of the upright will
        flourish.

15:11
Death and Destruction lie open before
    the LORD—
    how much more the hearts of men!

16:18
Pride goes before destruction,
a haughty spirit before a fall.

17:19
He who loves a quarrel loves sin;
he who builds a high gate invites
destruction.

18:9
One who is slack in his work
is brother to one who destroys.

21:28
A false witness will perish,
and whoever listens to him will be
destroyed forever.

22:8
He who sows wickedness reaps
trouble,
and the rod of his fury will be
destroyed.

24:21-22
Fear the LORD and the king, my son,
and do not join with the rebellious,
²²for those two will send sudden
destruction upon them,
and who knows what calamities they
can bring?

27:20
Death and Destruction are never
satisfied,
and neither are the eyes of man.

28:24
He who robs his father or mother
and says, "It's not wrong"—
he is partner to him who destroys.

29:1
A man who remains stiff-necked after
many rebukes
will suddenly be destroyed—without
remedy.

DETESTABLE THINGS
(See Abominations)

DISASTER
(Also see Destruction, Trouble)
1:26-27
I [wisdom] in turn will laugh at your
disaster;
I will mock when calamity overtakes
you—
²⁷when calamity overtakes you like a
storm,
when disaster sweeps over you like a
whirlwind,
when distress and trouble overwhelm
you.

3:25-26
Have no fear of sudden disaster
or of the ruin that overtakes the
wicked,
²⁶for the LORD will be your confidence
and will keep your foot from being
snared.

14:32
When calamity comes, the wicked are
brought down,
but even in death the righteous have
a refuge.

16:4
The LORD works out everything for his
own ends—
even the wicked for a day of disaster.

17:5
He who mocks the poor shows
contempt for their Maker;
whoever gloats over disaster will not
go unpunished.

21:23
He who guards his mouth and his
tongue
keeps himself from calamity.

24:16
for though a righteous man falls seven
times, he rises again,
but the wicked are brought down by
calamity.

27:10
Do not forsake your friend and the friend
of your father,
and do not go to your brother's house
when disaster strikes you—
better a neighbor nearby than a
brother far away.

DISCERNMENT
(Also see Advice, Discipline, Rebukes)
1:5
let the wise listen and add to their
learning,
and let the discerning get guidance—

3:21
My son, preserve sound judgment and
discernment,
do not let them out of your sight...

8:8-9
All the words of my [wisdom's] mouth
are just;
none of them is crooked or perverse.
⁹To the discerning all of them are right;
they are faultless to those who have
knowledge.

8:12
I, wisdom, dwell together with prudence;
I possess knowledge and discretion.

10:13
Wisdom is found on the lips of the
discerning,
but a rod is for the back of him who
lacks judgment.

10:21
The lips of the righteous nourish many,
but fools die for lack of judgment.

11:12
A man who lacks judgment derides his
neighbor,
but a man of understanding holds his
tongue.

11:22
Like a gold ring in a pig's snout

is a beautiful woman who shows no
discretion.

12:11
He who works his land will have
abundant food,
but he who chases fantasies lacks
judgment.

12:15
The way of a fool seems right to him,
but a wise man listens to advice.

13:15
Good understanding wins favor,
but the way of the unfaithful is hard.

14:6
The mocker seeks wisdom and finds
none,
but knowledge comes easily to the
discerning.

14:8
The wisdom of the prudent is to give
thought to their ways,
but the folly of fools is deception.

14:15
A simple man believes anything,
but a prudent man gives thought to
his steps.

14:33
Wisdom reposes in the heart of the
discerning
and even among fools she lets herself
be known.

15:5
A fool spurns his father's discipline,
but whoever heeds correction shows
prudence.

15:14
The discerning heart seeks knowledge,
but the mouth of a fool feeds on folly.

15:21
Folly delights a man who lacks
judgment,

but a man of understanding keeps a
straight course.

15:28
The heart of the righteous weighs its
answers,
but the mouth of the wicked gushes
evil.

16:21
The wise in heart are called discerning,
and pleasant words promote
instruction.

17:10
A rebuke impresses a man of discernment
more than a hundred lashes a fool.

17:18
A man lacking in judgment strikes
hands in pledge
and puts up security for his neighbor.

17:24
A discerning man keeps wisdom in view,
but a fool's eyes wander to the ends of
the earth.

17:28 - 18:1
Even a fool is thought wise if he keeps
silent,
and discerning if he holds his tongue.

18:1An unfriendly man pursues selfish
ends;
he defies all sound judgment.

18:15
The heart of the discerning acquires
knowledge;
the ears of the wise seek it out.

18:17
The first to present his case seems right,
till another comes forward and
questions him.

19:8
He who gets wisdom loves his own soul;
he who cherishes understanding
prospers.

19:25
Flog a mocker, and the simple will
learn prudence;
rebuke a discerning man, and he will
gain knowledge.

20:16
Take the garment of one who puts up
security for a stranger;
hold it in pledge if he does it for a
wayward woman.

25:7b-8
What you have seen with your eyes
8do not bring hastily to court,
for what will you do in the end
if your neighbor puts you to shame?

25:20
Like one who takes away a garment on
a cold day,
or like vinegar poured on soda,
is one who sings songs to a heavy
heart.

28:7
He who keeps the law is a discerning
son,
but a companion of gluttons
disgraces his father.

28:11
A rich man may be wise in his own eyes,
but a poor man who has discernment
sees through him.

28:16
A tyrannical ruler lacks judgment,
but he who hates ill-gotten gain will
enjoy a long life.

DISCIPLINE
(Also see Advice, Discernment, Hard
Work, Laziness, Rebukes)
1:1-3
The proverbs of Solomon son of David,
king of Israel:

2for attaining wisdom and discipline;
for understanding words of insight;

³for acquiring a disciplined and prudent
life,
doing what is right and just and fair...

1:7
The fear of the LORD is the beginning of
knowledge,
but fools despise wisdom and
discipline.

1:29-31
"Since they hated knowledge
and did not choose to fear the LORD,
³⁰since they would not accept my
[wisdom's] advice
and spurned my rebuke,
³¹they will eat the fruit of their ways
and be filled with the fruit of their
schemes."

3:11-12
My son, do not despise the LORD's
discipline
and do not resent his rebuke,
¹²because the LORD disciplines those he
loves,
as a father the son he delights in.

5:12
You will say, "How I hated discipline!
How my heart spurned correction!"

5:23
He will die for lack of discipline,
led astray by his own great folly.

6:23
For these commands are a lamp,
this teaching is a light,
and the corrections of discipline
are the way to life...

9:13
The woman Folly is loud;
she is undisciplined and without
knowledge.

10:17
He who heeds discipline shows the
way to life,
but whoever ignores correction leads
others astray.

12:1
Whoever loves discipline loves
knowledge,
but he who hates correction is stupid.

13:1
A wise son heeds his father's instruction,
but a mocker does not listen to rebuke.

13:18
He who ignores discipline comes to
poverty and shame,
but whoever heeds correction is
honored.

13:24
He who spares the rod hates his son,
but he who loves him is careful to
discipline him.

15:5
A fool spurns his father's discipline,
but whoever heeds correction shows
prudence.

15:10
Stern discipline awaits him who leaves
the path;
he who hates correction will die.

15:12
A mocker resents correction;
he will not consult the wise.

15:31-32
He who listens to a life-giving rebuke
will be at home among the wise.

³²He who ignores discipline despises
himself,
but whoever heeds correction gains
understanding.

18:6
A fool's lips bring him strife,
and his mouth invites a beating.

19:18
Discipline your son, for in that there is
hope;
do not be a willing party to his death.

19:25
Flog a mocker, and the simple will
learn prudence;
rebuke a discerning man, and he will
gain knowledge.

19:29
Penalties are prepared for mockers,
and beatings for the backs of fools.

20:11
Even a child is known by his actions,
by whether his conduct is pure and
right.

20:30
Blows and wounds cleanse away evil,
and beatings purge the inmost being.

22:6
Train a child in the way he should go,
and when he is old he will not turn
from it.

22:15
Folly is bound up in the heart of a
child,
but the rod of discipline will drive it
far from him.

23:13-14
Do not withhold discipline from a
child;
if you punish him with the rod, he
will not die.
[14]Punish him with the rod
and save his soul from death.

23:22-23
Listen to your father, who gave you life,
and do not despise your mother
when she is old.
[23]Buy the truth and do not sell it;
get wisdom, discipline and understanding.

25:28
Like a city whose walls are broken
down
is a man who lacks self-control.

26:3
A whip for the horse, a halter for the
donkey,
and a rod for the backs of fools!

27:5
Better is open rebuke
than hidden love.

29:15
The rod of correction imparts wisdom,
but a child left to himself disgraces
his mother.

29:17-19
Discipline your son, and he will give
you peace;
he will bring delight to your soul.

[18]Where there is no revelation, the
people cast off restraint;
but blessed is he who keeps the law.

[19]A servant cannot be corrected by
mere words;
though he understands, he will not
respond.

29:21
If a man pampers his servant from
youth,
he will bring grief in the end.

30:17
"The eye that mocks a father,
that scorns obedience to a mother,
will be pecked out by the ravens of the
valley,
will be eaten by the vultures."

DISGRACE
(Also see Shame)
6:33
Blows and disgrace are his [a thief's]
lot,
and his shame will never be wiped
away...

11:2
When pride comes, then comes disgrace,
but with humility comes wisdom.

13:5
The righteous hate what is false,
  but the wicked bring shame and
    disgrace.

14:34
Righteousness exalts a nation,
  but sin is a disgrace to any people.

18:3
When wickedness comes, so does
    contempt,
  and with shame comes disgrace.

19:26
He who robs his father and drives out
    his mother
  is a son who brings shame and
    disgrace.

28:7
He who keeps the law is a discerning
    son,
  but a companion of gluttons
    disgraces his father.

29:15
The rod of correction imparts wisdom,
  but a child left to himself disgraces
    his mother.

DISSENSION
(Also see Mocker, Strife)
6:14
[A scoundrel and villain] who plots evil
    with deceit in his heart—
  he always stirs up dissension.

6:19
[Six things the LORD hates, seven that
    are detestable]
  a false witness who pours out lies
  and a man who stirs up dissension
    among brothers.

10:12
Hatred stirs up dissension,
  but love covers over all wrongs.

15:18
A hot-tempered man stirs up dissension,

but a patient man calms a quarrel.

16:28
A perverse man stirs up dissension,
  and a gossip separates close friends.

17:11
An evil man is bent only on rebellion;
  a merciless official will be sent
    against him.

17:14
Starting a quarrel is like breaching a dam;
  so drop the matter before a dispute
    breaks out.

18:8
The words of a gossip are like choice
    morsels;
  they go down to a man's inmost
    parts.

18:18-19
Casting the lot settles disputes
  and keeps strong opponents apart.

[19]An offended brother is more
    unyielding than a fortified city,
  and disputes are like the barred gates
    of a citadel.

19:13
A foolish son is his father's ruin,
  and a quarrelsome wife is like a
    constant dripping.

20:3
It is to a man's honor to avoid strife,
  but every fool is quick to quarrel.
21:10
The wicked man craves evil;
  his neighbor gets no mercy from him.

23:29-35
Who has woe? Who has sorrow?
  Who has strife? Who has complaints?
  Who has needless bruises? Who has
    bloodshot eyes?
[30]Those who linger over wine,
  who go to sample bowls of mixed
    wine.

[31]Do not gaze at wine when it is red,
    when it sparkles in the cup,
    when it goes down smoothly!
[32]In the end it bites like a snake
    and poisons like a viper.
[33]Your eyes will see strange sights
    and your mind imagine confusing
        things.
[34]You will be like one sleeping on the
        high seas,
    lying on top of the rigging.
[35]"They hit me," you will say, "but I'm
        not hurt!
    They beat me, but I don't feel it!
When will I wake up
    so I can find another drink?"

24:21-22

Fear the LORD and the king, my son,
    and do not join with the rebellious,
[22]for those two will send sudden
        destruction upon them,
    and who knows what calamities they
        can bring?

28:25

A greedy man stirs up dissension,
    but he who trusts in the LORD will
        prosper.

29:22

An angry man stirs up dissension,
    and a hot-tempered one commits
        many sins.

30:33

"For as churning the milk produces
        butter,
    and as twisting the nose produces
        blood,
    so stirring up anger produces strife."

DRUNKENNESS
(See Alcohol)

DUPLICITY
(Also see Integrity)
11:3
The integrity of the upright guides
    them,

but the unfaithful are destroyed by
    their duplicity.

EAR
(Also see Teachable)
2:2
...turning your ear to wisdom
    and applying your heart to under-
        standing...

18:15
The heart of the discerning acquires
        knowledge;
    the ears of the wise seek it out.

20:12
Ears that hear and eyes that see—
    the LORD has made them both.

21:13
If a man shuts his ears to the cry of the
        poor,
    he too will cry out and not be
        answered.

21:28
A false witness will perish,
    and whoever listens to him will be
        destroyed forever.

23:12
Apply your heart to instruction
    and your ears to words of knowledge.

25:12
Like an earring of gold or an ornament
        of fine gold
    is a wise man's rebuke to a listening
        ear.
25:20
Like one who takes away a garment on
        a cold day,
    or like vinegar poured on soda,
    is one who sings songs to a heavy
        heart.

25:25
Like cold water to a weary soul
    is good news from a distant land.

26:17
Like one who seizes a dog by the ears
is a passer-by who meddles in a
quarrel not his own.

28:9
If anyone turns a deaf ear to the law,
even his prayers are detestable.

ENCOURAGEMENT
27:2
Let another praise you, and not your
own mouth;
someone else, and not your own lips.

ENEMY
(Also see Wicked)
16:7
When a man's ways are pleasing to the
LORD,
he makes even his enemies live at
peace with him.

24:17-18
Do not gloat when your enemy falls;
when he stumbles, do not let your
heart rejoice,
[18]or the LORD will see and disapprove
and turn his wrath away from him.

25:21
If your enemy is hungry, give him food
to eat;
if he is thirsty, give him water to
drink.

27:6
Wounds from a friend can be trusted,
but an enemy multiplies kisses.
29:24
The accomplice of a thief is his own
enemy;
he is put under oath and dare not
testify.

ENVY
(Also see Jealousy)
3:31-32
Do not envy a violent man
or choose any of his ways,

[32]for the LORD detests a perverse man
but takes the upright into his
confidence.

14:30
A heart at peace gives life to the body,
but envy rots the bones.

23:17
Do not let your heart envy sinners,
but always be zealous for the fear of
the LORD.

24:1-2
Do not envy wicked men,
do not desire their company;
[2]for their hearts plot violence,
and their lips talk about making
trouble.

24:19-20
Do not fret because of evil men
or be envious of the wicked,
[20]for the evil man has no future hope,
and the lamp of the wicked will be
snuffed out.

ETERNITY
(Also see Spirit)
8:23
"I [wisdom] was appointed from
eternity,
from the beginning, before the world
began..."

12:28
In the way of righteousness there is life;
along that path is immortality.

EVANGELISM
(Also see Zeal)
11:30
The fruit of the righteous is a tree of life,
and he who wins souls is wise.

28:1
The wicked man flees though no one
pursues,
but the righteous are as bold as a
lion.

29:25
Fear of man will prove to be a snare,
    but whoever trusts in the LORD is kept
        safe.

EVIL
(Also see Wickedness)
3:7
Do not be wise in your own eyes;
    fear the LORD and shun evil.

4:27
Do not swerve to the right or the left;
    keep your foot from evil.

5:22
The evil deeds of a wicked man
        ensnare him;
    the cords of his sin hold him fast.

8:13
"To fear the LORD is to hate evil;
    I [wisdom] hate pride and arrogance,
    evil behavior and perverse speech."

10:23
A fool finds pleasure in evil conduct,
    but a man of understanding delights
        in wisdom.

11:6
The righteousness of the upright
        delivers them,
    but the unfaithful are trapped by evil
        desires.

11:19
The truly righteous man attains life,
    but he who pursues evil goes to his
        death.

11:27
He who seeks good finds goodwill,
    but evil comes to him who searches
        for it.

12:13
An evil man is trapped by his sinful
        talk,
    but a righteous man escapes trouble.

12:20
There is deceit in the hearts of those
        who plot evil,
    but joy for those who promote peace.

13:19
A longing fulfilled is sweet to the soul,
    but fools detest turning from evil.

14:16
A wise man fears the LORD and shuns
        evil,
    but a fool is hotheaded and reckless.

14:22
Do not those who plot evil go astray?
    But those who plan what is good
        find love and faithfulness.

15:6
The house of the righteous contains
        great treasure,
    but the income of the wicked brings
        them trouble.

15:28
The heart of the righteous weighs its
        answers,
    but the mouth of the wicked gushes
        evil.

16:6
Through love and faithfulness sin is
        atoned for;
    through the fear of the LORD a man
        avoids evil.

16:17
The highway of the upright avoids evil;
    he who guards his way guards his
        life.

16:27-28
A scoundrel plots evil,
    and his speech is like a scorching
        fire.

[28]A perverse man stirs up dissension,
    and a gossip separates close friends.

16:30
He who winks with his eye is plotting
        perversity;
    he who purses his lips is bent on
        evil.

17:11
An evil man is bent only on rebellion;
    a merciless official will be sent
        against him.

17:13
If a man pays back evil for good,
    evil will never leave his house.

20:8
When a king sits on his throne to judge,
    he winnows out all evil with his eyes.

20:30
Blows and wounds cleanse away evil,
    and beatings purge the inmost being.

21:10
The wicked man craves evil;
    his neighbor gets no mercy from him.

21:27
The sacrifice of the wicked is detest-
        able—
    how much more so when brought
        with evil intent!

24:8
He who plots evil
    will be known as a schemer.

24:20
for the evil man has no future hope,
    and the lamp of the wicked will be
        snuffed out.

26:23
Like a coating of glaze over earthen-
        ware
    are fervent lips with an evil heart.

28:5
Evil men do not understand justice,
    but those who seek the Lord
        understand it fully.

29:6
An evil man is snared by his own sin,
    but a righteous one can sing and be
        glad.

30:32
"If you have played the fool and
        exalted yourself,
    or if you have planned evil,
    clap your hand over your mouth!"

EYES
4:25
Let your eyes look straight ahead,
    fix your gaze directly before you.

6:4
[If you have put security up for your
        neighbor]
allow no sleep to your eyes,
    no slumber to your eyelids.

6:17
[Seven things that are detestable to the
        Lord]
    haughty eyes,
    a lying tongue,
    hands that shed innocent blood...

17:24
A discerning man keeps wisdom in
        view,
    but a fool's eyes wander to the ends
        of the earth.

21:4
Haughty eyes and a proud heart,
    the lamp of the wicked, are sin!

23:26
My son, give me your heart
    and let your eyes keep to my ways...

FAITH
(Also see Trustworthy, Unfaithful)
2:8
For he [the Lord] guards the course of
        the just
    and protects the way of his faithful
        ones.

3:3-6

Let love and faithfulness never leave
    you;
    bind them around your neck,
    write them on the tablet of your heart.
⁴Then you will win favor and a good
        name
    in the sight of God and man.

⁵Trust in the LORD with all your heart
    and lean not on your own under-
        standing;
⁶in all your ways acknowledge him,
    and he will make your paths straight.

14:22

Do not those who plot evil go astray?
    But those who plan what is good
        find love and faithfulness.

16:6

Through love and faithfulness sin is
        atoned for;
    through the fear of the LORD a man
        avoids evil.

16:20

Whoever gives heed to instruction
        prospers,
    and blessed is he who trusts in the
        LORD.

20:6

Many a man claims to have unfailing
        love,
    but a faithful man who can find?

20:28

Love and faithfulness keep a king safe;
    through love his throne is made
        secure.

27:6

Wounds from a friend can be trusted,
    but an enemy multiplies kisses.

28:20

A faithful man will be richly blessed,
    but one eager to get rich will not go
        unpunished.

FALL

11:14

For lack of guidance a nation falls,
    but many advisers make victory sure.

11:28

Whoever trusts in his riches will fall,
    but the righteous will thrive like a
        green leaf.

13:17

A wicked messenger falls into trouble,
    but a trustworthy envoy brings
        healing.

16:18

Pride goes before destruction,
    a haughty spirit before a fall.

22:14

The mouth of an adulteress is a deep
        pit;
    he who is under the LORD's wrath will
        fall into it.

24:16-18

...for though a righteous man falls
        seven times, he rises again,
    but the wicked are brought down by
        calamity.

¹⁷Do not gloat when your enemy falls;
    when he stumbles, do not let your
        heart rejoice,
¹⁸or the LORD will see and disapprove
    and turn his wrath away from him.

26:27

If a man digs a pit, he will fall into it;
    if a man rolls a stone, it will roll back
        on him.

28:10

He who leads the upright along an evil
        path
    will fall into his own trap,
    but the blameless will receive a good
        inheritance.

28:14
Blessed is the man who always fears
    the LORD,
  but he who hardens his heart falls
    into trouble.

28:18
He whose walk is blameless is kept
    safe,
  but he whose ways are perverse will
    suddenly fall.

FALSE WITNESS
(Also see Lying)
6:19
[Seven things that are detestable to the
    LORD]
  a false witness who pours out lies
  and a man who stirs up dissension
    among brothers.

12:17
A truthful witness gives honest
    testimony,
  but a false witness tells lies.

13:5
The righteous hate what is false,
  but the wicked bring shame and
    disgrace.

14:5
A truthful witness does not deceive,
  but a false witness pours out lies.

19:5
A false witness will not go unpunished,
  and he who pours out lies will not go
    free.

19:9
A false witness will not go unpunished,
  and he who pours out lies will
    perish.

21:28
A false witness will perish,
  and whoever listens to him will be
    destroyed forever.

25:18
Like a club or a sword or a sharp arrow
  is the man who gives false testimony
    against his neighbor.

FAMILY
(Also see Children, Home, Parents)
3:3
Let love and faithfulness never leave
    you;
  bind them around your neck,
  write them on the tablet of your heart.

11:29
He who brings trouble on his family
    will inherit only wind,
  and the fool will be servant to the
    wise.

12:7
Wicked men are overthrown and are
    no more,
  but the house of the righteous stands
    firm.

14:1
The wise woman builds her house,
  but with her own hands the foolish
    one tears hers down.

14:11
The house of the wicked will be
    destroyed,
  but the tent of the upright will
    flourish.

15:6
The house of the righteous contains
    great treasure,
  but the income of the wicked brings
    them trouble.

15:25
The LORD tears down the proud man's
    house
  but he keeps the widow's boundaries
    intact.

15:27
A greedy man brings trouble to his
    family,
  but he who hates bribes will live.

17:1
Better a dry crust with peace and quiet
than a house full of feasting, with
strife.

17:13
If a man pays back evil for good,
evil will never leave his house.

21:9
Better to live on a corner of the roof
than share a house with a quarrelsome wife.

21:12
The Righteous One takes note of the
house of the wicked
and brings the wicked to ruin.

21:20
In the house of the wise are stores of
choice food and oil,
but a foolish man devours all he has.

24:3-4
By wisdom a house is built,
and through understanding it is
established;
⁴through knowledge its rooms are filled
with rare and beautiful treasures.

24:15
Do not lie in wait like an outlaw
against a righteous man's
house,
do not raid his dwelling place...

24:27
Finish your outdoor work
and get your fields ready;
after that, build your house.

25:17
Seldom set foot in your neighbor's
house—
too much of you, and he will hate
you.

25:25
Like cold water to a weary soul
is good news from a distant land.

27:8
Like a bird that strays from its nest
is a man who strays from his home.

28:10
He who leads the upright along an evil
path
will fall into his own trap,
but the blameless will receive a good
inheritance.

FATHER
(See Parents)

FEAR OF THE LORD
(Also see Trustworthy, Unfaithful)
1:7
The fear of the LORD is the beginning of
knowledge,
but fools despise wisdom and
discipline.

1:29-31
"Since they hated knowledge
and did not choose to fear the LORD,
³⁰since they would not accept my
[wisdom's] advice
and spurned my rebuke,
³¹they will eat the fruit of their ways
and be filled with the fruit of their
schemes."

2:1-8
My son, if you accept my words
and store up my commands within
you,
²turning your ear to wisdom
and applying your heart to understanding,
³and if you call out for insight
and cry aloud for understanding,
⁴and if you look for it as for silver
and search for it as for hidden
treasure,
⁵then you will understand the fear of
the LORD
and find the knowledge of God.
⁶For the LORD gives wisdom,
and from his mouth come knowledge
and understanding.
⁷He holds victory in store for the
upright,

he is a shield to those whose walk is
blameless,
[8]for he guards the course of the just
and protects the way of his faithful
ones.

3:7-8
Do not be wise in your own eyes;
fear the LORD and shun evil.
[8]This will bring health to your body
and nourishment to your bones.

8:13
"To fear the LORD is to hate evil;
I [wisdom] hate pride and arrogance,
evil behavior and perverse speech."

9:10
"The fear of the LORD is the beginning
of wisdom,
and knowledge of the Holy One is
understanding."

10:27
The fear of the LORD adds length to life,
but the years of the wicked are cut
short.

14:2
He whose walk is upright fears the LORD,
but he whose ways are devious
despises him.

14:16
A wise man fears the LORD and shuns
evil,
but a fool is hotheaded and reckless.

14:26-27
He who fears the LORD has a secure
fortress,
and for his children it will be a refuge.

[27]The fear of the LORD is a fountain of life,
turning a man from the snares of
death.

15:16
Better a little with the fear of the LORD
than great wealth with turmoil.

15:33
The fear of the LORD teaches a man
wisdom,
and humility comes before honor.

16:6
Through love and faithfulness sin is
atoned for;
through the fear of the LORD a man
avoids evil.

19:23
The fear of the LORD leads to life:
Then one rests content, untouched
by trouble.

22:4
Humility and the fear of the LORD
bring wealth and honor and life.

23:17
Do not let your heart envy sinners,
but always be zealous for the fear of
the LORD.

24:21-22
Fear the LORD and the king, my son,
and do not join with the rebellious,
[22]for those two will send sudden
destruction upon them,
and who knows what calamities they
can bring?

28:14
Blessed is the man who always fears
the LORD,
but he who hardens his heart falls
into trouble.

FINANCIAL MATTERS
(Also see Generosity, Hard Work,
Integrity, Laziness, Poverty,
Prosperity, Selfishness)

Bargain Driver
20:14
"It's no good, it's no good!" says the
buyer;
then off he goes and boasts about his
purchase.

Bribes

6:35
He [the jealous husband] will not accept
any compensation;
he will refuse the bribe, however
great it is.

15:27
A greedy man brings trouble to his
family,
but he who hates bribes will live.

17:8
A bribe is a charm to the one who
gives it;
wherever he turns, he succeeds.

17:23
A wicked man accepts a bribe in secret
to pervert the course of justice.

21:14
A gift given in secret soothes anger,
and a bribe concealed in the cloak
pacifies great wrath.

28:16
A tyrannical ruler lacks judgment,
but he who hates ill-gotten gain will
enjoy a long life.

29:4
By justice a king gives a country stability,
but one who is greedy for bribes tears
it down.

Inheritance

3:35
The wise inherit honor,
but fools he [the LORD] holds up to
shame.

11:29
He who brings trouble on his family
will inherit only wind,
and the fool will be servant to the
wise.

13:22
A good man leaves an inheritance for
his children's children,

but a sinner's wealth is stored up for
the righteous.

14:18
The simple inherit folly,
but the prudent are crowned with
knowledge.

17:2
A wise servant will rule over a
disgraceful son,
and will share the inheritance as one
of the brothers.

19:14
Houses and wealth are inherited from
parents,
but a prudent wife is from the LORD.

20:21
An inheritance quickly gained at the
beginning
will not be blessed at the end.

28:10
He who leads the upright along an evil
path
will fall into his own trap,
but the blameless will receive a good
inheritance.

Integrity

1:18-19
These men lie in wait for their own
blood;
they waylay only themselves!
[19]Such is the end of all who go after ill-
gotten gain;
it takes away the lives of those who
get it.

10:2
Ill-gotten treasures are of no value,
but righteousness delivers from
death.

11:18
The wicked man earns deceptive
wages,
but he who sows righteousness reaps
a sure reward.

13:11
Dishonest money dwindles away,
    but he who gathers money little by
        little makes it grow.

21:6
A fortune made by a lying tongue
    is a fleeting vapor and a deadly
        snare.

28:6
Better a poor man whose walk is
        blameless
than a rich man whose ways are
        perverse.

Interest
28:8
He who increases his wealth by
        exorbitant interest
amasses it for another, who will be
        kind to the poor.

Loans
11:15
He who puts up security for another
        will surely suffer,
but whoever refuses to strike hands
        in pledge is safe.

22:26-27
Do not be a man who strikes hands in
        pledge
or puts up security for debts;
²⁷if you lack the means to pay,
    your very bed will be snatched from
        under you.

27:13
Take the garment of one who puts up
        security for a stranger;
hold it in pledge if he does it for a
        wayward woman.

28:8
He who increases his wealth by
        exorbitant interest
amasses it for another, who will be
        kind to the poor.

30:15
"The leech has two daughters.
    'Give! Give!' they cry.

"There are three things that are never
        satisfied,
    four that never say, 'Enough!'"

Lots
16:33
The lot is cast into the lap,
    but its every decision is from the Lord.

18:18
Casting the lot settles disputes
and keeps strong opponents apart.

Savings
11:26
People curse the man who hoards
        grain,
    but blessing crowns him who is
        willing to sell.

13:11
Dishonest money dwindles away,
    but he who gathers money little by
        little makes it grow.
21:20
In the house of the wise are stores of
        choice food and oil,
    but a foolish man devours all he has.

27:23-27
Be sure you know the condition of
        your flocks,
    give careful attention to your herds;
²⁴for riches do not endure forever,
    and a crown is not secure for all
        generations.
²⁵When the hay is removed and new
        growth appears
    and the grass from the hills is
        gathered in,
²⁶the lambs will provide you with
        clothing,
    and the goats with the price of a
        field.
²⁷You will have plenty of goats' milk
    to feed you and your family
    and to nourish your servant girls.

FIRE
6:27-29
Can a man scoop fire into his lap
without his clothes being burned?
²⁸Can a man walk on hot coals
without his feet being scorched?
²⁹So is he who sleeps with another
man's wife;
no one who touches her will go
unpunished.

16:27
A scoundrel plots evil,
and his speech is like a scorching fire.

26:18-21
Like a madman shooting
firebrands or deadly arrows
¹⁹is a man who deceives his neighbor
and says, "I was only joking!"

²⁰Without wood a fire goes out;
without gossip a quarrel dies down.

²¹As charcoal to embers and as wood to
fire,
so is a quarrelsome man for kindling
strife.

30:15-16
"The leech has two daughters.
'Give! Give!' they cry.

"There are three things that are never
satisfied,
four that never say, 'Enough!':
¹⁶the grave, the barren womb,
land, which is never satisfied with
water,
and fire, which never says, 'Enough!'"

FOOL
(Also see Wisdom, Folly)
8:5
"You who are simple, gain prudence;
you who are foolish, gain understanding."

9:4-6
"Let all who are simple come in here!"

she [wisdom] says to those who lack
judgment.
⁵"Come, eat my food
and drink the wine I have mixed.
⁶Leave your simple ways and you will
live;
walk in the way of understanding."

9:13-18
The woman Folly is loud;
she is undisciplined and without
knowledge.
¹⁴She sits at the door of her house,
on a seat at the highest point of the
city,
¹⁵calling out to those who pass by,
who go straight on their way.
¹⁶"Let all who are simple come in here!"
she says to those who lack judgment.
¹⁷"Stolen water is sweet;
food eaten in secret is delicious!"
¹⁸But little do they know that the dead
are there,
that her guests are in the depths of
the grave.

10:10
He who winks maliciously causes grief,
and a chattering fool comes to ruin.

10:18
He who conceals his hatred has lying
lips,
and whoever spreads slander is a fool.

10:21
The lips of the righteous nourish many,
but fools die for lack of judgment.

13:19
A longing fulfilled is sweet to the soul,
but fools detest turning from evil.

14:9
Fools mock at making amends for sin,
but goodwill is found among the
upright.

14:15
A simple man believes anything,

but a prudent man gives thought to
his steps.

14:17

A quick-tempered man does foolish
things,
and a crafty man is hated.

17:7

Arrogant lips are unsuited to a fool—
how much worse lying lips to a ruler!

17:21

To have a fool for a son brings grief;
there is no joy for the father of a fool.

17:24-25

A discerning man keeps wisdom in view,
but a fool's eyes wander to the ends of
the earth.

[25]A foolish son brings grief to his father
and bitterness to the one who bore
him.

17:28

Even a fool is thought wise if he keeps
silent,
and discerning if he holds his tongue.

18:2

A fool finds no pleasure in understanding
but delights in airing his own
opinions.

18:6-7

A fool's lips bring him strife,
and his mouth invites a beating.

[7]A fool's mouth is his undoing,
and his lips are a snare to his soul.

18:13

He who answers before listening—
that is his folly and his shame.

19:1

Better a poor man whose walk is
blameless
than a fool whose lips are perverse.

19:3

A man's own folly ruins his life,
yet his heart rages against the Lord.

19:10

It is not fitting for a fool to live in
luxury—
how much worse for a slave to rule
over princes!

20:1

Wine is a mocker and beer a brawler;
whoever is led astray by them is not
wise.

20:3

It is to a man's honor to avoid strife,
but every fool is quick to quarrel.

22:15

Folly is bound up in the heart of a
child,

but the rod of discipline will drive it
far from him.

24:7

Wisdom is too high for a fool;
in the assembly at the gate he has
nothing to say.

24:9

The schemes of folly are sin,
and men detest a mocker.

26:1

Like snow in summer or rain in harvest,
honor is not fitting for a fool.

26:3-12

A whip for the horse, a halter for the
donkey,
and a rod for the backs of fools!

[4]Do not answer a fool according to his
folly,
or you will be like him yourself.

[5]Answer a fool according to his folly,
or he will be wise in his own eyes.

⁶Like cutting off one's feet or drinking
    violence
  is the sending of a message by the
    hand of a fool.

⁷Like a lame man's legs that hang limp
  is a proverb in the mouth of a fool.

⁸Like tying a stone in a sling
  is the giving of honor to a fool.

⁹Like a thornbush in a drunkard's hand
  is a proverb in the mouth of a fool.

¹⁰Like an archer who wounds at
    random
  is he who hires a fool or any passer-
    by.

¹¹As a dog returns to its vomit,
  so a fool repeats his folly.

¹²Do you see a man wise in his own
    eyes?
  There is more hope for a fool than
    for him.

27:3
Stone is heavy and sand a burden,
  but provocation by a fool is heavier
    than both.

27:22
Though you grind a fool in a mortar,
  grinding him like grain with a pestle,
  you will not remove his folly from him.

29:20
Do you see a man who speaks in haste?
  There is more hope for a fool than
    for him.

30:21-23
"Under three things the earth trembles,
  under four it cannot bear up:
²²a servant who becomes king,
  a fool who is full of food,
²³an unloved woman who is married,
  and a maidservant who displaces her
    mistress."

30:32
"If you have played the fool and
    exalted yourself,
  or if you have planned evil,
  clap your hand over your mouth!"

FORGIVENESS
(Also see Reconciliation)
16:6
Through love and faithfulness sin is
    atoned for;
  through the fear of the LORD a man
    avoids evil.

17:9
He who covers over an offense
    promotes love,
  but whoever repeats the matter
    separates close friends.

19:11
A man's wisdom gives him patience;
  it is to his glory to overlook an
    offense.
20:22
Do not say, "I'll pay you back for this
    wrong!"
  Wait for the LORD, and he will deliver
    you.

21:10
The wicked man craves evil;
  his neighbor gets no mercy from him.

FOUR THINGS
30:15-16
"The leech has two daughters.
  'Give! Give!' they cry.

"There are three things that are never
    satisfied,
  four that never say, 'Enough!':
¹⁶the grave, the barren womb,
  land, which is never satisfied with
    water,
  and fire, which never says, 'Enough!'"

30:18-19
"There are three things that are too
    amazing for me,

four that I do not understand:
[19]the way of an eagle in the sky,
 the way of a snake on a rock,
the way of a ship on the high seas,
 and the way of a man with a
  maiden."

30:21-31

"Under three things the earth trembles,
 under four it cannot bear up:
[22]a servant who becomes king,
 a fool who is full of food,
[23]an unloved woman who is married,
 and a maidservant who displaces her
  mistress.

[24]"Four things on earth are small,
 yet they are extremely wise:
[25]Ants are creatures of little strength,
 yet they store up their food in the
  summer;
[26]coneys are creatures of little power,
 yet they make their home in the
  crags;
[27]locusts have no king,
 yet they advance together in ranks;
[28]a lizard can be caught with the hand,
 yet it is found in kings' palaces.

[29]"There are three things that are stately
 in their stride,
 four that move with stately bearing:
[30]a lion, mighty among beasts,
 who retreats before nothing;
[31]a strutting rooster, a he-goat,
 and a king with his army around
  him."

FRIENDSHIP

(Also see Neighbors)
12:26

A righteous man is cautious in
 friendship,
 but the way of the wicked leads them
  astray.

13:20

He who walks with the wise grows wise,
 but a companion of fools suffers harm.

14:20

The poor are shunned even by their
  neighbors,
 but the rich have many friends.

16:28

A perverse man stirs up dissension,
 and a gossip separates close friends.

17:9

He who covers over an offense
 promotes love,
 but whoever repeats the matter
  separates close friends.

17:17

A friend loves at all times,
 and a brother is born for adversity.

18:1

An unfriendly man pursues selfish ends;
 he defies all sound judgment.
18:24

A man of many companions may come
 to ruin,
 but there is a friend who sticks closer
  than a brother.

19:4

Wealth brings many friends,
 but a poor man's friend deserts him.

19:6-7

Many curry favor with a ruler,
 and everyone is the friend of a man
  who gives gifts.

[7]A poor man is shunned by all his
  relatives—
 how much more do his friends avoid
  him!
Though he pursues them with pleading,
 they are nowhere to be found.

22:11

He who loves a pure heart and whose
  speech is gracious
 will have the king for his friend.

22:24-25
Do not make friends with a hot-
tempered man,
do not associate with one easily
angered,
²⁵or you may learn his ways
and get yourself ensnared.

23:20
Do not join those who drink too much
wine
or gorge themselves on meat...

24:1-2
Do not envy wicked men,
do not desire their company;
²for their hearts plot violence,
and their lips talk about making
trouble.

24:21-22
Fear the LORD and the king, my son,
and do not join with the rebellious,
²²for those two will send sudden
destruction upon them,
and who knows what calamities they
can bring?

27:6
Wounds from a friend can be trusted,
but an enemy multiplies kisses.

27:9-10
Perfume and incense bring joy to the
heart,
and the pleasantness of one's friend
springs from his earnest
counsel.

¹⁰Do not forsake your friend and the
friend of your father,
and do not go to your brother's
house when disaster strikes
you—
better a neighbor nearby than a
brother far away.

27:17
As iron sharpens iron,
so one man sharpens another.

GENEROSITY
(Also see Gifts, Selfishness)
3:27-28
Do not withhold good from those who
deserve it,
when it is in your power to act.
²⁸Do not say to your neighbor,
"Come back later; I'll give it
tomorrow"—
when you now have it with you.

11:24-26
One man gives freely, yet gains even
more;
another withholds unduly, but comes
to poverty.

²⁵A generous man will prosper;
he who refreshes others will himself
be refreshed.

²⁶People curse the man who hoards
grain,
but blessing crowns him who is
willing to sell.

18:16
A gift opens the way for the giver
and ushers him into the presence of
the great.

19:12
A king's rage is like the roar of a lion,
but his favor is like dew on the grass.

19:17
He who is kind to the poor lends to the
LORD,
and he will reward him for what he
has done.

21:26
All day long he [the sluggard] craves for
more,
but the righteous give without
sparing.

22:7
The rich rule over the poor,
and the borrower is servant to the
lender.

22:9
A generous man will himself be
blessed,
for he shares his food with the poor.

28:27
He who gives to the poor will lack
nothing,
but he who closes his eyes to them
receives many curses.

GIFTS
(Also see Generosity)
18:16
A gift opens the way for the giver
and ushers him into the presence of
the great.

19:6
Many curry favor with a ruler,
and everyone is the friend of a man
who gives gifts.

21:14
A gift given in secret soothes anger,
and a bribe concealed in the cloak
pacifies great wrath.

22:16
He who oppresses the poor to increase
his wealth
and he who gives gifts to the rich—
both come to poverty.

25:14
Like clouds and wind without rain
is a man who boasts of gifts he does
not give.

GLORY
(Also see Honor)
14:28
A large population is a king's glory,
but without subjects a prince is
ruined.

19:11
A man's wisdom gives him patience;
it is to his glory to overlook an
offense.

20:29
The glory of young men is their
strength,
gray hair the splendor of the old.

25:2
It is the glory of God to conceal a
matter;
to search out a matter is the glory of
kings.

GLUTTONY
*(Also see Discipline, Hard Work,
Laziness)*
23:1-3
When you sit to dine with a ruler,
note well what is before you,
²and put a knife to your throat
if you are given to gluttony.
³Do not crave his delicacies,
for that food is deceptive.

23:19-21
Listen, my son, and be wise,
and keep your heart on the right
path.
²⁰Do not join those who drink too
much wine
or gorge themselves on meat,
²¹for drunkards and gluttons become
poor,
and drowsiness clothes them in rags.

28:7
He who keeps the law is a discerning
son,
but a companion of gluttons
disgraces his father.

GOD
(Also see Lord)
15:3
The eyes of the Lord are everywhere,
keeping watch on the wicked and
the good.

16:4
The Lord works out everything for his
own ends—
even the wicked for a day of disaster.

20:12
Ears that hear and eyes that see—
the Lord has made them both.

30:4-6
"Who has gone up to heaven and come
down?
Who has gathered up the wind in the
hollow of his hands?
Who has wrapped up the waters in his
cloak?
Who has established all the ends of
the earth?
What is his name, and the name of his
son?
Tell me if you know!

5"Every word of God is flawless;
he is a shield to those who take
refuge in him.
6Do not add to his words,
or he will rebuke you and prove you
a liar."

GODLESS
11:9
With his mouth the godless destroys
his neighbor,
but through knowledge the righteous
escape.

GOLD
(Also see Prosperity)
3:14
For she [wisdom] is more profitable
than silver
and yields better returns than gold.

8:10
"Choose my [wisdom's] instruction
instead of silver,
knowledge rather than choice gold..."

8:19
"My [wisdom's] fruit is better than fine
gold;
what I yield surpasses choice silver."

11:22
Like a gold ring in a pig's snout

is a beautiful woman who shows no
discretion.

16:16
How much better to get wisdom than
gold,
to choose understanding rather than
silver!

17:3
The crucible for silver and the furnace
for gold,
but the Lord tests the heart.

20:15
Gold there is, and rubies in abundance,
but lips that speak knowledge are a
rare jewel.

22:1
A good name is more desirable than
great riches;
to be esteemed is better than silver or
gold.

25:11-12
A word aptly spoken
is like apples of gold in settings of
silver.

12Like an earring of gold or an
ornament of fine gold
is a wise man's rebuke to a listening
ear.

27:21
The crucible for silver and the furnace
for gold,
but man is tested by the praise he
receives.

GOOD NAME
3:3-4
Let love and faithfulness never leave
you;
bind them around your neck,
write them on the tablet of your
heart.
4Then you will win favor and a good
name
in the sight of God and man.

22:1
A good name is more desirable than
   great riches;
  to be esteemed is better than silver or
   gold.

25:9-10
If you argue your case with a neighbor,
  do not betray another man's
   confidence,
[10]or he who hears it may shame you
  and you will never lose your bad
   reputation.

GOODNESS
2:20
Thus you will walk in the ways of good
   men
  and keep to the paths of the
   righteous.

3:27
Do not withhold good from those who
   deserve it,
  when it is in your power to act.

11:23
The desire of the righteous ends only in
   good,
  but the hope of the wicked only in
   wrath.

11:27
He who seeks good finds goodwill,
  but evil comes to him who searches
   for it.

12:2
A good man obtains favor from the
   LORD,
  but the LORD condemns a crafty man.

12:14
From the fruit of his lips a man is filled
   with good things
  as surely as the work of his hands
   rewards him.

13:2
From the fruit of his lips a man enjoys
   good things,

but the unfaithful have a craving for
   violence.

13:22
A good man leaves an inheritance for
   his children's children,
  but a sinner's wealth is stored up for
   the righteous.

14:9
Fools mock at making amends for sin,
  but goodwill is found among the
   upright.

14:14
The faithless will be fully repaid for
   their ways,
  and the good man rewarded for his.

14:19
Evil men will bow down in the
   presence of the good,
  and the wicked at the gates of the
   righteous.

14:22
Do not those who plot evil go astray?
  But those who plan what is good
   find love and faithfulness.

15:3
The eyes of the LORD are everywhere,
  keeping watch on the wicked and
   the good.

15:23
A man finds joy in giving an apt
   reply—
  and how good is a timely word!

15:30
A cheerful look brings joy to the heart,
  and good news gives health to the
   bones.

16:29
A violent man entices his neighbor
  and leads him down a path that is
   not good.

17:13
If a man pays back evil for good,
    evil will never leave his house.

17:22
A cheerful heart is good medicine,
    but a crushed spirit dries up the
        bones.

17:26
It is not good to punish an innocent
        man,
    or to flog officials for their integrity.

18:5
It is not good to be partial to the
        wicked
    or to deprive the innocent of justice.

18:22
He who finds a wife finds what is good
    and receives favor from the LORD.

19:2
It is not good to have zeal without
        knowledge,
    nor to be hasty and miss the way.

20:14
"It's no good, it's no good!" says the
        buyer;
    then off he goes and boasts about his
        purchase.

24:13
Eat honey, my son, for it is good;
    honey from the comb is sweet to
        your taste.

24:23
These also are sayings of the wise:

    To show partiality in judging is not
        good...

25:25
Like cold water to a weary soul
    is good news from a distant land.

25:27
It is not good to eat too much honey,
    nor is it honorable to seek one's own
        honor.

28:10
He who leads the upright along an evil
        path
    will fall into his own trap,
    but the blameless will receive a good
        inheritance.

28:21
To show partiality is not good—
    yet a man will do wrong for a piece
        of bread.

31:12
She [a wife of noble character] brings
        him good, not harm,
    all the days of her life.

GOSSIP
(See Dissension, Tongue, Strife)

GRAVE
(Also see Death, Life)
5:5
Her [the adulteress'] feet go down to
        death;
    her steps lead straight to the grave.

7:27
Her [the adulteress'] house is a highway
        to the grave,
    leading down to the chambers of
        death.

9:18
But little do they know that the dead
        are there,
    that her [folly's] guests are in the
        depths of the grave.

15:24
The path of life leads upward for the
        wise
    to keep him from going down to the
        grave.

30:15-16
"The leech has two daughters.
'Give! Give!' they cry.
"There are three things that are never
satisfied,
four that never say, 'Enough!':
[16]the grave, the barren womb,
land, which is never satisfied with
water,
and fire, which never says, 'Enough!'"

GREED
(See Selfishness)

GRIEF
(Also see Joy)
10:1
The proverbs of Solomon:

A wise son brings joy to his father,
but a foolish son grief to his mother.

10:10
He who winks maliciously causes grief,
and a chattering fool comes to ruin.

14:13
Even in laughter the heart may ache,
and joy may end in grief.

17:21
To have a fool for a son brings grief;
there is no joy for the father of a fool.

17:25
A foolish son brings grief to his father
and bitterness to the one who bore him.

29:21
If a man pampers his servant from
youth,
he will bring grief in the end.

GUILT
(Also see Shame)
17:15
Acquitting the guilty and condemning
the innocent—
the LORD detests them both.

21:8
The way of the guilty is devious,
but the conduct of the innocent is
upright.
24:24-25
Whoever says to the guilty, "You are
innocent"—
peoples will curse him and nations
denounce him.
[25]But it will go well with those who
convict the guilty,
and rich blessing will come upon
them.

HARD WORK
(Also see Discipline, Laziness)
10:4-5
Lazy hands make a man poor,
but diligent hands bring wealth.

[5]He who gathers crops in summer is a
wise son,
but he who sleeps during harvest is a
disgraceful son.

12:11
He who works his land will have
abundant food,
but he who chases fantasies lacks
judgment.

12:14
From the fruit of his lips a man is filled
with good things
as surely as the work of his hands
rewards him.

12:24
Diligent hands will rule,
but laziness ends in slave labor.

12:27
The lazy man does not roast his game,
but the diligent man prizes his
possessions.

13:4
The sluggard craves and gets nothing,
but the desires of the diligent are
fully satisfied.

14:4
Where there are no oxen, the manger is
empty,
but from the strength of an ox comes
an abundant harvest.

14:23
All hard work brings a profit,
but mere talk leads only to poverty.

16:26
The laborer's appetite works for him;
his hunger drives him on.

18:9
One who is slack in his work
is brother to one who destroys.

20:13
Do not love sleep or you will grow poor;
stay awake and you will have food to
spare.

21:5
The plans of the diligent lead to profit
as surely as haste leads to poverty.

22:29
Do you see a man skilled in his work?
He will serve before kings;
he will not serve before obscure men.

24:27
Finish your outdoor work
and get your fields ready;
after that, build your house.

27:18
He who tends a fig tree will eat its fruit,
and he who looks after his master
will be honored.

27:23-27
Be sure you know the condition of
your flocks,
give careful attention to your herds;
²⁴for riches do not endure forever,
and a crown is not secure for all
generations.
²⁵When the hay is removed and new
growth appears

and the grass from the hills is
gathered in,
²⁶the lambs will provide you with
clothing,
and the goats with the price of a
field.
²⁷You will have plenty of goats' milk
to feed you and your family
and to nourish your servant girls.

28:19
He who works his land will have
abundant food,
but the one who chases fantasies will
have his fill of poverty.

HARVEST
6:6-8
Go to the ant, you sluggard;
consider its ways and be wise!
⁷It has no commander,
no overseer or ruler,
⁸yet it stores its provisions in summer
and gathers its food at harvest.

10:5
He who gathers crops in summer is a
wise son,
but he who sleeps during harvest is a
disgraceful son.

14:4
Where there are no oxen, the manger is
empty,
but from the strength of an ox comes
an abundant harvest.

18:20
From the fruit of his mouth a man's
stomach is filled;
with the harvest from his lips he is
satisfied.

20:4
A sluggard does not plow in season;
so at harvest time he looks but finds
nothing.

25:13
Like the coolness of snow at harvest
time

is a trustworthy messenger to those
who send him;
he refreshes the spirit of his masters.

26:1
Like snow in summer or rain in harvest,
honor is not fitting for a fool.

HATE
1:22
"How long will you simple ones love
your simple ways?
How long will mockers delight in
mockery
and fools hate knowledge?"

6:16
There are six things the LORD hates,
seven that are detestable to him...

8:13
"To fear the LORD is to hate evil;
I [wisdom] hate pride and arrogance,
evil behavior and perverse speech."

8:36
"But whoever fails to find me harms
himself;
all who hate me love death."

9:8
Do not rebuke a mocker or he will hate
you;
rebuke a wise man and he will love
you.

10:12
Hatred stirs up dissension,
but love covers over all wrongs.

10:18
He who conceals his hatred has lying
lips,
and whoever spreads slander is a
fool.

12:1
Whoever loves discipline loves
knowledge,
but he who hates correction is stupid.

13:5
The righteous hate what is false,
but the wicked bring shame and
disgrace.

13:24
He who spares the rod hates his son,
but he who loves him is careful to
discipline him.

14:17
A quick-tempered man does foolish
things,
and a crafty man is hated.

15:10
Stern discipline awaits him who leaves
the path;
he who hates correction will die.

15:17
Better a meal of vegetables where there
is love
than a fattened calf with hatred.

15:27
A greedy man brings trouble to his
family,
but he who hates bribes will live.

24:17-18
Do not gloat when your enemy falls;
when he stumbles, do not let your
heart rejoice,
[18]or the LORD will see and disapprove
and turn his wrath away from him.

25:17
Seldom set foot in your neighbor's
house—
too much of you, and he will hate
you.

26:28
A lying tongue hates those it hurts,
and a flattering mouth works ruin.

28:16
A tyrannical ruler lacks judgment,
but he who hates ill-gotten gain will
enjoy a long life.

29:10
Bloodthirsty men hate a man of
   integrity
and seek to kill the upright.

HEALTH
3:7-8
Do not be wise in your own eyes;
   fear the LORD and shun evil.
⁸This will bring health to your body
   and nourishment to your bones.

4:20-22
My son, pay attention to what I
   [wisdom] say;
   listen closely to my words.
²¹Do not let them out of your sight,
   keep them within your heart;
²²for they are life to those who find
   them
   and health to a man's whole body.

12:18
Reckless words pierce like a sword,
   but the tongue of the wise brings
      healing.

13:17
A wicked messenger falls into trouble,
   but a trustworthy envoy brings
      healing.

15:4
The tongue that brings healing is a tree
   of life,
   but a deceitful tongue crushes the
      spirit.

15:30
A cheerful look brings joy to the heart,
   and good news gives health to the
      bones.

16:24
Pleasant words are a honeycomb,
   sweet to the soul and healing to the
      bones.

17:22
A cheerful heart is good medicine,

but a crushed spirit dries up the
   bones.

18:14
A man's spirit sustains him in sickness,
   but a crushed spirit who can bear?

HEART
(Also see Spirit)
3:1-6
My son, do not forget my teaching,
   but keep my commands in your
      heart,
²for they will prolong your life many
   years
   and bring you prosperity.

³Let love and faithfulness never leave
   you;
   bind them around your neck,
   write them on the tablet of your
      heart.
⁴Then you will win favor and a good
   name
   in the sight of God and man.

⁵Trust in the LORD with all your heart
   and lean not on your own under-
      standing;
⁶in all your ways acknowledge him,
   and he will make your paths straight.

4:23
Above all else, guard your heart,
   for it is the wellspring of life.

10:20
The tongue of the righteous is choice
   silver,
   but the heart of the wicked is of little
      value.

11:20
The LORD detests men of perverse heart
   but he delights in those whose ways
      are blameless.

12:20
There is deceit in the hearts of those
   who plot evil,
   but joy for those who promote peace.

12:23
A prudent man keeps his knowledge to
himself,
but the heart of fools blurts out folly.

12:25
An anxious heart weighs a man down,
but a kind word cheers him up.

13:12
Hope deferred makes the heart sick,
but a longing fulfilled is a tree of life.

13:25
The righteous eat to their hearts' content,
but the stomach of the wicked goes
hungry.

14:10
Each heart knows its own bitterness,
and no one else can share its joy.

14:13
Even in laughter the heart may ache,
and joy may end in grief.

14:33
Wisdom reposes in the heart of the
discerning
and even among fools she lets herself
be known.

15:7
The lips of the wise spread knowledge;
not so the hearts of fools.

15:11
Death and Destruction lie open before
the LORD—
how much more the hearts of men!

15:13-15
A happy heart makes the face cheerful,
but heartache crushes the spirit.

¹⁴The discerning heart seeks knowledge,
but the mouth of a fool feeds on folly.

¹⁵All the days of the oppressed are
wretched,

but the cheerful heart has a continual
feast.

15:28
The heart of the righteous weighs its
answers,
but the mouth of the wicked gushes
evil.

15:30
A cheerful look brings joy to the heart,
and good news gives health to the
bones.

16:1
To man belong the plans of the heart,
but from the LORD comes the reply of
the tongue.

16:5
The LORD detests all the proud of heart.
Be sure of this: They will not go
unpunished.

16:9
In his heart a man plans his course,
but the LORD determines his steps.

16:21
The wise in heart are called discerning,
and pleasant words promote
instruction.

16:23
A wise man's heart guides his mouth,
and his lips promote instruction.

17:3
The crucible for silver and the furnace
for gold,
but the LORD tests the heart.

17:20
A man of perverse heart does not
prosper;
he whose tongue is deceitful falls
into trouble.

17:22
A cheerful heart is good medicine,
but a crushed spirit dries up the
bones.

18:12
Before his downfall a man's heart is
   proud,
   but humility comes before honor.

18:15
The heart of the discerning acquires
   knowledge;
   the ears of the wise seek it out.

19:3
A man's own folly ruins his life,
   yet his heart rages against the LORD.

19:21
Many are the plans in a man's heart,
   but it is the LORD's purpose that
   prevails.

20:5
The purposes of a man's heart are deep
   waters,
   but a man of understanding draws
   them out.

20:9
Who can say, "I have kept my heart
   pure;
   I am clean and without sin"?

21:1
The king's heart is in the hand of the
   LORD;
   he directs it like a watercourse
   wherever he pleases.

21:4
Haughty eyes and a proud heart,
   the lamp of the wicked, are sin!

22:11
He who loves a pure heart and whose
   speech is gracious
   will have the king for his friend.

23:12
Apply your heart to instruction
   and your ears to words of knowledge.

23:15
My son, if your heart is wise,
   then my heart will be glad...

23:17
Do not let your heart envy sinners,
   but always be zealous for the fear of
   the LORD.

24:1-2
Do not envy wicked men,
   do not desire their company;
   ²for their hearts plot violence,
   and their lips talk about making
   trouble.

24:12
If you say, "But we knew nothing
   about this,"
   does not he who weighs the heart
   perceive it?
Does not he who guards your life
   know it?
   Will he not repay each person
   according to what he has done?

24:32
I applied my heart to what I observed
   and learned a lesson from what I
   saw...

25:3
As the heavens are high and the earth
   is deep,
   so the hearts of kings are
   unsearchable.

25:20
Like one who takes away a garment on
   a cold day,
   or like vinegar poured on soda,
   is one who sings songs to a heavy
   heart.

26:23-25
Like a coating of glaze over earthen-
   ware
   are fervent lips with an evil heart.

²⁴A malicious man disguises himself
   with his lips,
   but in his heart he harbors deceit.
²⁵Though his speech is charming, do
   not believe him,
   for seven abominations fill his heart.

27:9

Perfume and incense bring joy to the heart,
and the pleasantness of one's friend springs from his earnest counsel.

27:19

As water reflects a face,
so a man's heart reflects the man.

28:14

Blessed is the man who always fears the LORD,
but he who hardens his heart falls into trouble.

29:1

A man who remains stiff-necked after many rebukes
will suddenly be destroyed—without remedy.

HOME

(Also see Children, Family, Parents)

3:33

The LORD's curse is on the house of the wicked,
but he blesses the home of the righteous.

7:11

She [the adulteress] is loud and defiant, her feet never stay at home...

7:14

[The adulteress says,] "I have fellowship offerings at home;
today I fulfilled my vows."

7:19-20

"My husband is not at home;
he has gone on a long journey.
²⁰He took his purse filled with money
and will not be home till full moon."

14:1

The wise woman builds her house,
but with her own hands the foolish one tears hers down.

15:31

He who listens to a life-giving rebuke
will be at home among the wise.

24:15-16

Do not lie in wait like an outlaw against a righteous man's house,
do not raid his dwelling place;
¹⁶for though a righteous man falls seven times, he rises again,
but the wicked are brought down by calamity.

24:27

Finish your outdoor work
and get your fields ready;
after that, build your house.

24:33-34

A little sleep, a little slumber,
a little folding of the hands to rest—
³⁴and poverty will come on you like a bandit
and scarcity like an armed man.

27:8

Like a bird that strays from its nest
is a man who strays from his home.

30:26

"Coneys are creatures of little power,
yet they make their home in the crags..."

HONESTY

(Also see Integrity, Lying)

12:17

A truthful witness gives honest testimony,
but a false witness tells lies.

12:19

Truthful lips endure forever,
but a lying tongue lasts only a moment.

12:22

The LORD detests lying lips,
but he delights in men who are truthful.

14:5
A truthful witness does not deceive,
but a false witness pours out lies.

14:25
A truthful witness saves lives,
but a false witness is deceitful.

16:13
Kings take pleasure in honest lips;
they value a man who speaks the
truth.

23:23
Buy the truth and do not sell it;
get wisdom, discipline and understanding.

24:26
An honest answer
is like a kiss on the lips.

HONOR
(Also see Glory)
3:9-10
Honor the LORD with your wealth,
with the firstfruits of all your crops;
[10]then your barns will be filled to
overflowing,
and your vats will brim over with
new wine.

3:35
The wise inherit honor,
but fools he [the LORD] holds up to
shame.

4:8
Esteem her [wisdom], and she will exalt
you;
embrace her, and she will honor you.

8:18
"With me [wisdom] are riches and honor,
enduring wealth and prosperity."

15:33
The fear of the LORD teaches a man
wisdom,
and humility comes before honor.

18:12
Before his downfall a man's heart is
proud,
but humility comes before honor.

20:3
It is to a man's honor to avoid strife,
but every fool is quick to quarrel.

21:21
He who pursues righteousness and love
finds life, prosperity and honor.

22:4
Humility and the fear of the LORD
bring wealth and honor and life.
25:27
It is not good to eat too much honey,
nor is it honorable to seek one's own
honor.

26:1
Like snow in summer or rain in harvest,
honor is not fitting for a fool.

26:8
Like tying a stone in a sling
is the giving of honor to a fool.

29:23
A man's pride brings him low,
but a man of lowly spirit gains honor.

HOPE
(Also see Patience)
11:7
When a wicked man dies, his hope
perishes;
all he expected from his power
comes to nothing.

11:23
The desire of the righteous ends only in
good,
but the hope of the wicked only in
wrath.

13:12
Hope deferred makes the heart sick,
but a longing fulfilled is a tree of life.

19:18
Discipline your son, for in that there is
    hope;
    do not be a willing party to his death.

23:18
There is surely a future hope for you,
    and your hope will not be cut off.

24:14
Know also that wisdom is sweet to
    your soul;
    if you find it, there is a future hope
        for you,
    and your hope will not be cut off.
24:20
...for the evil man has no future hope,
    and the lamp of the wicked will be
        snuffed out.

26:12
Do you see a man wise in his own eyes?
    There is more hope for a fool than for
        him.

29:20
Do you see a man who speaks in haste?
    There is more hope for a fool than
        for him.

HUMILITY
(Also see Pride)
3:34
He mocks proud mockers
    but gives grace to the humble.

6:3
Then do this, my son, to free yourself,
    since you have fallen into your
        neighbor's hands:
Go and humble yourself;
    press your plea with your neighbor!

11:2
When pride comes, then comes
    disgrace,
    but with humility comes wisdom.

15:33
The fear of the Lord teaches a man
    wisdom,

and humility comes before honor.

16:19
Better to be lowly in spirit and among
    the oppressed
    than to share plunder with the proud.

18:12
Before his downfall a man's heart is
    proud,
    but humility comes before honor.

22:4
Humility and the fear of the Lord
    bring wealth and honor and life.
25:6-7B
Do not exalt yourself in the king's
    presence,
    and do not claim a place among
        great men;
7it is better for him to say to you,
    "Come up here,"
    than for him to humiliate you before
        a nobleman.

25:27
It is not good to eat too much honey,
    nor is it honorable to seek one's own
        honor.

29:23
A man's pride brings him low,
    but a man of lowly spirit gains honor.

HUNGER
(Also see Justice, Poverty, Prosperity)
6:30
Men do not despise a thief if he steals
    to satisfy his hunger when he is
        starving.

10:3
The Lord does not let the righteous go
    hungry
    but he thwarts the craving of the
        wicked.

13:25
The righteous eat to their hearts'
    content,

but the stomach of the wicked goes
    hungry.

16:26
The laborer's appetite works for him;
    his hunger drives him on.

19:15
Laziness brings on deep sleep,
    and the shiftless man goes hungry.

25:21
If your enemy is hungry, give him food
        to eat;
    if he is thirsty, give him water to
        drink.

27:7
He who is full loathes honey,
    but to the hungry even what is bitter
        tastes sweet.

IMPETUOUSNESS
19:2
It is not good to have zeal without
        knowledge,
    nor to be hasty and miss the way.

20:21
An inheritance quickly gained at the
        beginning
    will not be blessed at the end.

20:25
It is a trap for a man to dedicate
        something rashly
    and only later to consider his vows.

INHERITANCE
(See Financial Matters)

INJUSTICE
(See Justice)

INNOCENCE
6:16-17
There are six things the LORD hates,
    seven that are detestable to him:
        [17]haughty eyes,
        a lying tongue,
        hands that shed innocent blood...

16:2
All a man's ways seem innocent to him,
    but motives are weighed by the LORD.

17:15
Acquitting the guilty and condemning
        the innocent—
    the LORD detests them both.

17:26
It is not good to punish an innocent
        man,
    or to flog officials for their integrity.

18:5
It is not good to be partial to the
        wicked
    or to deprive the innocent of justice.

21:8
The way of the guilty is devious,
    but the conduct of the innocent is
        upright.

24:24
Whoever says to the guilty, "You are
        innocent"—
    peoples will curse him and nations
        denounce him.

INTEGRITY
(Also see Duplicity)
10:9
The man of integrity walks securely,
    but he who takes crooked paths will
        be found out.

11:3
The integrity of the upright guides
        them,
    but the unfaithful are destroyed by
        their duplicity.

12:17
A truthful witness gives honest
        testimony,
    but a false witness tells lies.

13:6
Righteousness guards the man of
        integrity,

but wickedness overthrows the
sinner.

13:11
Dishonest money dwindles away,
but he who gathers money little by
little makes it grow.

17:26
It is not good to punish an innocent
man,
or to flog officials for their integrity.

22:28
Do not move an ancient boundary
stone
set up by your forefathers.

24:28
Do not testify against your neighbor
without cause,
or use your lips to deceive.

25:9-10
If you argue your case with a neighbor,
do not betray another man's
confidence,
[10]or he who hears it may shame you
and you will never lose your bad
reputation.

25:13
Like the coolness of snow at harvest time
is a trustworthy messenger to those
who send him;
he refreshes the spirit of his masters.

25:19
Like a bad tooth or a lame foot
is reliance on the unfaithful in times
of trouble.

25:26-27
Like a muddied spring or a polluted
well
is a righteous man who gives way to
the wicked.

[27]It is not good to eat too much honey,
nor is it honorable to seek one's own
honor.

29:10
Bloodthirsty men hate a man of
integrity
and seek to kill the upright.

INTEREST
(See Financial Matters)

JEALOUSY
(Also see Envy)
6:34
...for jealousy arouses a husband's fury,
and he will show no mercy when he
takes revenge.

27:4
Anger is cruel and fury overwhelming,
but who can stand before jealousy?

JOY
(Also See Laughter, Pleasure)
10:1
The proverbs of Solomon:

A wise son brings joy to his father,
but a foolish son grief to his mother.

10:28
The prospect of the righteous is joy,
but the hopes of the wicked come to
nothing.

11:10
When the righteous prosper, the city
rejoices;
when the wicked perish, there are
shouts of joy.

12:20
There is deceit in the hearts of those
who plot evil,
but joy for those who promote peace.

14:10
Each heart knows its own bitterness,
and no one else can share its joy.

14:13
Even in laughter the heart may ache,
and joy may end in grief.

15:13
A happy heart makes the face cheerful,
but heartache crushes the spirit.

15:20
A wise son brings joy to his father,
but a foolish man despises his
mother.

15:23
A man finds joy in giving an apt
reply—
and how good is a timely word!

15:30
A cheerful look brings joy to the heart,
and good news gives health to the
bones.

17:21
To have a fool for a son brings grief;
there is no joy for the father of a fool.

21:15
When justice is done, it brings joy to
the righteous
but terror to evildoers.

23:24
The father of a righteous man has great
joy;
he who has a wise son delights in
him.

27:9
Perfume and incense bring joy to the
heart,
and the pleasantness of one's friend
springs from his earnest
counsel.

27:11
Be wise, my son, and bring joy to my
heart;
then I can answer anyone who treats
me with contempt.

29:3
A man who loves wisdom brings joy to
his father,

but a companion of prostitutes
squanders his wealth.

JUDGEMENT
(See Discernment)

JUSTICE
*(See Compassion, Poverty, Oppression,
Rulers)*

8:8
"All the words of my [wisdom's] mouth
are just;
none of them is crooked or perverse."

8:20-21
"I [wisdom] walk in the way of
righteousness,
along the paths of justice,
[21]bestowing wealth on those who love
me
and making their treasuries full."

11:1
The Lord abhors dishonest scales,
but accurate weights are his delight.

13:23
A poor man's field may produce
abundant food,
but injustice sweeps it away.

15:25
The Lord tears down the proud man's
house
but he keeps the widow's boundaries
intact.

16:8
Better a little with righteousness
than much gain with injustice.

16:10-11
The lips of a king speak as an oracle,
and his mouth should not betray
justice.

[11]Honest scales and balances are from
the Lord;
all the weights in the bag are of his
making.

17:15
Acquitting the guilty and condemning
    the innocent—
    the LORD detests them both.

17:23
A wicked man accepts a bribe in secret
    to pervert the course of justice.

17:26
It is not good to punish an innocent
    man,
    or to flog officials for their integrity.

18:5
It is not good to be partial to the
    wicked
    or to deprive the innocent of justice.

18:17
The first to present his case seems right,
    till another comes forward and
    questions him.

18:23
A poor man pleads for mercy,
    but a rich man answers harshly.

19:5
A false witness will not go unpunished,
    and he who pours out lies will not go
    free.

19:28
A corrupt witness mocks at justice,
    and the mouth of the wicked gulps
    down evil.

20:8
When a king sits on his throne to
    judge,
    he winnows out all evil with his eyes.

20:10
Differing weights and differing
    measures—
    the LORD detests them both.

20:22-23
Do not say, "I'll pay you back for this
    wrong!"

Wait for the LORD, and he will deliver
    you.
[23]The LORD detests differing weights,
    and dishonest scales do not please
    him.

21:15
When justice is done, it brings joy to
    the righteous
    but terror to evildoers.

22:16
He who oppresses the poor to increase
    his wealth
    and he who gives gifts to the rich—
    both come to poverty.

22:22-23
Do not exploit the poor because they
    are poor
    and do not crush the needy in court,
[23]for the LORD will take up their case
    and will plunder those who plunder
    them.

23:10-11
Do not move an ancient boundary stone
    or encroach on the fields of the
    fatherless,
[11]for their Defender is strong;
    he will take up their case against you.

24:23-25
These also are sayings of the wise:

To show partiality in judging is not good:
[24]Whoever says to the guilty, "You are
    innocent"—
    peoples will curse him and nations
    denounce him.
[25]But it will go well with those who
    convict the guilty,
    and rich blessing will come upon
    them.

24:28-29
Do not testify against your neighbor
    without cause,
    or use your lips to deceive.
[29]Do not say, "I'll do to him as he has
    done to me;

I'll pay that man back for what he
did."

25:7b-10
What you have seen with your eyes
⁸do not bring hastily to court,
for what will you do in the end
if your neighbor puts you to shame?

⁹If you argue your case with a neighbor,
do not betray another man's confidence,
¹⁰or he who hears it may shame you
and you will never lose your bad
reputation.

28:3
A ruler who oppresses the poor
is like a driving rain that leaves no
crops.

28:5
Evil men do not understand justice,
but those who seek the LORD
understand it fully.

28:15-16
Like a roaring lion or a charging bear
is a wicked man ruling over a
helpless people.

¹⁶A tyrannical ruler lacks judgment,
but he who hates ill-gotten gain will
enjoy a long life.

28:21
To show partiality is not good—
yet a man will do wrong for a piece
of bread.

29:4
By justice a king gives a country
stability,
but one who is greedy for bribes
tears it down.

29:7
The righteous care about justice for the
poor,
but the wicked have no such
concern.

29:13-14
The poor man and the oppressor have
this in common:
The LORD gives sight to the eyes of
both.

¹⁴If a king judges the poor with fairness,
his throne will always be secure.

29:26
Many seek an audience with a ruler,
but it is from the LORD that man gets
justice.

31:4-5
"It is not for kings, O Lemuel—
not for kings to drink wine,
not for rulers to crave beer,
⁵lest they drink and forget what the law
decrees,
and deprive all the oppressed of their
rights."

31:8-9
"Speak up for those who cannot speak
for themselves,
for the rights of all who are destitute.
⁹Speak up and judge fairly;
defend the rights of the poor and
needy."

KINDNESS
(Also see Generosity)
11:16-17
A kindhearted woman gains respect,
but ruthless men gain only wealth.

¹⁷A kind man benefits himself,
but a cruel man brings trouble on
himself.

12:10
A righteous man cares for the needs of
his animal,
but the kindest acts of the wicked are
cruel.

12:25
An anxious heart weighs a man down,
but a kind word cheers him up.

14:21
He who despises his neighbor sins,
   but blessed is he who is kind to the
      needy.

14:31
He who oppresses the poor shows
      contempt for their Maker,
   but whoever is kind to the needy
      honors God.

15:1
A gentle answer turns away wrath,
   but a harsh word stirs up anger.

19:17
He who is kind to the poor lends to the
      LORD,
   and he will reward him for what he
      has done.

25:15
Through patience a ruler can be
      persuaded,
   and a gentle tongue can break a bone.

28:8
He who increases his wealth by
      exorbitant interest
   amasses it for another, who will be
      kind to the poor.

KINGS
(See Rulers)

KNOWLEDGE
1:4
[Proverbs] for giving prudence to the
      simple,
   knowledge and discretion to the
      young—

1:7
The fear of the LORD is the beginning of
      knowledge,
   but fools despise wisdom and
      discipline.

1:29
"Since they hated knowledge
   and did not choose to fear the LORD..."

2:1-6
My son, if you accept my words
   and store up my commands within
      you,
[2]turning your ear to wisdom
   and applying your heart to understand-
      ing,
[3]and if you call out for insight
   and cry aloud for understanding,
[4]and if you look for it as for silver
   and search for it as for hidden treasure,
[5]then you will understand the fear of the
      LORD
   and find the knowledge of God.
[6]For the LORD gives wisdom,
   and from his mouth come knowledge
      and understanding.

2:10
For wisdom will enter your heart,
   and knowledge will be pleasant to
      your soul.

3:19-20
By wisdom the LORD laid the earth's
      foundations,
   by understanding he set the heavens
      in place;
[20]by his knowledge the deeps were
      divided,
   and the clouds let drop the dew.

5:2
...that you may maintain discretion
   and your lips may preserve knowl-
      edge.

8:10
"Choose my [wisdom's] instruction
      instead of silver,
   knowledge rather than choice
      gold..."

9:10
"The fear of the LORD is the beginning
      of wisdom,
   and knowledge of the Holy One is
      understanding."

9:13
The woman Folly is loud;
    she is undisciplined and without
        knowledge.

10:14
Wise men store up knowledge,
    but the mouth of a fool invites ruin.

11:9
With his mouth the godless destroys his
        neighbor,
    but through knowledge the righteous
        escape.

12:1
Whoever loves discipline loves
        knowledge,
    but he who hates correction is stupid.

12:23
A prudent man keeps his knowledge to
        himself,
    but the heart of fools blurts out folly.

13:16
Every prudent man acts out of
        knowledge,
    but a fool exposes his folly.

14:6-7
The mocker seeks wisdom and finds
        none,
    but knowledge comes easily to the
        discerning.

⁷Stay away from a foolish man,
    for you will not find knowledge on
        his lips.

14:18
The simple inherit folly,
    but the prudent are crowned with
        knowledge.

15:2
The tongue of the wise commends
        knowledge,
    but the mouth of the fool gushes
        folly.

15:7
The lips of the wise spread knowledge;
    not so the hearts of fools.

15:14
The discerning heart seeks knowledge,
    but the mouth of a fool feeds on folly.

17:27
A man of knowledge uses words with
        restraint,
    and a man of understanding is even-
        tempered.

18:15
The heart of the discerning acquires
        knowledge;
    the ears of the wise seek it out.

19:2
It is not good to have zeal without
        knowledge,
    nor to be hasty and miss the way.

19:25
Flog a mocker, and the simple will
        learn prudence;
    rebuke a discerning man, and he will
        gain knowledge.

19:27
Stop listening to instruction, my son,
    and you will stray from the words of
        knowledge.

20:15
Gold there is, and rubies in abundance,
    but lips that speak knowledge are a
        rare jewel.

21:11
When a mocker is punished, the simple
        gain wisdom;
    when a wise man is instructed, he
        gets knowledge.

22:12
The eyes of the Lord keep watch over
        knowledge,
    but he frustrates the words of the
        unfaithful.

22:20
Have I not written thirty sayings for
you,
sayings of counsel and knowledge...

23:12
Apply your heart to instruction
and your ears to words of knowledge.

24:4
Through knowledge its rooms
[wisdom's house] are filled
with rare and beautiful treasures.

24:5
A wise man has great power,
and a man of knowledge increases
strength...

28:2
When a country is rebellious, it has
many rulers,
but a man of understanding and
knowledge maintains order.

30:3
"I [Agur son of Jakeh] have not learned
wisdom,
nor have I knowledge of the Holy
One."

LAUGHTER
(Also see Joy, Pleasure)
1:26
"I [wisdom] in turn will laugh at your
disaster;
I will mock when calamity overtakes
you—"

14:13
Even in laughter the heart may ache,
and joy may end in grief.

31:25
She [a wife of noble character] is
clothed with strength and
dignity;
she can laugh at the days to come.

LAW
(See Commands, Obedience)
8:15
By me [wisdom] kings reign
and rulers make laws that are just...

28:4
Those who forsake the law praise the
wicked,
but those who keep the law resist
them.

28:7
He who keeps the law is a discerning
son,
but a companion of gluttons
disgraces his father.

28:9
If anyone turns a deaf ear to the law,
even his prayers are detestable.

29:18
Where there is no revelation, the
people cast off restraint;
but blessed is he who keeps the law.

31:5
"...lest they drink and forget what the
law decrees,
and deprive all the oppressed of their
rights."

LAZINESS
(Also see Discipline, Hard Work)
6:6-11
Go to the ant, you sluggard;
consider its ways and be wise!
[7]It has no commander,
no overseer or ruler,
[8]yet it stores its provisions in summer
and gathers its food at harvest.

[9]How long will you lie there, you
sluggard?
When will you get up from your
sleep?
[10]A little sleep, a little slumber,
a little folding of the hands to rest—

[11]and poverty will come on you like a
     bandit
and scarcity like an armed man.

10:4-5
Lazy hands make a man poor,
     but diligent hands bring wealth.
[5]He who gathers crops in summer is
     a wise son,
but he who sleeps during harvest is a
     disgraceful son.

10:26
As vinegar to the teeth and smoke to
     the eyes,
so is a sluggard to those who send
     him.

12:11
He who works his land will have
     abundant food,
but he who chases fantasies lacks
     judgment.

12:24
Diligent hands will rule,
     but laziness ends in slave labor.

12:27
The lazy man does not roast his game,
     but the diligent man prizes his
     possessions.

13:4
The sluggard craves and gets nothing,
     but the desires of the diligent are
     fully satisfied.

14:23
All hard work brings a profit,
     but mere talk leads only to poverty.

15:19
The way of the sluggard is blocked
     with thorns,
but the path of the upright is a
     highway.

18:9
One who is slack in his work
     is brother to one who destroys.

19:15
Laziness brings on deep sleep,
     and the shiftless man goes hungry.

19:24
The sluggard buries his hand in the
     dish;
he will not even bring it back to his
     mouth!

20:4
A sluggard does not plow in season;
     so at harvest time he looks but finds
     nothing.

20:13
Do not love sleep or you will grow
     poor;
stay awake and you will have food to
     spare.

21:5
The plans of the diligent lead to profit
     as surely as haste leads to poverty.

21:17
He who loves pleasure will become
     poor;
whoever loves wine and oil will
     never be rich.

21:25-26
The sluggard's craving will be the death
     of him,
because his hands refuse to work.
[26]All day long he craves for more,
     but the righteous give without
     sparing.

22:13
The sluggard says, "There is a lion
     outside!"
or, "I will be murdered in the streets!"

23:21
...for drunkards and gluttons become
     poor,
and drowsiness clothes them in rags.

24:30-34
I went past the field of the sluggard,
  past the vineyard of the man who
    lacks judgment;
[31]thorns had come up everywhere,
  the ground was covered with weeds,
  and the stone wall was in ruins.
[32]I applied my heart to what I observed
  and learned a lesson from what I
    saw:
[33]A little sleep, a little slumber,
  a little folding of the hands to rest—
[34]and poverty will come on you like a
    bandit
  and scarcity like an armed man.

26:13-16
The sluggard says, "There is a lion in
    the road,
  a fierce lion roaming the streets!"

[14]As a door turns on its hinges,
  so a sluggard turns on his bed.

[15]The sluggard buries his hand in the
    dish;
  he is too lazy to bring it back to his
    mouth.

[16]The sluggard is wiser in his own eyes
  than seven men who answer
    discreetly.

28:19
He who works his land will have
    abundant food,
  but the one who chases fantasies will
    have his fill of poverty.

LEADING
2:18
For her [the adulteress'] house leads
    down to death
  and her paths to the spirits of the
    dead.

4:11
I guide you in the way of wisdom
  and lead you along straight paths.

5:5
Her [the adulteress'] feet go down to
    death;
  her steps lead straight to the grave.

7:27
Her [the adulteress'] house is a highway
    to the grave,
  leading down to the chambers of
    death.

8:3-4
...beside the gates leading into the city,
  at the entrances, she [wisdom] cries
    aloud:
[4]"To you, O men, I call out;
  I raise my voice to all mankind."

10:17
He who heeds discipline shows the
    way to life,
  but whoever ignores correction leads
    others astray.

12:26
A righteous man is cautious in
    friendship,
  but the way of the wicked leads them
    astray.

14:12
There is a way that seems right to a
    man,
  but in the end it leads to death.

14:23
All hard work brings a profit,
  but mere talk leads only to poverty.

15:24
The path of life leads upward for the
    wise
  to keep him from going down to the
    grave.

16:25
There is a way that seems right to a
    man,
  but in the end it leads to death.

16:29
A violent man entices his neighbor
and leads him down a path that is
not good.

19:23
The fear of the LORD leads to life:
Then one rests content, untouched
by trouble.

20:7
The righteous man leads a blameless
life;
blessed are his children after him.

21:5
The plans of the diligent lead to profit
as surely as haste leads to poverty.

28:10
He who leads the upright along an evil
path
will fall into his own trap,
but the blameless will receive a good
inheritance.

LIFE
(Also see Death, Grave)
2:19
None who go to her [the adulteress]
return
or attain the paths of life.

3:2
For they [the LORD's commands] will
prolong your life many years
and bring you prosperity.

3:22
They [the LORD's commands] will be life
for you,
an ornament to grace your neck.

4:10
Listen, my son, accept what I say,
and the years of your life will be
many.

4:13
Hold on to instruction, do not let it go;
guard it well, for it is your life.

4:22-23
For they [wisdom's words] are life to
those who find them
and health to a man's whole body.
²³Above all else, guard your heart,
for it is the wellspring of life.

5:6
She [the adulteress] gives no thought to
the way of life;
her paths are crooked, but she knows
it not.

5:11
At the end of your life you will groan,
when your flesh and body are spent.

6:23
For these commands are a lamp,
this teaching is a light,
and the corrections of discipline
are the way to life...

8:35
"For whoever finds me [wisdom] finds
life
and receives favor from the LORD."

9:11
"For through me [wisdom] your days
will be many,
and years will be added to your life."

10:11
The mouth of the righteous is a
fountain of life,
but violence overwhelms the mouth
of the wicked.

10:16-17
The wages of the righteous bring them
life,
but the income of the wicked brings
them punishment.

¹⁷He who heeds discipline shows the
way to life,
but whoever ignores correction leads
others astray.

10:27
The fear of the LORD adds length to life,
   but the years of the wicked are cut
      short.

11:19
The truly righteous man attains life,
   but he who pursues evil goes to his
      death.

11:30
The fruit of the righteous is a tree of life,
   and he who wins souls is wise.

12:28
In the way of righteousness there is life;
   along that path is immortality.

13:8
A man's riches may ransom his life,
   but a poor man hears no threat.

13:12
Hope deferred makes the heart sick,
   but a longing fulfilled is a tree of life.

13:14
The teaching of the wise is a fountain
      of life,
   turning a man from the snares of
      death.

14:27
The fear of the LORD is a fountain of life,
   turning a man from the snares of
      death.

14:30
A heart at peace gives life to the body,
   but envy rots the bones.

15:4
The tongue that brings healing is a tree
      of life,
   but a deceitful tongue crushes the
      spirit.

15:24
The path of life leads upward for the
      wise

to keep him from going down to the
      grave.

16:15
When a king's face brightens, it means
      life;
   his favor is like a rain cloud in
      spring.

16:22
Understanding is a fountain of life to
      those who have it,
   but folly brings punishment to fools.

16:31
Gray hair is a crown of splendor;
   it is attained by a righteous life.

18:21
The tongue has the power of life and
      death,
   and those who love it will eat its
      fruit.

19:3
A man's own folly ruins his life,
   yet his heart rages against the LORD.

19:23
The fear of the LORD leads to life:
   Then one rests content, untouched
      by trouble.

20:2
A king's wrath is like the roar of a lion;
   he who angers him forfeits his life.

20:7
The righteous man leads a blameless
      life;
   blessed are his children after him.

21:21
He who pursues righteousness and love
   finds life, prosperity and honor.

22:4
Humility and the fear of the LORD
   bring wealth and honor and life.

23:22
Listen to your father, who gave you life,
and do not despise your mother
when she is old.

24:12
If you say, "But we knew nothing
about this,"
does not he who weighs the heart
perceive it?
Does not he who guards your life know
it?
Will he not repay each person
according to what he has done?

28:16
A tyrannical ruler lacks judgment,
but he who hates ill-gotten gain will
enjoy a long life.

31:12
She [a wife of noble character] brings
him good, not harm,
all the days of her life.

LOANS
(See Financial Matters)

LORD
(Also see God*)*
1:7
The fear of the Lord is the beginning of
knowledge,
but fools despise wisdom and
discipline.

1:29-31
"Since they hated knowledge
and did not choose to fear the Lord,
30since they would not accept my
[wisdom's] advice
and spurned my rebuke,
31they will eat the fruit of their ways
and be filled with the fruit of their
schemes."

2:6-8
For the Lord gives wisdom,
and from his mouth come knowledge
and understanding.

7He holds victory in store for the
upright,
he is a shield to those whose walk is
blameless,
8for he guards the course of the just
and protects the way of his faithful
ones.

3:5-10
Trust in the Lord with all your heart
and lean not on your own understanding;
6in all your ways acknowledge him,
and he will make your paths straight.

7Do not be wise in your own eyes;
fear the Lord and shun evil.
8This will bring health to your body
and nourishment to your bones.

9Honor the Lord with your wealth,
with the firstfruits of all your crops;
10then your barns will be filled to
overflowing,
and your vats will brim over with
new wine.

3:19-21
By wisdom the Lord laid the earth's
foundations,
by understanding he set the heavens
in place;
20by his knowledge the deeps were
divided,
and the clouds let drop the dew.

21My son, preserve sound judgment and
discernment,
do not let them out of your sight...

3:25-26
Have no fear of sudden disaster
or of the ruin that overtakes the
wicked,
26for the Lord will be your confidence
and will keep your foot from being
snared.

3:31-32
Do not envy a violent man
or choose any of his ways,

³²for the LORD detests a perverse man
but takes the upright into his
confidence.

6:16-19
There are six things the LORD hates,
seven that are detestable to him:
¹⁷haughty eyes,
a lying tongue,
hands that shed innocent blood,
¹⁸a heart that devises wicked
schemes,
feet that are quick to rush into evil,
¹⁹a false witness who pours out lies
and a man who stirs up dissension
among brothers.

8:35
"For whoever finds me [wisdom] finds
life
and receives favor from the LORD."

9:10
"The fear of the LORD is the beginning
of wisdom,
and knowledge of the Holy One is
understanding."

11:1
The LORD abhors dishonest scales,
but accurate weights are his delight.

11:20
The LORD detests men of perverse heart
but he delights in those whose ways
are blameless.

12:2
A good man obtains favor from the LORD,
but the LORD condemns a crafty man.

12:22
The LORD detests lying lips,
but he delights in men who are
truthful.

14:26-27
He who fears the LORD has a secure
fortress,
and for his children it will be a
refuge.

²⁷The fear of the LORD is a fountain of
life,
turning a man from the snares of
death.

15:3
The eyes of the LORD are everywhere,
keeping watch on the wicked and
the good.

15:8-9
The LORD detests the sacrifice of the
wicked,
but the prayer of the upright pleases
him.

⁹The LORD detests the way of the
wicked
but he loves those who pursue
righteousness.

15:11
Death and Destruction lie open before
the LORD—
how much more the hearts of men!

15:25
The LORD tears down the proud man's
house
but he keeps the widow's boundaries
intact.

15:29
The LORD is far from the wicked
but he hears the prayer of the
righteous.

16:1-5
To man belong the plans of the heart,
but from the LORD comes the reply of
the tongue.

²All a man's ways seem innocent to him,
but motives are weighed by the LORD.

³Commit to the LORD whatever you do,
and your plans will succeed.

⁴The LORD works out everything for his
own ends—
even the wicked for a day of disaster.

⁵The LORD detests all the proud of heart.
Be sure of this: They will not go
unpunished.

16:9
In his heart a man plans his course,
but the LORD determines his steps.
16:11
Honest scales and balances are from
the LORD;
all the weights in the bag are of his
making.

16:33
The lot is cast into the lap,
but its every decision is from the
LORD.

17:3
The crucible for silver and the furnace
for gold,
but the LORD tests the heart.

17:15
Acquitting the guilty and condemning
the innocent—
the LORD detests them both.

19:21
Many are the plans in a man's heart,
but it is the LORD's purpose that
prevails.

20:10
Differing weights and differing
measures—
the LORD detests them both.

20:12
Ears that hear and eyes that see—
the LORD has made them both.

20:23
The LORD detests differing weights,
and dishonest scales do not please
him.

LOTS
(See Financial Matters)

LOVE
(Also see Hate)
3:3-4
Let love and faithfulness never leave
you;
bind them around your neck,
write them on the tablet of your
heart.
⁴Then you will win favor and a good
name
in the sight of God and man.

13:24
He who spares the rod hates his son,
but he who loves him is careful to
discipline him.

14:22
Do not those who plot evil go astray?
But those who plan what is good
find love and faithfulness.

15:9
The LORD detests the way of the wicked
but he loves those who pursue
righteousness.

15:17
Better a meal of vegetables where there
is love
than a fattened calf with hatred.

16:6
Through love and faithfulness sin is
atoned for;
through the fear of the LORD a man
avoids evil.

17:9
He who covers over an offense
promotes love,
but whoever repeats the matter
separates close friends.

17:17
A friend loves at all times,
and a brother is born for adversity.

19:8
He who gets wisdom loves his own soul;

he who cherishes understanding
    prospers.

19:12
A king's rage is like the roar of a lion,
    but his favor is like dew on the grass.

19:22
What a man desires is unfailing love;
    better to be poor than a liar.

20:6
Many a man claims to have unfailing
    love,
    but a faithful man who can find?

20:28
Love and faithfulness keep a king safe;
    through love his throne is made
    secure.

21:21
He who pursues righteousness and love
    finds life, prosperity and honor.

27:5
Better is open rebuke
    than hidden love.

LUST
(See Eyes, Sin, Temptation)

LYING
(Also see Tongue, False Witness)
10:18
He who conceals his hatred has lying
    lips,
    and whoever spreads slander is a
    fool.

12:5
The plans of the righteous are just,
    but the advice of the wicked is
    deceitful.

12:17
A truthful witness gives honest
    testimony,
    but a false witness tells lies.

12:19-20
Truthful lips endure forever,
    but a lying tongue lasts only a moment.

[20]There is deceit in the hearts of those
    who plot evil,
    but joy for those who promote peace.

12:22
The Lord detests lying lips,
    but he delights in men who are
    truthful.

14:5
A truthful witness does not deceive,
    but a false witness pours out lies.

14:8
The wisdom of the prudent is to give
    thought to their ways,
    but the folly of fools is deception.

14:25
A truthful witness saves lives,
    but a false witness is deceitful.

15:4
The tongue that brings healing is a tree
    of life,
    but a deceitful tongue crushes the
    spirit.

17:4
A wicked man listens to evil lips;
    a liar pays attention to a malicious
    tongue.

17:7
Arrogant lips are unsuited to a fool—
    how much worse lying lips to a ruler!

17:20
A man of perverse heart does not
    prosper;
    he whose tongue is deceitful falls
    into trouble.

19:5
A false witness will not go unpunished,
    and he who pours out lies will not go
    free.

19:8
He who gets wisdom loves his own
soul;
he who cherishes understanding
prospers.

19:22
What a man desires is unfailing love;
better to be poor than a liar.

20:17
Food gained by fraud tastes sweet to a
man,
but he ends up with a mouth full of
gravel.

21:6
A fortune made by a lying tongue
is a fleeting vapor and a deadly
snare.

21:28
A false witness will perish,
and whoever listens to him will be
destroyed forever.

24:28
Do not testify against your neighbor
without cause,
or use your lips to deceive.

25:14
Like clouds and wind without rain
is a man who boasts of gifts he does
not give.

25:18
Like a club or a sword or a sharp arrow
is the man who gives false testimony
against his neighbor.

26:18-19
Like a madman shooting
firebrands or deadly arrows
[19]is a man who deceives his neighbor
and says, "I was only joking!"

26:24-28
A malicious man disguises himself with
his lips,
but in his heart he harbors deceit.

[25]Though his speech is charming, do
not believe him,
for seven abominations fill his heart.
[26]His malice may be concealed by
deception,
but his wickedness will be exposed
in the assembly.

[27]If a man digs a pit, he will fall into it;
if a man rolls a stone, it will roll back
on him.

[28]A lying tongue hates those it hurts,
and a flattering mouth works ruin.

29:12
If a ruler listens to lies,
all his officials become wicked.

30:8
"Keep falsehood and lies far from me;
give me neither poverty nor riches,
but give me only my daily bread."

MASTERS
(Also see Rulers)
27:18
He who tends a fig tree will eat its
fruit,
and he who looks after his master
will be honored.

30:10
"Do not slander a servant to his master,
or he will curse you, and you will
pay for it."

MATERIALISM
(See Prosperity, Selfishness)

MEASUREMENTS
11:1
The LORD abhors dishonest scales,
but accurate weights are his delight.

16:11
Honest scales and balances are from
the LORD;
all the weights in the bag are of his
making.

20:10

Differing weights and differing
measures—
the LORD detests them both.

20:23

The LORD detests differing weights,
and dishonest scales do not please
him.

MESSAGE/MESSENGER

13:17

A wicked messenger falls into trouble,
but a trustworthy envoy brings
healing.

16:14

A king's wrath is a messenger of death,
but a wise man will appease it.

25:13

Like the coolness of snow at harvest
time
is a trustworthy messenger to those
who send him;
he refreshes the spirit of his masters.

26:6

Like cutting off one's feet or drinking
violence
is the sending of a message by the
hand of a fool.

MOCKER

(Also see Dissension, Strife, Tongue)
9:7-8

"Whoever corrects a mocker invites
insult;
whoever rebukes a wicked man
incurs abuse.
⁸Do not rebuke a mocker or he will
hate you;
rebuke a wise man and he will love
you."

9:12

"If you are wise, your wisdom will
reward you;
if you are a mocker, you alone will
suffer."

13:1

A wise son heeds his father's instruction,
but a mocker does not listen to
rebuke.

14:6

The mocker seeks wisdom and finds
none,
but knowledge comes easily to the
discerning.

14:9

Fools mock at making amends for sin,
but goodwill is found among the
upright.

15:12

A mocker resents correction;
he will not consult the wise.

19:25

Flog a mocker, and the simple will
learn prudence;
rebuke a discerning man, and he will
gain knowledge.

19:29

Penalties are prepared for mockers,
and beatings for the backs of fools.

20:1

Wine is a mocker and beer a brawler;
whoever is led astray by them is not
wise.

21:11

When a mocker is punished, the simple
gain wisdom;
when a wise man is instructed, he
gets knowledge.

21:24

The proud and arrogant man—
"Mocker" is his name;
he behaves with overweening pride.

22:10

Drive out the mocker, and out goes
strife;
quarrels and insults are ended.

24:8-9
He who plots evil
    will be known as a schemer.
⁹The schemes of folly are sin,
    and men detest a mocker.

29:8
Mockers stir up a city,
    but wise men turn away anger.

30:17
"The eye that mocks a father,
    that scorns obedience to a mother,
will be pecked out by the ravens of the
        valley,
    will be eaten by the vultures."

MONEY
*(See Financial Matters, Poverty,
    Prosperity)*

MOTHERS
(See Parents)

MOTIVES
16:2
All a man's ways seem innocent to him,
    but motives are weighed by the LORD.

MURDER
28:17
A man tormented by the guilt of murder
    will be a fugitive till death;
    let no one support him.

NATIONS
11:14
For lack of guidance a nation falls,
    but many advisers make victory sure.

14:34
Righteousness exalts a nation,
    but sin is a disgrace to any people.

24:24
Whoever says to the guilty, "You are
        innocent"—
peoples will curse him and nations
        denounce him.

NEIGHBOR
(Also see Friendship)
3:28-29
Do not say to your neighbor,
    "Come back later; I'll give it
        tomorrow"—
    when you now have it with you.
²⁹Do not plot harm against your
        neighbor,
    who lives trustfully near you.

6:1-5
My son, if you have put up security for
        your neighbor,
    if you have struck hands in pledge
        for another,
²if you have been trapped by what you
        said,
    ensnared by the words of your mouth,
³then do this, my son, to free yourself,
    since you have fallen into your
        neighbor's hands:
Go and humble yourself;
    press your plea with your neighbor!
⁴Allow no sleep to your eyes,
    no slumber to your eyelids.
⁵Free yourself, like a gazelle from the
        hand of the hunter,
    like a bird from the snare of the
        fowler.

11:9
With his mouth the godless destroys his
        neighbor,
    but through knowledge the righteous
        escape.

11:12
A man who lacks judgment derides his
        neighbor,
    but a man of understanding holds his
        tongue.

14:20-21
The poor are shunned even by their
        neighbors,
    but the rich have many friends.

²¹He who despises his neighbor sins,
    but blessed is he who is kind to the
        needy.

16:29

A violent man entices his neighbor
and leads him down a path that is
not good.

17:18

A man lacking in judgment strikes
hands in pledge
and puts up security for his neighbor.

21:10

The wicked man craves evil;
his neighbor gets no mercy from him.

24:28

Do not testify against your neighbor
without cause,
or use your lips to deceive.

25:7b-10

What you have seen with your eyes
[8]do not bring hastily to court,
for what will you do in the end
if your neighbor puts you to shame?

[9]If you argue your case with a
neighbor,
do not betray another man's
confidence,
[10]or he who hears it may shame you
and you will never lose your bad
reputation.

25:17-18

Seldom set foot in your neighbor's
house—
too much of you, and he will hate
you.

[18]Like a club or a sword or a sharp
arrow
is the man who gives false testimony
against his neighbor.

26:18-19

Like a madman shooting
firebrands or deadly arrows
[19]is a man who deceives his neighbor
and says, "I was only joking!"

27:10

Do not forsake your friend and the
friend of your father,
and do not go to your brother's
house when disaster strikes
you—
better a neighbor nearby than a
brother far away.

27:14

If a man loudly blesses his neighbor
early in the morning,
it will be taken as a curse.

29:5

Whoever flatters his neighbor
is spreading a net for his feet.

OBEDIENCE
(Also see Commands, Law)

4:5

Get wisdom, get understanding;
do not forget my words or swerve
from them.

5:13

[A ruined man at the end of his life says,]
"I would not obey my teachers
or listen to my instructors."

7:1

My son, keep my words
and store up my commands within
you.

19:16

He who obeys instructions guards his
life,
but he who is contemptuous of his
ways will die.

28:4

Those who forsake the law praise the
wicked,
but those who keep the law resist
them.

28:7

He who keeps the law is a discerning
son,

but a companion of gluttons
disgraces his father.

28:9
If anyone turns a deaf ear to the law,
even his prayers are detestable.

29:18
Where there is no revelation, the
people cast off restraint;
but blessed is he who keeps the law.

30:6
"Do not add to his words,
or he will rebuke you and prove you
a liar."

30:17
"The eye that mocks a father,
that scorns obedience to a mother,
will be pecked out by the ravens of the
valley,
will be eaten by the vultures."

31:5
[Kings are not to drink wine or rulers
crave beer]
"lest they drink and forget what the law
decrees,
and deprive all the oppressed of their
rights."

OPPRESSION
(Also see Justice, Rulers)
14:31
He who oppresses the poor shows
contempt for their Maker,
but whoever is kind to the needy
honors God.

15:15
All the days of the oppressed are
wretched,
but the cheerful heart has a continual
feast.

16:19
Better to be lowly in spirit and among
the oppressed
than to share plunder with the proud.

22:16
He who oppresses the poor to increase
his wealth
and he who gives gifts to the rich—
both come to poverty.

28:3
A ruler who oppresses the poor
is like a driving rain that leaves no
crops.

31:5
"...lest they drink and forget what the
law decrees,
and deprive all the oppressed of their
rights."

PARENTS
(Also see Children, Family)
1:8-9
Listen, my son, to your father's
instruction
and do not forsake your mother's
teaching.
⁹They will be a garland to grace your
head
and a chain to adorn your neck.

4:1-4
Listen, my sons, to a father's instruction;
pay attention and gain understanding.
²I give you sound learning,
so do not forsake my teaching.
³When I was a boy in my father's
house,
still tender, and an only child of my
mother,
⁴he taught me and said,
"Lay hold of my words with all your
heart;
keep my commands and you will
live."

4:10
Listen, my son, accept what I say,
and the years of your life will be many.

4:20-22
My son, pay attention to what I say;
listen closely to my words.

[21]Do not let them out of your sight,
   keep them within your heart;
[22]for they are life to those who find
   them
and health to a man's whole body.

6:20-24

My son, keep your father's commands
   and do not forsake your mother's
   teaching.
[21]Bind them upon your heart forever;
   fasten them around your neck.
[22]When you walk, they will guide you;
   when you sleep, they will watch over
   you;
   when you awake, they will speak to
   you.
[23]For these commands are a lamp,
   this teaching is a light,
and the corrections of discipline
are the way to life,
[24]keeping you from the immoral
   woman,
from the smooth tongue of the
   wayward wife.

10:1

The proverbs of Solomon:

A wise son brings joy to his father,
   but a foolish son grief to his mother.

13:1

A wise son heeds his father's instruction,
   but a mocker does not listen to
   rebuke.

13:22

A good man leaves an inheritance for
   his children's children,
   but a sinner's wealth is stored up for
   the righteous.

14:26

He who fears the LORD has a secure
   fortress,
   and for his children it will be a
   refuge.

15:5

A fool spurns his father's discipline,
   but whoever heeds correction shows
   prudence.

15:20

A wise son brings joy to his father,
   but a foolish man despises his
   mother.

17:6

Children's children are a crown to the
   aged,
   and parents are the pride of their
   children.

17:21

To have a fool for a son brings grief;
   there is no joy for the father of a fool.

17:25

A foolish son brings grief to his father
   and bitterness to the one who bore
   him.

19:13-14

A foolish son is his father's ruin,
   and a quarrelsome wife is like a
   constant dripping.

[14]Houses and wealth are inherited from
   parents,
   but a prudent wife is from the LORD.

19:26

He who robs his father and drives out
   his mother
is a son who brings shame and
   disgrace.

23:15

My son, if your heart is wise,
   then my heart will be glad...

23:19

Listen, my son, and be wise,
   and keep your heart on the right
   path.

23:22
Listen to your father, who gave you life,
and do not despise your mother
when she is old.

23:24-27
The father of a righteous man has great
joy;
he who has a wise son delights in
him.
[25]May your father and mother be glad;
may she who gave you birth rejoice!

[26]My son, give me your heart
and let your eyes keep to my ways,
[27]for a prostitute is a deep pit
and a wayward wife is a narrow well.

24:13
Eat honey, my son, for it is good;
honey from the comb is sweet to
your taste.

24:21
Fear the LORD and the king, my son,
and do not join with the rebellious...

25:24
Better to live on a corner of the roof
than share a house with a quarrelsome wife.

27:10-11
Do not forsake your friend and the
friend of your father,
and do not go to your brother's
house when disaster strikes
you—
better a neighbor nearby than a
brother far away.

[11]Be wise, my son, and bring joy to my
heart;
then I can answer anyone who treats
me with contempt.

27:15
A quarrelsome wife is like
a constant dripping on a rainy day...

28:7
He who keeps the law is a discerning
son,
but a companion of gluttons
disgraces his father.

28:24
He who robs his father or mother
and says, "It's not wrong"—
he is partner to him who destroys.

29:3
A man who loves wisdom brings joy to
his father,
but a companion of prostitutes
squanders his wealth.

29:15
The rod of correction imparts wisdom,
but a child left to himself disgraces
his mother.

30:17
"The eye that mocks a father,
that scorns obedience to a mother,
will be pecked out by the ravens of the
valley,
will be eaten by the vultures."

THE PATH
1:15
...my son, do not go along with them
[sinners],
do not set foot on their paths...

2:8
For he [the LORD] guards the course of
the just
and protects the way of his faithful
ones.

2:12-15
Wisdom will save you from the ways of
wicked men,
from men whose words are perverse,
[13]who leave the straight paths
to walk in dark ways,
[14]who delight in doing wrong
and rejoice in the perverseness of evil,
[15]whose paths are crooked
and who are devious in their ways.

2:18-20

For her [the adulteress'] house leads
    down to death
    and her paths to the spirits of the
    dead.
[19]None who go to her return
    or attain the paths of life.

[20]Thus you will walk in the ways of
    good men
    and keep to the paths of the
    righteous.

3:6

...in all your ways acknowledge him
    [the LORD],
    and he will make your paths straight.

3:16-17

Long life is in her [wisdom's] right
    hand;
    in her left hand are riches and honor.
Her ways are pleasant ways,
    and all her paths are peace.

3:22-23

They [sound judgment and discern-
    ment] will be life for you,
    an ornament to grace your neck.
[23]Then you will go on your way in
    safety,
    and your foot will not stumble...

4:11

I [wisdom] guide you in the way of
    wisdom
    and lead you along straight paths.

4:14-15

Do not set foot on the path of the
    wicked
    or walk in the way of evil men.
[15]Avoid it, do not travel on it;
    turn from it and go on your way.

4:18-19

The path of the righteous is like the
    first gleam of dawn,
    shining ever brighter till the full light
    of day.

[19]But the way of the wicked is like
    deep darkness;
    they do not know what makes them
    stumble.

4:26

Make level paths for your feet
    and take only ways that are firm.

5:6

She [the adulteress] gives no thought to
    the way of life;
    her paths are crooked, but she knows
    it not.

5:21

For a man's ways are in full view of the
    LORD,
    and he examines all his paths.

7:25

Do not let your heart turn to her [the
    adulteress'] ways
    or stray into her paths.

8:2

On the heights along the way,
    where the paths meet, she [wisdom]
    takes her stand...

8:20

"I [wisdom] walk in the way of
    righteousness,
    along the paths of justice..."

9:6

"Leave your simple ways and you will
    live;
    walk in the way of understanding."

9:15

[Folly is] calling out to those who pass
    by,
    who go straight on their way.

10:9

The man of integrity walks securely,
    but he who takes crooked paths will
    be found out.

10:17
He who heeds discipline shows the
way to life,
but whoever ignores correction leads
others astray.

10:29
The way of the LORD is a refuge for the
righteous,
but it is the ruin of those who do
evil.

11:5
The righteousness of the blameless
makes a straight way for them,
but the wicked are brought down by
their own wickedness.

12:12
The wicked desire the plunder of evil
men,
but the root of the righteous
flourishes.

12:26
A righteous man is cautious in
friendship,
but the way of the wicked leads them
astray.

12:28
In the way of righteousness there is life;
along that path is immortality.

13:15
Good understanding wins favor,
but the way of the unfaithful is hard.

14:12
There is a way that seems right to a
man,
but in the end it leads to death.

15:9
The LORD detests the way of the wicked
but he loves those who pursue
righteousness.

15:19
The way of the sluggard is blocked
with thorns,

but the path of the upright is a
highway.

15:21
Folly delights a man who lacks
judgment,
but a man of understanding keeps a
straight course.

16:9
In his heart a man plans his course,
but the LORD determines his steps.

16:17
The highway of the upright avoids evil;
he who guards his way guards his
life.

16:25
There is a way that seems right to a
man,
but in the end it leads to death.

17:23
A wicked man accepts a bribe in secret
to pervert the course of justice.

18:16
A gift opens the way for the giver
and ushers him into the presence of
the great.

19:2
It is not good to have zeal without
knowledge,
nor to be hasty and miss the way.

20:24
A man's steps are directed by the LORD.
How then can anyone understand his
own way?

21:8
The way of the guilty is devious,
but the conduct of the innocent is
upright.

22:5-6
In the paths of the wicked lie thorns
and snares,
but he who guards his soul stays far
from them.

⁶Train a child in the way he should go,
and when he is old he will not turn
from it.

25:26
Like a muddied spring or a polluted
well
is a righteous man who gives way to
the wicked.

30:18-20
"There are three things that are too
amazing for me,
four that I do not understand:
¹⁹the way of an eagle in the sky,
the way of a snake on a rock,
the way of a ship on the high seas,
and the way of a man with a maiden.

²⁰"This is the way of an adulteress:
She eats and wipes her mouth
and says, 'I've done nothing wrong.'"

PATIENCE
(Also see Hope)
14:29
A patient man has great understanding,
but a quick-tempered man displays
folly.

15:18
A hot-tempered man stirs up dissension,
but a patient man calms a quarrel.

16:32
Better a patient man than a warrior,
a man who controls his temper than
one who takes a city.

19:11
A man's wisdom gives him patience;
it is to his glory to overlook an
offense.

25:15
Through patience a ruler can be
persuaded,
and a gentle tongue can break a
bone.

PEACE
(Also see Refuge, Safety)
3:17
Her ways are pleasant ways,
and all her paths are peace.

12:20
There is deceit in the hearts of those
who plot evil,
but joy for those who promote peace.

14:30
A heart at peace gives life to the body,
but envy rots the bones.

16:7
When a man's ways are pleasing to the
LORD,
he makes even his enemies live at
peace with him.

17:1
Better a dry crust with peace and quiet
than a house full of feasting, with
strife.

29:9
If a wise man goes to court with a fool,
the fool rages and scoffs, and there is
no peace.

29:17
Discipline your son, and he will give
you peace;
he will bring delight to your soul.

PLANS
(Also see Advice, Purpose)
12:5
The plans of the righteous are just,
but the advice of the wicked is
deceitful.

14:22
Do not those who plot evil go astray?
But those who plan what is good
find love and faithfulness.

15:22
Plans fail for lack of counsel,
but with many advisers they succeed.

16:1
To man belong the plans of the heart,
but from the LORD comes the reply of
the tongue.

16:3
Commit to the LORD whatever you do,
and your plans will succeed.

16:9
In his heart a man plans his course,
but the LORD determines his steps.

19:21
Many are the plans in a man's heart,
but it is the LORD's purpose that
prevails.

20:18
Make plans by seeking advice;
if you wage war, obtain guidance.

21:5
The plans of the diligent lead to profit
as surely as haste leads to poverty.

21:30
There is no wisdom, no insight, no plan
that can succeed against the LORD.

24:6
...for waging war you need guidance,
and for victory many advisers.

24:27
Finish your outdoor work
and get your fields ready;
after that, build your house.

PLEASURE
(Also see Joy, Laughter)
10:23
A fool finds pleasure in evil conduct,
but a man of understanding delights
in wisdom.

16:13
Kings take pleasure in honest lips;
they value a man who speaks the
truth.

18:2
A fool finds no pleasure in understanding
but delights in airing his own
opinions.

21:1
The king's heart is in the hand of the
LORD;
he directs it like a watercourse
wherever he pleases.

21:17
He who loves pleasure will become
poor;
whoever loves wine and oil will
never be rich.

POOR
(See Poverty)

POVERTY
*(Also see Compassion, Justice,
Oppression, Prosperity)*
6:6-11
Go to the ant, you sluggard;
consider its ways and be wise!
[7]It has no commander,
no overseer or ruler,
[8]yet it stores its provisions in summer
and gathers its food at harvest.

[9]How long will you lie there, you
sluggard?
When will you get up from your
sleep?
[10]A little sleep, a little slumber,
a little folding of the hands to rest—
[11]and poverty will come on you like a
bandit
and scarcity like an armed man.

10:4
Lazy hands make a man poor,
but diligent hands bring wealth.

10:15
The wealth of the rich is their fortified
city,
but poverty is the ruin of the poor.

11:24
One man gives freely, yet gains even
more;
another withholds unduly, but comes
to poverty.

12:9
Better to be a nobody and yet have a
servant
than pretend to be somebody and
have no food.

13:7-8
One man pretends to be rich, yet has
nothing;
another pretends to be poor, yet has
great wealth.

[8]A man's riches may ransom his life,
but a poor man hears no threat.

13:18
He who ignores discipline comes to
poverty and shame,
but whoever heeds correction is
honored.

13:23
A poor man's field may produce
abundant food,
but injustice sweeps it away.

13:25
The righteous eat to their hearts'
content,
but the stomach of the wicked goes
hungry.

14:20-21
The poor are shunned even by their
neighbors,
but the rich have many friends.
[21]He who despises his neighbor sins,
but blessed is he who is kind to the
needy.

14:23
All hard work brings a profit,
but mere talk leads only to poverty.

14:31
He who oppresses the poor shows
contempt for their Maker,
but whoever is kind to the needy
honors God.

15:15
All the days of the oppressed are
wretched,
but the cheerful heart has a continual
feast.

17:5
He who mocks the poor shows
contempt for their Maker;
whoever gloats over disaster will not
go unpunished.

18:23
A poor man pleads for mercy,
but a rich man answers harshly.

19:1
Better a poor man whose walk is
blameless
than a fool whose lips are perverse.

19:4
Wealth brings many friends,
but a poor man's friend deserts him.

19:7
A poor man is shunned by all his
relatives—
how much more do his friends avoid
him!
Though he pursues them with pleading,
they are nowhere to be found.

19:15
Laziness brings on deep sleep,
and the shiftless man goes hungry.

19:17
He who is kind to the poor lends to the
LORD,
and he will reward him for what he
has done.

19:22
What a man desires is unfailing love;
    better to be poor than a liar.

21:5
The plans of the diligent lead to profit
    as surely as haste leads to poverty.

21:13
If a man shuts his ears to the cry of the
        poor,
    he too will cry out and not be
        answered.

21:17
He who loves pleasure will become
        poor;
    whoever loves wine and oil will
        never be rich.

22:2
Rich and poor have this in common:
    The LORD is the Maker of them all.

22:7
The rich rule over the poor,
    and the borrower is servant to the
        lender.

22:9
A generous man will himself be blessed,
    for he shares his food with the poor.

22:16
He who oppresses the poor to increase
        his wealth
    and he who gives gifts to the rich—
        both come to poverty.

22:22-23
Do not exploit the poor because they
        are poor
    and do not crush the needy in court,
²³for the LORD will take up their case
    and will plunder those who plunder
        them.

23:21
...for drunkards and gluttons become
        poor,
    and drowsiness clothes them in rags.

24:33-34
A little sleep, a little slumber,
    a little folding of the hands to rest—
³⁴and poverty will come on you like a
        bandit
    and scarcity like an armed man.

27:7
He who is full loathes honey,
    but to the hungry even what is bitter
        tastes sweet.

28:3
A ruler who oppresses the poor
    is like a driving rain that leaves no
        crops.

28:6
Better a poor man whose walk is
        blameless
    than a rich man whose ways are
        perverse.

28:8
He who increases his wealth by
        exorbitant interest
    amasses it for another, who will be
        kind to the poor.

28:11
A rich man may be wise in his own
        eyes,
    but a poor man who has discernment
        sees through him.

28:19
He who works his land will have
        abundant food,
    but the one who chases fantasies will
        have his fill of poverty.

28:21-22
To show partiality is not good—
    yet a man will do wrong for a piece
        of bread.

²²A stingy man is eager to get rich
    and is unaware that poverty awaits
        him.

28:27
He who gives to the poor will lack
    nothing,
    but he who closes his eyes to them
    receives many curses.

29:7
The righteous care about justice for the
    poor,
    but the wicked have no such
    concern.

29:13-14
The poor man and the oppressor have
    this in common:
    The Lord gives sight to the eyes of
    both.

[14]If a king judges the poor with fairness,
his throne will always be secure.

30:7-9
"Two things I [Agur son of Jakeh] ask of
    you, O Lord;
    do not refuse me before I die:
[8]Keep falsehood and lies far from me;
    give me neither poverty nor riches,
    but give me only my daily bread.
[9]Otherwise, I may have too much
    and disown you and say, 'Who is the
    Lord?'
Or I may become poor and steal,
    and so dishonor the name of my
    God."

30:14
"[There are] those whose teeth are
    swords
    and whose jaws are set with knives
to devour the poor from the earth,
    the needy from among mankind."

31:6-9
"Give beer to those who are perishing,
    wine to those who are in anguish;
[7]let them drink and forget their poverty
    and remember their misery no more.

[8]"Speak up for those who cannot speak
    for themselves,
    for the rights of all who are destitute.

[9]Speak up and judge fairly;
    defend the rights of the poor and
    needy."

PRACTICAL JOKING
(Also see Folly)
26:18-19
Like a madman shooting
    firebrands or deadly arrows
[19]is a man who deceives his neighbor
    and says, "I was only joking!"

PRAYER
15:8
The Lord detests the sacrifice of the
    wicked,
    but the prayer of the upright pleases
    him.

15:29
The Lord is far from the wicked
    but he hears the prayer of the
    righteous.

28:9
If anyone turns a deaf ear to the law,
    even his prayers are detestable.

PRIDE
8:13
"To fear the Lord is to hate evil;
    I [wisdom] hate pride and arrogance,
    evil behavior and perverse speech."

11:2
When pride comes, then comes
    disgrace,
    but with humility comes wisdom.

13:10
Pride only breeds quarrels,
    but wisdom is found in those who
    take advice.

15:25
The Lord tears down the proud man's
    house
    but he keeps the widow's boundaries
    intact.

16:5
The LORD detests all the proud of heart.
Be sure of this: They will not go
unpunished.

16:18-19
Pride goes before destruction,
a haughty spirit before a fall.

19Better to be lowly in spirit and among
the oppressed
than to share plunder with the proud.

17:7
Arrogant lips are unsuited to a fool—
how much worse lying lips to a ruler!

17:19
He who loves a quarrel loves sin;
he who builds a high gate invites
destruction.

18:12
Before his downfall a man's heart is
proud,
but humility comes before honor.

21:4
Haughty eyes and a proud heart,
the lamp of the wicked, are sin!

21:24
The proud and arrogant man—
"Mocker" is his name;
he behaves with overweening pride.

26:12
Do you see a man wise in his own eyes?
There is more hope for a fool than for
him.

26:16
The sluggard is wiser in his own eyes
than seven men who answer
discreetly.

27:21
The crucible for silver and the furnace
for gold,
but man is tested by the praise he
receives.

29:23
A man's pride brings him low,
but a man of lowly spirit gains honor.

30:11-14
"There are those who curse their fathers
and do not bless their mothers;
12those who are pure in their own eyes
and yet are not cleansed of their filth;
13those whose eyes are ever so haughty,
whose glances are so disdainful;
14those whose teeth are swords
and whose jaws are set with knives
to devour the poor from the earth,
the needy from among mankind."

PRINCES
(See Rulers)

PROCRASTINATION
(Also see Laziness)
3:28
Do not say to your neighbor,
"Come back later; I'll give it
tomorrow"—
when you now have it with you.

PROSPERITY
*(Also see Financial Matters, Justice,
Poverty, Oppression)*
3:1-2
My son, do not forget my teaching,
but keep my commands in your heart,
2for they will prolong your life many
years
and bring you prosperity.

3:9-10
Honor the LORD with your wealth,
with the firstfruits of all your crops;
10then your barns will be filled to
overflowing,
and your vats will brim over with
new wine.

3:13-18
Blessed is the man who finds wisdom,
the man who gains understanding,
14for she is more profitable than silver
and yields better returns than gold.

[15]She is more precious than rubies;
  nothing you desire can compare with
    her.
[16]Long life is in her right hand;
  in her left hand are riches and honor.
[17]Her ways are pleasant ways,
  and all her paths are peace.
[18]She is a tree of life to those who
    embrace her;
  those who lay hold of her will be
    blessed.

4:10-13

Listen, my son, accept what I say,
  and the years of your life will be
    many.
[11]I guide you in the way of wisdom
  and lead you along straight paths.
[12]When you walk, your steps will not
    be hampered;
  when you run, you will not stumble.
[13]Hold on to instruction, do not let it
    go;
  guard it well, for it is your life.

8:18-21

"With me [wisdom] are riches and
    honor,
  enduring wealth and prosperity.
[19]My fruit is better than fine gold;
  what I yield surpasses choice silver.
[20]I walk in the way of righteousness,
  along the paths of justice,
[21]bestowing wealth on those who love
    me
  and making their treasuries full."

9:10-11

"The fear of the LORD is the beginning
    of wisdom,
  and knowledge of the Holy One is
    understanding.
[11]For through me [wisdom] your days
    will be many,
  and years will be added to your life."

10:2

Ill-gotten treasures are of no value,
  but righteousness delivers from
    death.

10:4

Lazy hands make a man poor,
  but diligent hands bring wealth.

10:15

The wealth of the rich is their fortified
    city,
  but poverty is the ruin of the poor.

10:22

The blessing of the LORD brings wealth,
  and he adds no trouble to it.

10:24

What the wicked dreads will overtake
    him;
  what the righteous desire will be
    granted.

10:27

The fear of the LORD adds length to life,
  but the years of the wicked are cut
    short.

11:4

Wealth is worthless in the day of wrath,
  but righteousness delivers from
    death.

11:7

When a wicked man dies, his hope
    perishes;
  all he expected from his power
    comes to nothing.

11:16

A kindhearted woman gains respect,
  but ruthless men gain only wealth.

11:25

A generous man will prosper;
  he who refreshes others will himself
    be refreshed.

11:28

Whoever trusts in his riches will fall,
  but the righteous will thrive like a
    green leaf.

12:3
A man cannot be established through
    wickedness,
    but the righteous cannot be uprooted.

12:7
Wicked men are overthrown and are
    no more,
    but the house of the righteous stands
    firm.

12:9
Better to be a nobody and yet have a
    servant
    than pretend to be somebody and
    have no food.

12:21
No harm befalls the righteous,
    but the wicked have their fill of
    trouble.

13:7-8
One man pretends to be rich, yet has
    nothing;
    another pretends to be poor, yet has
    great wealth.

⁸A man's riches may ransom his life,
    but a poor man hears no threat.

13:11
Dishonest money dwindles away,
    but he who gathers money little by
    little makes it grow.

13:21-22
Misfortune pursues the sinner,
    but prosperity is the reward of the
    righteous.

²²A good man leaves an inheritance for
    his children's children,
    but a sinner's wealth is stored up for
    the righteous.

14:4
Where there are no oxen, the manger is
    empty,
    but from the strength of an ox comes
    an abundant harvest.

14:11
The house of the wicked will be
    destroyed,
    but the tent of the upright will
    flourish.

14:20
The poor are shunned even by their
    neighbors,
    but the rich have many friends.

14:24
The wealth of the wise is their crown,
    but the folly of fools yields folly.

14:26
He who fears the LORD has a secure
    fortress,
    and for his children it will be a refuge.

15:6
The house of the righteous contains
    great treasure,
    but the income of the wicked brings
    them trouble.

15:16
Better a little with the fear of the LORD
    than great wealth with turmoil.

15:27
A greedy man brings trouble to his
    family,
    but he who hates bribes will live.

16:8
Better a little with righteousness
    than much gain with injustice.

16:16
How much better to get wisdom than
    gold,
    to choose understanding rather than
    silver!

16:19
Better to be lowly in spirit and among
    the oppressed
    than to share plunder with the proud.

17:5
He who mocks the poor shows
     contempt for their Maker;
   whoever gloats over disaster will not
     go unpunished.

17:16
Of what use is money in the hand of a
     fool,
   since he has no desire to get wisdom?

17:20
A man of perverse heart does not
     prosper;
   he whose tongue is deceitful falls
     into trouble.

18:11
The wealth of the rich is their fortified
     city;
   they imagine it an unscalable wall.

18:23
A poor man pleads for mercy,
   but a rich man answers harshly.

19:4
Wealth brings many friends,
   but a poor man's friend deserts him.

19:8
He who gets wisdom loves his own soul;
   he who cherishes understanding
     prospers.

20:15
Gold there is, and rubies in abundance,
   but lips that speak knowledge are a
     rare jewel.

21:5-6
The plans of the diligent lead to profit
   as surely as haste leads to poverty.

[6]A fortune made by a lying tongue
   is a fleeting vapor and a deadly snare.

21:20-21
In the house of the wise are stores of
     choice food and oil,
   but a foolish man devours all he has.

[21]He who pursues righteousness and
     love
   finds life, prosperity and honor.

22:1-2
A good name is more desirable than
     great riches;
   to be esteemed is better than silver or
     gold.

[2]Rich and poor have this in common:
   The Lord is the Maker of them all.

22:4
Humility and the fear of the Lord
   bring wealth and honor and life.

22:7
The rich rule over the poor,
   and the borrower is servant to the
     lender.

22:16
He who oppresses the poor to increase
     his wealth
   and he who gives gifts to the rich—
     both come to poverty.

23:4-5
Do not wear yourself out to get rich;
   have the wisdom to show restraint.
[5]Cast but a glance at riches, and they
     are gone,
   for they will surely sprout wings
   and fly off to the sky like an eagle.

24:25
But it will go well with those who
     convict the guilty,
   and rich blessing will come upon
     them.

27:7
He who is full loathes honey,
   but to the hungry even what is bitter
     tastes sweet.

27:24
...for riches do not endure forever,
   and a crown is not secure for all
     generations.

28:6
Better a poor man whose walk is
    blameless
than a rich man whose ways are
    perverse.

28:8
He who increases his wealth by
    exorbitant interest
amasses it for another, who will be
    kind to the poor.

28:11
A rich man may be wise in his own
    eyes,
but a poor man who has discernment
    sees through him.

28:20
A faithful man will be richly blessed,
but one eager to get rich will not go
    unpunished.

28:22
A stingy man is eager to get rich
    and is unaware that poverty awaits
    him.

29:3
A man who loves wisdom brings joy to
    his father,
but a companion of prostitutes
    squanders his wealth.

30:8
"Keep falsehood and lies far from me;
give me neither poverty nor riches,
but give me only my daily bread."

31:18
She [the wife of noble character] sees
    that her trading is profitable,
and her lamp does not go out at
    night.

PROVIDENCE
(Also see God, LORD)
5:21
For a man's ways are in full view of the
    LORD,
and he examines all his paths.

15:3
The eyes of the LORD are everywhere,
    keeping watch on the wicked and
    the good.

15:11
Death and Destruction lie open before
    the LORD—
how much more the hearts of men!

16:1-4
To man belong the plans of the heart,
    but from the LORD comes the reply of
    the tongue.

²All a man's ways seem innocent to him,
    but motives are weighed by the LORD.

³Commit to the LORD whatever you do,
    and your plans will succeed.

⁴The LORD works out everything for his
    own ends—
    even the wicked for a day of disaster.

16:9
In his heart a man plans his course,
    but the LORD determines his steps.

16:33
The lot is cast into the lap,
    but its every decision is from the LORD.

17:3
The crucible for silver and the furnace
    for gold,
but the LORD tests the heart.

19:21
Many are the plans in a man's heart,
    but it is the LORD's purpose that
    prevails.

20:12
Ears that hear and eyes that see—
    the LORD has made them both.

20:24
A man's steps are directed by the LORD.
How then can anyone understand his
    own way?

20:27
The lamp of the LORD searches the spirit
    of a man;
it searches out his inmost being.

21:2
All a man's ways seem right to him,
    but the LORD weighs the heart.

21:30-31
There is no wisdom, no insight, no plan
that can succeed against the LORD.

³¹The horse is made ready for the day
    of battle,
    but victory rests with the LORD.

22:2
Rich and poor have this in common:
The LORD is the Maker of them all.

24:12
If you say, "But we knew nothing
    about this,"
does not he who weighs the heart
    perceive it?
Does not he who guards your life
    know it?
Will he not repay each person
    according to what he has
    done?

29:13
The poor man and the oppressor have
    this in common:
The LORD gives sight to the eyes of
    both.

29:26
Many seek an audience with a ruler,
    but it is from the LORD that man gets
    justice.

PURITY
15:26
The LORD detests the thoughts of the
    wicked,
    but those of the pure are pleasing to
    him.

20:9
Who can say, "I have kept my heart pure;
    I am clean and without sin"?

20:11
Even a child is known by his actions,
    by whether his conduct is pure and
    right.

22:11
He who loves a pure heart and whose
    speech is gracious
    will have the king for his friend.

30:12
"[There are] those who are pure in their
    own eyes
    and yet are not cleansed of their
    filth..."

PURPOSE
(Also see Plans)
13:19
A longing fulfilled is sweet to the soul,
    but fools detest turning from evil.

RASHNESS
(See Impetuousness)

REBUKES
*(Also see Advice, Discernment,
        Discipline)*
9:7-8
"Whoever corrects a mocker invites
    insult;
    whoever rebukes a wicked man
    incurs abuse.
⁸Do not rebuke a mocker or he will
    hate you;
    rebuke a wise man and he will love
    you."

13:1
A wise son heeds his father's instruc-
    tion,
    but a mocker does not listen to
    rebuke.

15:31
He who listens to a life-giving rebuke
    will be at home among the wise.

17:5
He who mocks the poor shows
   contempt for their Maker;
whoever gloats over disaster will not
   go unpunished.

17:10
A rebuke impresses a man of discernment
more than a hundred lashes a fool.

19:25
Flog a mocker, and the simple will
   learn prudence;
rebuke a discerning man, and he will
   gain knowledge.

25:12
Like an earring of gold or an ornament
   of fine gold
is a wise man's rebuke to a listening
   ear.

27:5
Better is open rebuke
   than hidden love.

27:17
As iron sharpens iron,
   so one man sharpens another.

28:23
He who rebukes a man will in the end
   gain more favor
than he who has a flattering tongue.

29:1
A man who remains stiff-necked after
   many rebukes
will suddenly be destroyed—without
   remedy.

29:19
A servant cannot be corrected by mere
   words;
though he understands, he will not
   respond.

RECONCILIATION
(See Forgiveness)
6:1-5
My son, if you have put up security for
   your neighbor,
   if you have struck hands in pledge
      for another,
²if you have been trapped by what you
      said,
   ensnared by the words of your
      mouth,
³then do this, my son, to free yourself,
   since you have fallen into your
      neighbor's hands:
Go and humble yourself;
   press your plea with your neighbor!
⁴Allow no sleep to your eyes,
   no slumber to your eyelids.
⁵Free yourself, like a gazelle from the
   hand of the hunter,
like a bird from the snare of the
   fowler.

14:9
Fools mock at making amends for sin,
   but goodwill is found among the
      upright.

17:9
He who covers over an offense
   promotes love,
but whoever repeats the matter
   separates close friends.

20:22
Do not say, "I'll pay you back for this
   wrong!"
   Wait for the LORD, and he will deliver
      you.

REFUGE
(Also see Peace, Safety)
10:29
The way of the LORD is a refuge for the
   righteous,
   but it is the ruin of those who do
      evil.

14:26
He who fears the LORD has a secure
   fortress,

and for his children it will be a
refuge.

14:32
When calamity comes, the wicked are
brought down,
but even in death the righteous have
a refuge.

22:3
A prudent man sees danger and takes
refuge,
but the simple keep going and suffer
for it.

27:12
The prudent see danger and take
refuge,
but the simple keep going and suffer
for it.

30:5
"Every word of God is flawless;
he is a shield to those who take
refuge in him."

REPENTANCE
14:9
Fools mock at making amends for sin,
but goodwill is found among the
upright.

REPUTATION
(See Good Name)

RESPONSIBILITY
26:6
Like cutting off one's feet or drinking
violence
is the sending of a message by the
hand of a fool.
26:10
Like an archer who wounds at random
is he who hires a fool or any passer-by.

RETRIBUTION
11:31
If the righteous receive their due on
earth,
how much more the ungodly and the
sinner!

20:22
Do not say, "I'll pay you back for this
wrong!"
Wait for the LORD, and he will deliver
you.

24:11-12
Rescue those being led away to death;
hold back those staggering toward
slaughter.
[12]If you say, "But we knew nothing
about this,"
does not he who weighs the heart
perceive it?
Does not he who guards your life
know it?
Will he not repay each person
according to what he has
done?

24:28-29
Do not testify against your neighbor
without cause,
or use your lips to deceive.
[29]Do not say, "I'll do to him as he has
done to me;
I'll pay that man back for what he did."

25:21
If your enemy is hungry, give him food
to eat;
if he is thirsty, give him water to
drink.

RIGHTEOUS/WICKED
(Also see Righteousness, Wicked)
3:33
The LORD's curse is on the house of the
wicked,
but he blesses the home of the
righteous.

10:3
The LORD does not let the righteous go
hungry
but he thwarts the craving of the
wicked.

10:6-7
Blessings crown the head of the
righteous,

but violence overwhelms the mouth
of the wicked.

⁷The memory of the righteous will be
a blessing,
but the name of the wicked will rot.

10:11
The mouth of the righteous is a
fountain of life,
but violence overwhelms the mouth
of the wicked.

10:16
The wages of the righteous bring them
life,
but the income of the wicked brings
them punishment.

10:20
The tongue of the righteous is choice
silver,
but the heart of the wicked is of little
value.

10:24-25
What the wicked dreads will overtake
him;
what the righteous desire will be
granted.

²⁵When the storm has swept by, the
wicked are gone,
but the righteous stand firm forever.

10:28-32
The prospect of the righteous is joy,
but the hopes of the wicked come to
nothing.
²⁹The way of the Lord is a refuge for
the righteous,
but it is the ruin of those who do
evil.

³⁰The righteous will never be uprooted,
but the wicked will not remain in the
land.

³¹The mouth of the righteous brings
forth wisdom,
but a perverse tongue will be cut out.

³²The lips of the righteous know what is
fitting,
but the mouth of the wicked only
what is perverse.

11:5-6
The righteousness of the blameless
makes a straight way for them,
but the wicked are brought down by
their own wickedness.

⁶The righteousness of the upright
delivers them,
but the unfaithful are trapped by evil
desires.

11:8
The righteous man is rescued from
trouble,
and it comes on the wicked instead.

11:10-11
When the righteous prosper, the city
rejoices;
when the wicked perish, there are
shouts of joy.

¹¹Through the blessing of the upright a
city is exalted,
but by the mouth of the wicked it is
destroyed.

11:18-19
The wicked man earns deceptive
wages,
but he who sows righteousness reaps
a sure reward.
⁹The truly righteous man attains life,
but he who pursues evil goes to his
death.

11:21
Be sure of this: The wicked will not go
unpunished,
but those who are righteous will go
free.

11:23
The desire of the righteous ends only in
good,

but the hope of the wicked only in
wrath.

11:31
If the righteous receive their due on
earth,
how much more the ungodly and the
sinner!

12:2-3
A good man obtains favor from the LORD,
but the LORD condemns a crafty man.

³A man cannot be established through
wickedness,
but the righteous cannot be
uprooted.

12:5-7
The plans of the righteous are just,
but the advice of the wicked is
deceitful.

⁶The words of the wicked lie in wait for
blood,
but the speech of the upright rescues
them.

⁷Wicked men are overthrown and are
no more,
but the house of the righteous stands
firm.

12:10
A righteous man cares for the needs of
his animal,
but the kindest acts of the wicked are
cruel.

12:12-13
The wicked desire the plunder of evil
men,
but the root of the righteous
flourishes.

¹³An evil man is trapped by his sinful
talk,
but a righteous man escapes trouble.

12:21
No harm befalls the righteous,

but the wicked have their fill of
trouble.

12:26
A righteous man is cautious in friendship,
but the way of the wicked leads them
astray.

13:5-6
The righteous hate what is false,
but the wicked bring shame and
disgrace.

⁶Righteousness guards the man of
integrity,
but wickedness overthrows the
sinner.

13:9
The light of the righteous shines
brightly,
but the lamp of the wicked is snuffed
out.

13:25
The righteous eat to their hearts'
content,
but the stomach of the wicked goes
hungry.

14:11
The house of the wicked will be
destroyed,
but the tent of the upright will
flourish.

14:19
Evil men will bow down in the
presence of the good,
and the wicked at the gates of the
righteous.

14:32
When calamity comes, the wicked are
brought down,
but even in death the righteous have
a refuge.

15:6
The house of the righteous contains
great treasure,

but the income of the wicked brings them trouble.

15:8-9
The LORD detests the sacrifice of the wicked,
but the prayer of the upright pleases him.

⁹The LORD detests the way of the wicked
but he loves those who pursue righteousness.

15:28-29
The heart of the righteous weighs its answers,
but the mouth of the wicked gushes evil.

²⁹The LORD is far from the wicked
but he hears the prayer of the righteous.

17:13
If a man pays back evil for good,
evil will never leave his house.

21:12
The Righteous One takes note of the house of the wicked
and brings the wicked to ruin.

21:15
When justice is done, it brings joy to the righteous
but terror to evildoers.

21:18
The wicked become a ransom for the righteous,
and the unfaithful for the upright.

21:29
A wicked man puts up a bold front,
but an upright man gives thought to his ways.

24:15-16
Do not lie in wait like an outlaw against a righteous man's house,

do not raid his dwelling place;
¹⁶for though a righteous man falls seven times, he rises again,
but the wicked are brought down by calamity.

25:4-5
Remove the dross from the silver,
and out comes material for the silversmith;
⁵remove the wicked from the king's presence,
and his throne will be established through righteousness.

25:26
Like a muddied spring or a polluted well
is a righteous man who gives way to the wicked.

28:1
The wicked man flees though no one pursues,
but the righteous are as bold as a lion.

28:12
When the righteous triumph, there is great elation;
but when the wicked rise to power, men go into hiding.

28:18
He whose walk is blameless is kept safe,
but he whose ways are perverse will suddenly fall.

28:28
When the wicked rise to power, people go into hiding;
but when the wicked perish, the righteous thrive.

29:2
When the righteous thrive, the people rejoice;
when the wicked rule, the people groan.

29:6-7
An evil man is snared by his own sin,
but a righteous one can sing and be glad.

⁷The righteous care about justice for the
poor,
but the wicked have no such concern.

29:16
When the wicked thrive, so does sin,
but the righteous will see their
downfall.

29:27
The righteous detest the dishonest;
the wicked detest the upright.

RIGHTEOUSNESS
*(Also see Blameless, Righteous/Wicked,
Upright)*
4:18
The path of the righteous is like the
first gleam of dawn,
shining ever brighter till the full light
of day.

8:20-21
"I [wisdom] walk in the way of righteousness,
along the paths of justice,
²¹bestowing wealth on those who love me
and making their treasuries full."

9:9
"Instruct a wise man and he will be
wiser still;
teach a righteous man and he will
add to his learning."

10:2
Ill-gotten treasures are of no value,
but righteousness delivers from death.

10:21
The lips of the righteous nourish many,
but fools die for lack of judgment.

10:31
The mouth of the righteous brings forth
wisdom,
but a perverse tongue will be cut out.

11:4
Wealth is worthless in the day of wrath,
but righteousness delivers from
death.

11:9
With his mouth the godless destroys his
neighbor,
but through knowledge the righteous
escape.

11:28
Whoever trusts in his riches will fall,
but the righteous will thrive like a
green leaf.

11:30
The fruit of the righteous is a tree of
life,
and he who wins souls is wise.

12:28
In the way of righteousness there is life;
along that path is immortality.

13:22
A good man leaves an inheritance for
his children's children,
but a sinner's wealth is stored up for
the righteous.

14:9
Fools mock at making amends for sin,
but goodwill is found among the
upright.

14:34
Righteousness exalts a nation,
but sin is a disgrace to any people.

16:8
Better a little with righteousness
than much gain with injustice.

16:12
Kings detest wrongdoing,
for a throne is established through
righteousness.

16:31
Gray hair is a crown of splendor;
it is attained by a righteous life.

18:10
The name of the Lord is a strong tower;
the righteous run to it and are safe.

20:7
The righteous man leads a blameless life;
blessed are his children after him.

21:3
To do what is right and just
is more acceptable to the LORD than
sacrifice.

21:7-8
The violence of the wicked will drag
them away,
for they refuse to do what is right.

⁸The way of the guilty is devious,
but the conduct of the innocent is
upright.

21:21
He who pursues righteousness and love
finds life, prosperity and honor.

21:26
All day long he [the sluggard] craves for
more,
but the righteous give without
sparing.

23:24
The father of a righteous man has great
joy;
he who has a wise son delights in him.

28:10
He who leads the upright along an evil
path
will fall into his own trap,
but the blameless will receive a good
inheritance.

RULERS
(Also see Justice, Oppression)
6:7-8
It [the ant] has no commander,
no overseer or ruler,
⁸yet it stores its provisions in summer
and gathers its food at harvest.

8:15-16
"By me [wisdom] kings reign
and rulers make laws that are just;

¹⁶by me princes govern,
and all nobles who rule on earth."

12:24
Diligent hands will rule,
but laziness ends in slave labor.

14:28
A large population is a king's glory,
but without subjects a prince is
ruined.

14:35
A king delights in a wise servant,
but a shameful servant incurs his
wrath.

16:10
The lips of a king speak as an oracle,
and his mouth should not betray
justice.

16:12-15
Kings detest wrongdoing,
for a throne is established through
righteousness.
¹³Kings take pleasure in honest lips;
they value a man who speaks the
truth.

¹⁴A king's wrath is a messenger of
death,
but a wise man will appease it.

¹⁵When a king's face brightens, it means
life;
his favor is like a rain cloud in
spring.

17:7
Arrogant lips are unsuited to a fool—
how much worse lying lips to a ruler!

19:6
Many curry favor with a ruler,
and everyone is the friend of a man
who gives gifts.
19:10
It is not fitting for a fool to live in
luxury—

how much worse for a slave to rule
    over princes!

19:12
A king's rage is like the roar of a lion,
    but his favor is like dew on the grass.

20:2
A king's wrath is like the roar of a lion;
    he who angers him forfeits his life.

20:8
When a king sits on his throne to judge,
    he winnows out all evil with his eyes.

20:26
A wise king winnows out the wicked;
    he drives the threshing wheel over
        them.

20:28
Love and faithfulness keep a king safe;
    through love his throne is made
        secure.

21:1
The king's heart is in the hand of the
        LORD;
    he directs it like a watercourse
        wherever he pleases.

22:7
The rich rule over the poor,
    and the borrower is servant to the
        lender.

22:11
He who loves a pure heart and whose
        speech is gracious
    will have the king for his friend.

22:29-23:3
Do you see a man skilled in his work?
He will serve before kings;
    he will not serve before obscure men.

²³:¹When you sit to dine with a ruler,
    note well what is before you,
²and put a knife to your throat
    if you are given to gluttony.

³Do not crave his delicacies,
    for that food is deceptive.

24:21-22
Fear the LORD and the king, my son,
    and do not join with the rebellious,
²²for those two will send sudden
        destruction upon them,
    and who knows what calamities they
        can bring?

25:2-7a
It is the glory of God to conceal a
        matter;
    to search out a matter is the glory of
        kings.

³As the heavens are high and the earth
        is deep,
    so the hearts of kings are
        unsearchable.

⁴Remove the dross from the silver,
    and out comes material for the
        silversmith;
⁵remove the wicked from the king's
        presence,
    and his throne will be established
        through righteousness.
⁶Do not exalt yourself in the king's
        presence,
    and do not claim a place among
        great men;
⁷it is better for him to say to you,
        "Come up here,"
    than for him to humiliate you before
        a nobleman.

25:15
Through patience a ruler can be
        persuaded,
    and a gentle tongue can break a bone.

27:18
He who tends a fig tree will eat its fruit,
    and he who looks after his master
        will be honored.

28:2-3
When a country is rebellious, it has
        many rulers,

but a man of understanding and
knowledge maintains order.

3A ruler who oppresses the poor
is like a driving rain that leaves no
crops.

28:16
A tyrannical ruler lacks judgment,
but he who hates ill-gotten gain will
enjoy a long life.

29:2
When the righteous thrive, the people
rejoice;
when the wicked rule, the people
groan.

29:4
By justice a king gives a country stability,
but one who is greedy for bribes tears
it down.
29:12
If a ruler listens to lies,
all his officials become wicked.

29:14
If a king judges the poor with fairness,
his throne will always be secure.

29:26
Many seek an audience with a ruler,
but it is from the LORD that man gets
justice.

30:21-23
"Under three things the earth trembles,
under four it cannot bear up:
22a servant who becomes king,
a fool who is full of food,
23an unloved woman who is married,
and a maidservant who displaces her
mistress."

30:27-29
"Locusts have no king,
yet they advance together in ranks;
28a lizard can be caught with the hand,
yet it is found in kings' palaces.

29"There are three things that are stately
in their stride,
four that move with stately bearing:
30a lion, mighty among beasts,
who retreats before nothing;
31a strutting rooster, a he-goat,
and a king with his army around him."

31:1-9
The sayings of King Lemuel—an oracle
his mother taught him:

2"O my son, O son of my womb,
O son of my vows,
3do not spend your strength on women,
your vigor on those who ruin kings.

4"It is not for kings, O Lemuel—
not for kings to drink wine,
not for rulers to crave beer,
5lest they drink and forget what the law
decrees,
and deprive all the oppressed of their
rights.
6Give beer to those who are perishing,
wine to those who are in anguish;
7let them drink and forget their poverty
and remember their misery no more.

8"Speak up for those who cannot speak
for themselves,
for the rights of all who are destitute.
9Speak up and judge fairly;
defend the rights of the poor and
needy."

SACRIFICE
3:9-10
Honor the LORD with your wealth,
with the firstfruits of all your crops;
10then your barns will be filled to
overflowing,
and your vats will brim over with
new wine.

7:14
[The adulteress woman says,] "I have
fellowship offerings at home;
today I fulfilled my vows."

15:8
The LORD detests the sacrifice of the
    wicked,
    but the prayer of the upright pleases
        him.

21:3
To do what is right and just
    is more acceptable to the LORD than
        sacrifice.

21:27
The sacrifice of the wicked is detestable—
    how much more so when brought with
        evil intent!

SAFETY
(Also see Peace, Refuge)
1:33
"But whoever listens to me [wisdom]
    will live in safety
and be at ease, without fear of harm."

2:7
He [the LORD] holds victory in store for
    the upright,
    he is a shield to those whose walk is
        blameless...

3:21-23
My son, preserve sound judgment and
    discernment,
    do not let them out of your sight;
²²they will be life for you,
    an ornament to grace your neck.
²³Then you will go on your way in
    safety,
    and your foot will not stumble...

11:15
He who puts up security for another
    will surely suffer,
    but whoever refuses to strike hands
        in pledge is safe.

18:10
The name of the LORD is a strong tower;
    the righteous run to it and are safe.

20:28
Love and faithfulness keep a king safe;

through love his throne is made
    secure.

28:18
He whose walk is blameless is kept safe,
    but he whose ways are perverse will
        suddenly fall.

28:26
He who trusts in himself is a fool,
    but he who walks in wisdom is kept
        safe.

29:25
Fear of man will prove to be a snare,
    but whoever trusts in the LORD is kept
        safe.

30:5
"Every word of God is flawless;
    he is a shield to those who take
        refuge in him."

SAVINGS
(See Financial Matters)

SELF-CONTROL
(See also Patience, Tongue)
11:12-13
A man who lacks judgment derides his
    neighbor,
    but a man of understanding holds his
        tongue.

¹³A gossip betrays a confidence,
    but a trustworthy man keeps a secret.

12:16
A fool shows his annoyance at once,
    but a prudent man overlooks an
        insult.

12:23
A prudent man keeps his knowledge to
    himself,
    but the heart of fools blurts out folly.

13:3
He who guards his lips guards his life,
    but he who speaks rashly will come
        to ruin.

14:29
A patient man has great understanding,
but a quick-tempered man displays
folly.

17:27-28
A man of knowledge uses words with
restraint,
and a man of understanding is even-
tempered.

²⁸Even a fool is thought wise if he
keeps silent,
and discerning if he holds his tongue.

25:28
Like a city whose walls are broken
down
is a man who lacks self-control.

29:11
A fool gives full vent to his anger,
but a wise man keeps himself under
control.

29:20
Do you see a man who speaks in haste?
There is more hope for a fool than
for him.

SELFISHNESS
(Also see Generosity)
11:24
One man gives freely, yet gains even
more;
another withholds unduly, but comes
to poverty.

11:26
People curse the man who hoards grain,
but blessing crowns him who is willing
to sell.

15:27
A greedy man brings trouble to his
family,
but he who hates bribes will live.

18:1
An unfriendly man pursues selfish ends;
he defies all sound judgment.

21:13
If a man shuts his ears to the cry of the
poor,
he too will cry out and not be
answered.

21:25-26
The sluggard's craving will be the death
of him,
because his hands refuse to work.
²⁶All day long he craves for more,
but the righteous give without
sparing.

22:7
The rich rule over the poor,
and the borrower is servant to the
lender.

23:6-8
Do not eat the food of a stingy man,
do not crave his delicacies;
⁷for he is the kind of man
who is always thinking about the
cost.
"Eat and drink," he says to you,
but his heart is not with you.
⁸You will vomit up the little you have
eaten
and will have wasted your compliments.

25:14
Like clouds and wind without rain
is a man who boasts of gifts he does
not give.

25:16
If you find honey, eat just enough—
too much of it, and you will vomit.

28:22
A stingy man is eager to get rich
and is unaware that poverty awaits
him.

28:25
A greedy man stirs up dissension,
but he who trusts in the LORD will
prosper.

29:4
By justice a king gives a country
    stability,
  but one who is greedy for bribes
    tears it down.

SERVANT
(See Slavery)

SEXUAL IMMORALITY
(See Adultery)

SHAME
(Also see Disgrace)
3:35
The wise inherit honor,
  but fools he holds up to shame.

6:33
Blows and disgrace are his lot,
  and his shame will never be wiped
    away...
13:5
The righteous hate what is false,
  but the wicked bring shame and
    disgrace.

13:18
He who ignores discipline comes to
    poverty and shame,
  but whoever heeds correction is
    honored.

18:3
When wickedness comes, so does
    contempt,
  and with shame comes disgrace.

18:13
He who answers before listening—
  that is his folly and his shame.

19:26
He who robs his father and drives out
    his mother
is a son who brings shame and
    disgrace.

25:7b-8
What you have seen with your eyes
  ⁸do not bring hastily to court,

for what will you do in the end
  if your neighbor puts you to shame?

SILVER
(See Gold)

THE SIMPLE
(See Fool)

SIN
1:10
My son, if sinners entice you,
  do not give in to them.

1:15-16
My son, do not go along with them,
  do not set foot on their paths;
  ¹⁶for their feet rush into sin,
    they are swift to shed blood.

5:22
The evil deeds of a wicked man
    ensnare him;
  the cords of his sin hold him fast.

10:19
When words are many, sin is not
    absent,
  but he who holds his tongue is wise.

11:31
If the righteous receive their due on
    earth,
  how much more the ungodly and the
    sinner!

12:13
An evil man is trapped by his sinful
    talk,
  but a righteous man escapes trouble.

13:6
Righteousness guards the man of
    integrity,
  but wickedness overthrows the
    sinner.

13:21-22
Misfortune pursues the sinner,
  but prosperity is the reward of the
    righteous.

[22]A good man leaves an inheritance for
his children's children,
but a sinner's wealth is stored up for
the righteous.

14:9
Fools mock at making amends for sin,
but goodwill is found among the
upright.

14:21
He who despises his neighbor sins,
but blessed is he who is kind to the
needy.

16:6
Through love and faithfulness sin is
atoned for;
through the fear of the LORD a man
avoids evil.

17:19
He who loves a quarrel loves sin;
he who builds a high gate invites
destruction.

20:9
Who can say, "I have kept my heart
pure;
I am clean and without sin"?

21:4
Haughty eyes and a proud heart,
the lamp of the wicked, are sin!

23:17
Do not let your heart envy sinners,
but always be zealous for the fear of
the LORD.

24:9
The schemes of folly are sin,
and men detest a mocker.

28:13
He who conceals his sins does not
prosper,
but whoever confesses and re-
nounces them finds mercy.

29:6
An evil man is snared by his own sin,
but a righteous one can sing and be
glad.

29:16
When the wicked thrive, so does sin,
but the righteous will see their
downfall.

29:22
An angry man stirs up dissension,
and a hot-tempered one commits
many sins.

SLANDER
(See Mocker)

SLAVERY
(Also see Masters, Rulers)

11:29
He who brings trouble on his family
will inherit only wind,
and the fool will be servant to the
wise.

12:9
Better to be a nobody and yet have a
servant
than pretend to be somebody and
have no food.

12:24
Diligent hands will rule,
but laziness ends in slave labor.

14:35
A king delights in a wise servant,
but a shameful servant incurs his
wrath.

17:2
A wise servant will rule over a
disgraceful son,
and will share the inheritance as one
of the brothers.

22:7
The rich rule over the poor,
and the borrower is servant to the
lender.

27:27
You will have plenty of goats' milk
    to feed you and your family
    and to nourish your servant girls.

29:19
A servant cannot be corrected by mere
        words;
    though he understands, he will not
        respond.

29:21
If a man pampers his servant from
        youth,
    he will bring grief in the end.

30:10
"Do not slander a servant to his master,
    or he will curse you, and you will
        pay for it."

30:21-22
"Under three things the earth trembles,
    under four it cannot bear up:
²²a servant who becomes king,
    a fool who is full of food…"

31:15
She gets up while it is still dark;
    she provides food for her family
    and portions for her servant girls.

SLEEP
3:21-24
My son, preserve sound judgment and
        discernment,
    do not let them out of your sight;
²²they will be life for you,
    an ornament to grace your neck.
²³Then you will go on your way in
        safety,
    and your foot will not stumble;
²⁴when you lie down, you will not be
        afraid;
    when you lie down, your sleep will
        be sweet.

4:16
For they [the wicked] cannot sleep till
        they do evil;

they are robbed of slumber till they
        make someone fall.

6:4
[When freeing oneself from sin] allow
    no sleep to your eyes,
    no slumber to your eyelids.

6:9-11
How long will you lie there, you
        sluggard?
    When will you get up from your
        sleep?
¹⁰A little sleep, a little slumber,
    a little folding of the hands to rest—
¹¹and poverty will come on you like a
        bandit
    and scarcity like an armed man.

6:22
When you walk, they [your parent's
        commands] will guide you;
    when you sleep, they will watch over
        you;
    when you awake, they will speak to
        you.

10:5
He who gathers crops in summer is a
        wise son,
    but he who sleeps during harvest is a
        disgraceful son.

19:15
Laziness brings on deep sleep,
    and the shiftless man goes hungry.

20:13
Do not love sleep or you will grow
        poor;
    stay awake and you will have food to
        spare.

23:34
You will be like one sleeping on the
        high seas,
    lying on top of the rigging.

24:33-34
A little sleep, a little slumber,
    a little folding of the hands to rest—

[34]and poverty will come on you like a
    bandit
and scarcity like an armed man.

SOUL
(Also see Eternity)
13:3
He who guards his lips guards his life,
    but he who speaks rashly will come
    to ruin.

13:19
A longing fulfilled is sweet to the soul,
    but fools detest turning from evil.

15:4
The tongue that brings healing is a tree
    of life,
    but a deceitful tongue crushes the
    spirit.

15:13
A happy heart makes the face cheerful,
    but heartache crushes the spirit.

16:17-19
The highway of the upright avoids evil;
    he who guards his way guards his life.

[18]Pride goes before destruction,
    a haughty spirit before a fall.

[19]Better to be lowly in spirit and among
    the oppressed
than to share plunder with the proud.

16:24
Pleasant words are a honeycomb,
    sweet to the soul and healing to the
    bones.

17:22
A cheerful heart is good medicine,
    but a crushed spirit dries up the
    bones.

18:6
A fool's lips bring him strife,
    and his mouth invites a beating.

18:14
A man's spirit sustains him in sickness,
    but a crushed spirit who can bear?

19:8
He who gets wisdom loves his own
    soul;
    he who cherishes understanding
    prospers.

20:27
The lamp of the LORD searches the spirit
    of a man;
    it searches out his inmost being.

22:5
In the paths of the wicked lie thorns
    and snares,
    but he who guards his soul stays far
    from them.

23:13-14
Do not withhold discipline from a
    child;
    if you punish him with the rod, he
    will not die.
[14]Punish him with the rod
    and save his soul from death.

24:14
Know also that wisdom is sweet to
    your soul;
    if you find it, there is a future hope
    for you,
    and your hope will not be cut off.

25:13
Like the coolness of snow at harvest
    time
    is a trustworthy messenger to those
    who send him;
    he refreshes the spirit of his masters.

25:25
Like cold water to a weary soul
    is good news from a distant land.

29:17
Discipline your son, and he will give
    you peace;
    he will bring delight to your soul.

29:23
A man's pride brings him low,
  but a man of lowly spirit gains honor.

SPEECH
(See Tongue)

SPIRIT
(See Soul)

STRENGTH
5:7-9
Now then, my sons, listen to me;
  do not turn aside from what I say.
[8]Keep to a path far from her [the
      adulteress],
  do not go near the door of her house,
[9]lest you give your best strength to
      others
  and your years to one who is cruel...

14:4
Where there are no oxen, the manger is
      empty,
  but from the strength of an ox comes
      an abundant harvest.

18:10
The name of the LORD is a strong tower;
  the righteous run to it and are safe.

18:18
Casting the lot settles disputes
  and keeps strong opponents apart.

21:29
A wicked man puts up a bold front,
  but an upright man gives thought to
      his ways.

23:10-11
Do not move an ancient boundary stone
  or encroach on the fields of the
      fatherless,
[11]for their Defender is strong;
  he will take up their case against you.

24:5
A wise man has great power,
  and a man of knowledge increases
      strength...

24:10
If you falter in times of trouble,
  how small is your strength!

30:25
"Ants are creatures of little strength,
  yet they store up their food in the
      summer..."

31:2-3
"O my son, O son of my womb,
  O son of my vows,
[3]do not spend your strength on women,
  your vigor on those who ruin kings."

31:17
She [a wife of noble character] sets
      about her work vigorously;
  her arms are strong for her tasks.

STRIFE
(See Dissension, Mocker)

SUCCESS
(See Victory)

TEACHABLE
(Also see Ear)
7:2
Keep my commands and you will live;
  guard my teachings as the apple of
      your eye.

9:9
"Instruct a wise man and he will be
      wiser still;
  teach a righteous man and he will
      add to his learning."

13:14
The teaching of the wise is a fountain
      of life,
  turning a man from the snares of
      death.

15:33
The fear of the LORD teaches a man
      wisdom,
  and humility comes before honor.

22:19
So that your trust may be in the LORD,
I teach you today, even you.

22:21
...teaching you true and reliable words,
so that you can give sound answers
to him who sent you...

TEACHINGS
(Also see Commands, Law)
7:2
Keep my commands and you will live;
guard my teachings as the apple of
your eye.

9:9
"Instruct a wise man and he will be
wiser still;
teach a righteous man and he will
add to his learning."

13:14
The teaching of the wise is a fountain
of life,
turning a man from the snares of
death.

15:33
The fear of the LORD teaches a man
wisdom,
and humility comes before honor.

22:19
So that your trust may be in the LORD,
I teach you today, even you.

22:21
...teaching you true and reliable words,
so that you can give sound answers
to him who sent you...

TEMPER
(Also see Anger)
14:16-17
A wise man fears the LORD and shuns
evil,
but a fool is hotheaded and reckless.

[17]A quick-tempered man does foolish
things,
and a crafty man is hated.

14:29
A patient man has great understanding,
but a quick-tempered man displays
folly.

15:1
A gentle answer turns away wrath,
but a harsh word stirs up anger.

15:18
A hot-tempered man stirs up dissension,
but a patient man calms a quarrel.

16:14
A king's wrath is a messenger of death,
but a wise man will appease it.

16:32
Better a patient man than a warrior,
a man who controls his temper than
one who takes a city.

19:12
A king's rage is like the roar of a lion,
but his favor is like dew on the grass.

19:19
A hot-tempered man must pay the
penalty;
if you rescue him, you will have to
do it again.

20:2
A king's wrath is like the roar of a lion;
he who angers him forfeits his life.

21:14
A gift given in secret soothes anger,
and a bribe concealed in the cloak
pacifies great wrath.

21:19
Better to live in a desert
than with a quarrelsome and ill-
tempered wife.

22:14
The mouth of an adulteress is a deep pit;
he who is under the LORD's wrath will
fall into it.

22:24-25
Do not make friends with a hot-
tempered man,
do not associate with one easily
angered,
²⁵or you may learn his ways
and get yourself ensnared.

27:4
Anger is cruel and fury overwhelming,
but who can stand before jealousy?

29:8
Mockers stir up a city,
but wise men turn away anger.

29:11
A fool gives full vent to his anger,
but a wise man keeps himself under
control.

29:22
An angry man stirs up dissension,
and a hot-tempered one commits
many sins.

30:33
"For as churning the milk produces
butter,
and as twisting the nose produces
blood,
so stirring up anger produces strife."

TEMPTATION
(Also see Eyes, Lust, Sin)
1:10-19
My son, if sinners entice you,
do not give in to them.
¹¹If they say, "Come along with us;
let's lie in wait for someone's blood,
let's waylay some harmless soul;
¹²let's swallow them alive, like the grave,
and whole, like those who go down
to the pit;
¹³we will get all sorts of valuable things
and fill our houses with plunder;
¹⁴throw in your lot with us,
and we will share a common purse"—
¹⁵my son, do not go along with them,
do not set foot on their paths;

¹⁶for their feet rush into sin,
they are swift to shed blood.
¹⁷How useless to spread a net
in full view of all the birds!
¹⁸These men lie in wait for their own
blood;
they waylay only themselves!
¹⁹Such is the end of all who go after ill-
gotten gain;
it takes away the lives of those who
get it.

2:12-15
Wisdom will save you from the ways of
wicked men,
from men whose words are perverse,
¹³who leave the straight paths
to walk in dark ways,
¹⁴who delight in doing wrong
and rejoice in the perverseness of
evil,
¹⁵whose paths are crooked
and who are devious in their ways.

3:29-30
Do not plot harm against your
neighbor,
who lives trustfully near you.
³⁰Do not accuse a man for no reason—
when he has done you no harm.

4:14-15
Do not set foot on the path of the
wicked
or walk in the way of evil men.
¹⁵Avoid it, do not travel on it;
turn from it and go on your way.

4:25-27
Let your eyes look straight ahead,
fix your gaze directly before you.
²⁶Make level paths for your feet
and take only ways that are firm.
²⁷Do not swerve to the right or the left;
keep your foot from evil.

6:12-13
A scoundrel and villain,
who goes about with a corrupt
mouth,

¹³who winks with his eye,
signals with his feet
and motions with his fingers,

7:21-23
With persuasive words she [the
adulteress] led him astray;
she seduced him with her smooth
talk.
²²All at once he followed her
like an ox going to the slaughter,
like a deer stepping into a noose
²³till an arrow pierces his liver,
like a bird darting into a snare,
little knowing it will cost him his life.

27:20
Death and Destruction are never
satisfied,
and neither are the eyes of man.

28:21
To show partiality is not good—
yet a man will do wrong for a piece
of bread.

THIEF
6:30-31
Men do not despise a thief if he steals
to satisfy his hunger when he is
starving.
³¹Yet if he is caught, he must pay
sevenfold,
though it costs him all the wealth of
his house.

29:24
The accomplice of a thief is his own
enemy;
he is put under oath and dare not
testify.

TONGUE
4:24
Put away perversity from your mouth;
keep corrupt talk far from your lips.

8:13
"To fear the LORD is to hate evil;
I [wisdom] hate pride and arrogance,
evil behavior and perverse speech."

10:11
The mouth of the righteous is a
fountain of life,
but violence overwhelms the mouth
of the wicked.

10:14
Wise men store up knowledge,
but the mouth of a fool invites ruin.

10:18-21
He who conceals his hatred has lying
lips,
and whoever spreads slander is a
fool.
¹⁹When words are many, sin is not
absent,
but he who holds his tongue is wise.

²⁰The tongue of the righteous is choice
silver,
but the heart of the wicked is of little
value.

²¹The lips of the righteous nourish
many,
but fools die for lack of judgment.

10:31-32
The mouth of the righteous brings forth
wisdom,
but a perverse tongue will be cut out.

³²The lips of the righteous know what is
fitting,
but the mouth of the wicked only
what is perverse.

11:9
With his mouth the godless destroys his
neighbor,
but through knowledge the righteous
escape.

11:11-13
Through the blessing of the upright a
city is exalted,
but by the mouth of the wicked it is
destroyed.

[12]A man who lacks judgment derides
his neighbor,
but a man of understanding holds his
tongue.

[13]A gossip betrays a confidence,
but a trustworthy man keeps a secret.

12:13-14
An evil man is trapped by his sinful talk,
but a righteous man escapes trouble.

[14]From the fruit of his lips a man is
filled with good things
as surely as the work of his hands
rewards him.

12:17-19
A truthful witness gives honest testimony,
but a false witness tells lies.

[18]Reckless words pierce like a sword,
but the tongue of the wise brings
healing.

[19]Truthful lips endure forever,
but a lying tongue lasts only a
moment.

12:22-23
The LORD detests lying lips,
but he delights in men who are
truthful.

[23]A prudent man keeps his knowledge
to himself,
but the heart of fools blurts out folly.

12:25
An anxious heart weighs a man down,
but a kind word cheers him up.

13:2-3
From the fruit of his lips a man enjoys
good things,
but the unfaithful have a craving for
violence.

[3]He who guards his lips guards his life,
but he who speaks rashly will come
to ruin.

14:3
A fool's talk brings a rod to his back,
but the lips of the wise protect them.

14:5
A truthful witness does not deceive,
but a false witness pours out lies.

14:7
Stay away from a foolish man,
for you will not find knowledge on
his lips.

14:23
All hard work brings a profit,
but mere talk leads only to poverty.

14:25
A truthful witness saves lives,
but a false witness is deceitful.

15:1-2
A gentle answer turns away wrath,
but a harsh word stirs up anger.

[2]The tongue of the wise commends
knowledge,
but the mouth of the fool gushes
folly.

15:4
The tongue that brings healing is a tree
of life,
but a deceitful tongue crushes the
spirit.

15:7
The lips of the wise spread knowledge;
not so the hearts of fools.

15:14
The discerning heart seeks knowledge,
but the mouth of a fool feeds on folly.

15:28
The heart of the righteous weighs its
answers,
but the mouth of the wicked gushes
evil.

16:1
To man belong the plans of the heart,

but from the LORD comes the reply of the tongue.

16:10
The lips of a king speak as an oracle, and his mouth should not betray justice.

16:13
Kings take pleasure in honest lips; they value a man who speaks the truth.

16:21
The wise in heart are called discerning, and pleasant words promote instruction.

16:23-24
A wise man's heart guides his mouth, and his lips promote instruction.

24Pleasant words are a honeycomb, sweet to the soul and healing to the bones.

16:27-28
A scoundrel plots evil,

and his speech is like a scorching fire.

28A perverse man stirs up dissension, and a gossip separates close friends.

17:4
A wicked man listens to evil lips; a liar pays attention to a malicious tongue.

17:7
Arrogant lips are unsuited to a fool— how much worse lying lips to a ruler!

17:9
He who covers over an offense promotes love, but whoever repeats the matter separates close friends.

17:14
Starting a quarrel is like breaching a dam;

so drop the matter before a dispute breaks out.

17:19-20
He who loves a quarrel loves sin; he who builds a high gate invites destruction.

20A man of perverse heart does not prosper; he whose tongue is deceitful falls into trouble.

17:27-28
A man of knowledge uses words with restraint, and a man of understanding is even-tempered.

28Even a fool is thought wise if he keeps silent, and discerning if he holds his tongue.

18:2
A fool finds no pleasure in understanding but delights in airing his own opinions.

18:4
The words of a man's mouth are deep waters, but the fountain of wisdom is a bubbling brook.

18:6-8
A fool's lips bring him strife, and his mouth invites a beating.

7A fool's mouth is his undoing, and his lips are a snare to his soul.

8The words of a gossip are like choice morsels; they go down to a man's inmost parts.

18:13
He who answers before listening— that is his folly and his shame.

18:20-21
From the fruit of his mouth a man's
    stomach is filled;
with the harvest from his lips he is
    satisfied.

[21]The tongue has the power of life and
    death,
and those who love it will eat its
    fruit.

18:23
A poor man pleads for mercy,
but a rich man answers harshly.

19:1
Better a poor man whose walk is
    blameless
than a fool whose lips are perverse.

19:9
A false witness will not go unpunished,
and he who pours out lies will
    perish.

19:24
The sluggard buries his hand in the
    dish;
he will not even bring it back to his
    mouth!

19:27-28
Stop listening to instruction, my son,
and you will stray from the words of
    knowledge.

[28]A corrupt witness mocks at justice,
and the mouth of the wicked gulps
    down evil.

20:15
Gold there is, and rubies in abundance,
but lips that speak knowledge are a
    rare jewel.

20:19-20
A gossip betrays a confidence;
so avoid a man who talks too much.

[20]If a man curses his father or mother,
his lamp will be snuffed out in pitch
    darkness.

21:6
A fortune made by a lying tongue
is a fleeting vapor and a deadly snare.

21:19
Better to live in a desert
than with a quarrelsome and ill-
    tempered wife.

21:23
He who guards his mouth and his
    tongue
keeps himself from calamity.

22:10-12
Drive out the mocker, and out goes
    strife;
quarrels and insults are ended.

[11]He who loves a pure heart and whose
    speech is gracious
will have the king for his friend.

[12]The eyes of the LORD keep watch over
    knowledge,
but he frustrates the words of the
    unfaithful.

23:16
...my [the parent's] inmost being will
    rejoice
when your lips speak what is right.

24:1-2
Do not envy wicked men,
    do not desire their company;
[2]for their hearts plot violence,
    and their lips talk about making
    trouble.

24:7
Wisdom is too high for a fool;
in the assembly at the gate he has
    nothing to say.

24:26
An honest answer
is like a kiss on the lips.

24:28-29
Do not testify against your
    neighbor without cause,

or use your lips to deceive.
²⁹Do not say, "I'll do to him as he
has done to me;
I'll pay that man back for what
he did."

25:11
A word aptly spoken
is like apples of gold in settings of
silver.

25:15
Through patience a ruler can be
persuaded,
and a gentle tongue can break a
bone.

25:23
As a north wind brings rain,
so a sly tongue brings angry looks.

26:4-5
Do not answer a fool according to his
folly,
or you will be like him yourself.

⁵Answer a fool according to his folly,
or he will be wise in his own eyes.

26:7
Like a lame man's legs that hang limp
is a proverb in the mouth of a fool.

26:9
Like a thornbush in a drunkard's hand
is a proverb in the mouth of a fool.

26:16
The sluggard is wiser in his own eyes
than seven men who answer
discreetly.

26:20-28
Without wood a fire goes out;
without gossip a quarrel dies down.

²¹As charcoal to embers and as wood to
fire,
so is a quarrelsome man for kindling
strife.

²²The words of a gossip are like choice
morsels;
they go down to a man's inmost
parts.

²³Like a coating of glaze over earthen-
ware
are fervent lips with an evil heart.

²⁴A malicious man disguises himself
with his lips,
but in his heart he harbors deceit.
²⁵Though his speech is charming, do
not believe him,
for seven abominations fill his heart.
²⁶His malice may be concealed by
deception,
but his wickedness will be exposed
in the assembly.

²⁷If a man digs a pit, he will fall into it;
if a man rolls a stone, it will roll back
on him.

²⁸A lying tongue hates those it hurts,
and a flattering mouth works ruin.

27:2
Let another praise you, and not your
own mouth;
someone else, and not your own lips.

27:14-16
If a man loudly blesses his neighbor
early in the morning,
it will be taken as a curse.

¹⁵A quarrelsome wife is like
a constant dripping on a rainy day;
¹⁶restraining her is like restraining the
wind
or grasping oil with the hand.

28:23
He who rebukes a man will in the end
gain more favor
than he who has a flattering tongue.

29:5
Whoever flatters his neighbor
is spreading a net for his feet.

29:9
If a wise man goes to court with a fool,
the fool rages and scoffs, and there is
no peace.

29:20
Do you see a man who speaks in haste?
There is more hope for a fool than
for him.

30:10-14
"Do not slander a servant to his
master,
or he will curse you, and you will
pay for it.

[11]"There are those who curse their
fathers
and do not bless their mothers;
[12]those who are pure in their own eyes
and yet are not cleansed of their
filth;
[13]those whose eyes are ever so
haughty,
whose glances are so disdainful;
[14]those whose teeth are swords
and whose jaws are set with knives
to devour the poor from the earth,
the needy from among mankind."

TROUBLE
(Also see Destruction, Disaster)
10:22
The blessing of the LORD brings wealth,
and he adds no trouble to it.

11:8
The righteous man is rescued from
trouble,
and it comes on the wicked instead.

11:29
He who brings trouble on his family
will inherit only wind,
and the fool will be servant to the
wise.

12:13
An evil man is trapped by his sinful
talk,
but a righteous man escapes trouble.

12:21
No harm befalls the righteous,
but the wicked have their fill of
trouble.

13:15
Good understanding wins favor,
but the way of the unfaithful is hard.

13:17
A wicked messenger falls into trouble,
but a trustworthy envoy brings
healing.

15:6
The house of the righteous contains
great treasure,
but the income of the wicked brings
them trouble.

15:27
A greedy man brings trouble to his
family,
but he who hates bribes will live.

17:20
A man of perverse heart does not
prosper;
he whose tongue is deceitful falls
into trouble.

19:23
The fear of the LORD leads to life:
Then one rests content, untouched
by trouble.

22:8
He who sows wickedness reaps
trouble,
and the rod of his fury will be
destroyed.

24:2
...for their [wicked men's] hearts plot
violence,
and their lips talk about making
trouble.

24:10
If you falter in times of trouble,
how small is your strength!

25:19
Like a bad tooth or a lame foot
   is reliance on the unfaithful in times
      of trouble.
28:14
Blessed is the man who always fears
      the Lord,
   but he who hardens his heart falls
      into trouble.

TRUST
(Also see Faith)
11:13
A gossip betrays a confidence,
   but a trustworthy man keeps a secret.

13:17
A wicked messenger falls into trouble,
   but a trustworthy envoy brings
      healing.

16:20
Whoever gives heed to instruction
      prospers,
   and blessed is he who trusts in the
      Lord.

23:23
Buy the truth and do not sell it;
   get wisdom, discipline and under-
      standing.

25:13
Like the coolness of snow at harvest
      time
   is a trustworthy messenger to those
      who send him;
   he refreshes the spirit of his masters.

29:25
Fear of man will prove to be a snare,
   but whoever trusts in the Lord is kept
      safe.

TRUTH
(Also see Integrity)
12:17
A truthful witness gives honest
      testimony,
   but a false witness tells lies.

12:19
Truthful lips endure forever,
   but a lying tongue lasts only a
      moment.

14:5
A truthful witness does not deceive,
   but a false witness pours out lies.

14:25
A truthful witness saves lives,
   but a false witness is deceitful.

16:13
Kings take pleasure in honest lips;
   they value a man who speaks the
      truth.

23:23
Buy the truth and do not sell it;
   get wisdom, discipline and under-
      standing.

UNFAITHFUL
(Also see Faith, Trust)
2:22
...but the wicked will be cut off from
      the land,
   and the unfaithful will be torn from
      it.

11:3
The integrity of the upright guides
      them,
   but the unfaithful are destroyed by
      their duplicity.

11:6
The righteousness of the upright
      delivers them,
   but the unfaithful are trapped by evil
      desires.

13:2
From the fruit of his lips a man enjoys
      good things,
   but the unfaithful have a craving for
      violence.

13:15
Good understanding wins favor,
    but the way of the unfaithful is hard.

21:18
The wicked become a ransom for the
        righteous,
    and the unfaithful for the upright.

22:12
The eyes of the LORD keep watch over
        knowledge,
    but he frustrates the words of the
        unfaithful.

23:28
Like a bandit she [the adulteress] lies in
        wait,
    and multiplies the unfaithful among
        men.

25:19
Like a bad tooth or a lame foot
    is reliance on the unfaithful in times
        of trouble.

UPRIGHT
(Also see Blameless, Righteousness)
2:7
He holds victory in store for the
        upright,
    he is a shield to those whose walk is
        blameless,

2:21
For the upright will live in the land,
    and the blameless will remain in it...

3:32
...for the LORD detests a perverse man
    but takes the upright into his
        confidence.

11:3
The integrity of the upright guides
        them,
    but the unfaithful are destroyed by
        their duplicity.
11:6
The righteousness of the upright
    delivers them,

but the unfaithful are trapped by evil
        desires.

11:11
Through the blessing of the upright a
        city is exalted,
    but by the mouth of the wicked it is
        destroyed.

12:6
The words of the wicked lie in wait for
        blood,
    but the speech of the upright rescues
        them.

14:2
He whose walk is upright fears the LORD,
    but he whose ways are devious
        despises him.

14:9
Fools mock at making amends for sin,
    but goodwill is found among the
        upright.

14:11
The house of the wicked will be
        destroyed,
    but the tent of the upright will
        flourish.

15:8
The LORD detests the sacrifice of the
        wicked,
    but the prayer of the upright pleases
        him.

15:19
The way of the sluggard is blocked
        with thorns,
    but the path of the upright is a
        highway.

16:17
The highway of the upright avoids evil;
    he who guards his way guards his
        life.
21:8
The way of the guilty is devious,
    but the conduct of the innocent is
        upright.

21:18
The wicked become a ransom for the
    righteous,
and the unfaithful for the upright.

21:29
A wicked man puts up a bold front,
    but an upright man gives thought to
    his ways.

28:10
He who leads the upright along an evil
    path
will fall into his own trap,
but the blameless will receive a good
    inheritance.

29:10
Bloodthirsty men hate a man of
    integrity
and seek to kill the upright.

29:27
The righteous detest the dishonest;
    the wicked detest the upright.

VICTORY
(Also see Success)
2:7
He holds victory in store for the
    upright,
    he is a shield to those whose walk is
    blameless...

11:14
For lack of guidance a nation falls,
    but many advisers make victory sure.

15:22
Plans fail for lack of counsel,
    but with many advisers they succeed.

16:3
Commit to the LORD whatever you do,
    and your plans will succeed.

17:8
A bribe is a charm to the one who
    gives it;
    wherever he turns, he succeeds.

21:30-31
There is no wisdom, no insight, no plan
    that can succeed against the LORD.

[31]The horse is made ready for the day
    of battle,
but victory rests with the LORD.

24:6
...for waging war you need guidance,
    and for victory many advisers.

VIOLENCE
3:31
Do not envy a violent man
    or choose any of his ways...

4:17
They [the wicked] eat the bread of
    wickedness
and drink the wine of violence.

10:6
Blessings crown the head of the
    righteous,
    but violence overwhelms the mouth
    of the wicked.

10:11
The mouth of the righteous is a
    fountain of life,
    but violence overwhelms the mouth
    of the wicked.

13:2
From the fruit of his lips a man enjoys
    good things,
    but the unfaithful have a craving for
    violence.

16:29
A violent man entices his neighbor
    and leads him down a path that is
    not good.

21:7
The violence of the wicked will drag
    them away,
    for they refuse to do what is right.

24:2

For their [wicked men's] hearts plot
    violence,
and their lips talk about making
    trouble.

26:6

Like cutting off one's feet or drinking
    violence
is the sending of a message by the
    hand of a fool.

VOWS
20:25

It is a trap for a man to dedicate
    something rashly
and only later to consider his vows.

THE WAY
(See The Path)

WICKED
(Also see Evil, Righteous/Wicked)
3:33

The LORD'S curse is on the house of the
    wicked,
but he blesses the home of the
    righteous.

4:14-17

Do not set foot on the path of the
    wicked
or walk in the way of evil men.
[15]Avoid it, do not travel on it;
    turn from it and go on your way.
[16]For they cannot sleep till they do evil;
    they are robbed of slumber till they
        make someone fall.
[17]They eat the bread of wickedness
and drink the wine of violence.

4:19

But the way of the wicked is like deep
    darkness;
they do not know what makes them
    stumble.

6:12

A scoundrel and villain,
    who goes about with a corrupt
        mouth...

8:7

"My [wisdom's] mouth speaks what is
    true,
for my lips detest wickedness."

9:7

"Whoever corrects a mocker invites
    insult;
whoever rebukes a wicked man
    incurs abuse."

10:27

The fear of the LORD adds length to life,
    but the years of the wicked are cut
        short.

11:7

When a wicked man dies, his hope
    perishes;
all he expected from his power
    comes to nothing.

11:17

A kind man benefits himself,
    but a cruel man brings trouble on
        himself.

13:17

A wicked messenger falls into trouble,
    but a trustworthy envoy brings healing.

14:2

He whose walk is upright fears the LORD,
    but he whose ways are devious
        despises him.

15:3

The eyes of the LORD are everywhere,
    keeping watch on the wicked and
        the good.

15:26

The LORD detests the thoughts of the
    wicked,
but those of the pure are pleasing to
    him.

16:4

The LORD works out everything for his
    own ends—
even the wicked for a day of disaster.

17:4
A wicked man listens to evil lips;
    a liar pays attention to a malicious
        tongue.

17:11
An evil man is bent only on rebellion;
    a merciless official will be sent
        against him.

17:23
A wicked man accepts a bribe in secret
    to pervert the course of justice.

18:3
When wickedness comes, so does
        contempt,
    and with shame comes disgrace.

18:5
It is not good to be partial to the
        wicked
    or to deprive the innocent of justice.

19:28
A corrupt witness mocks at justice,
    and the mouth of the wicked gulps
        down evil.

20:26
A wise king winnows out the wicked;
    he drives the threshing wheel over
        them.

21:4
Haughty eyes and a proud heart,
    the lamp of the wicked, are sin!

21:7
The violence of the wicked will drag
        them away,
    for they refuse to do what is right.

21:10
The wicked man craves evil;
    his neighbor gets no mercy from him.

21:27
The sacrifice of the wicked is detestable—
    how much more so when brought with
        evil intent!

22:5
In the paths of the wicked lie thorns
        and snares,
    but he who guards his soul stays far
        from them.

22:8
He who sows wickedness reaps trouble,
    and the rod of his fury will be
        destroyed.

24:1-2
Do not envy wicked men,
    do not desire their company;
²for their hearts plot violence,
    and their lips talk about making
        trouble.

24:19-20
Do not fret because of evil men
    or be envious of the wicked,
²⁰for the evil man has no future hope,
    and the lamp of the wicked will be
        snuffed out.

26:24-26
A malicious man disguises himself with
        his lips,
    but in his heart he harbors deceit.
²⁵Though his speech is charming, do
        not believe him,
    for seven abominations fill his heart.
²⁶His malice may be concealed by
        deception,
    but his wickedness will be exposed
        in the assembly.

28:4
Those who forsake the law praise the
        wicked,
    but those who keep the law resist
        them.

28:15
Like a roaring lion or a charging bear
    is a wicked man ruling over a
        helpless people.

28:28
When the wicked rise to power, people
    go into hiding;

but when the wicked perish, the
righteous thrive.

29:12
If a ruler listens to lies,
all his officials become wicked.

WIDOWS
15:25
The LORD tears down the proud man's
house
but he keeps the widow's boundaries
intact.

WIFE
2:16
It [wisdom] will save you also from the
adulteress,
from the wayward wife with her
seductive words...

5:18
May your fountain be blessed,
and may you rejoice in the wife of
your youth.

5:20
Why be captivated, my son, by an
adulteress?
Why embrace the bosom of another
man's wife?

6:24
[These commands are] keeping you
from the immoral woman,
from the smooth tongue of the
wayward wife.

6:29
So is he who sleeps with another man's
wife;
no one who touches her will go
unpunished.

7:5
They [wisdom's commands] will keep
you from the adulteress,
from the wayward wife with her
seductive words.

12:4
A wife of noble character is her
husband's crown,
but a disgraceful wife is like decay in
his bones.

18:22
He who finds a wife finds what is good
and receives favor from the LORD.

19:13-14
A foolish son is his father's ruin,
and a quarrelsome wife is like a
constant dripping.

¹⁴Houses and wealth are inherited from
parents,
but a prudent wife is from the LORD.

21:9
Better to live on a corner of the roof
than share a house with a quarrelsome wife.

21:19
Better to live in a desert
than with a quarrelsome and ill-
tempered wife.

23:27-28
...for a prostitute is a deep pit
and a wayward wife is a narrow well.
²⁸Like a bandit she lies in wait,
and multiplies the unfaithful among
men.

25:24
Better to live on a corner of the roof
than share a house with a quarrelsome wife.

27:15-16
A quarrelsome wife is like
a constant dripping on a rainy day;
¹⁶restraining her is like restraining the
wind
or grasping oil with the hand.

30:21-23
"Under three things the earth trembles,
under four it cannot bear up:

²²a servant who becomes king,
a fool who is full of food,
²³an unloved woman who is married,
and a maidservant who displaces her
mistress."

31:10-31
A wife of noble character who can
find?
She is worth far more than rubies.
¹¹Her husband has full confidence in
her
and lacks nothing of value.
¹²She brings him good, not harm,
all the days of her life.
¹³She selects wool and flax
and works with eager hands.
¹⁴She is like the merchant ships,
bringing her food from afar.
¹⁵She gets up while it is still dark;
she provides food for her family
and portions for her servant girls.
¹⁶She considers a field and buys it;
out of her earnings she plants a
vineyard.
¹⁷She sets about her work vigorously;
her arms are strong for her tasks.
¹⁸She sees that her trading is profitable,
and her lamp does not go out at
night.
¹⁹In her hand she holds the distaff
and grasps the spindle with her
fingers.
²⁰She opens her arms to the poor
and extends her hands to the needy.
²¹When it snows, she has no fear for
her household;
for all of them are clothed in scarlet.
²²She makes coverings for her bed;
she is clothed in fine linen and
purple.
²³Her husband is respected at the city
gate,
where he takes his seat among the
elders of the land.
²⁴She makes linen garments and sells
them,
and supplies the merchants with
sashes.
²⁵She is clothed with strength and
dignity;

she can laugh at the days to come.
²⁶She speaks with wisdom,
and faithful instruction is on her
tongue.
²⁷She watches over the affairs of her
household
and does not eat the bread of
idleness.
²⁸Her children arise and call her
blessed;
her husband also, and he praises her:
²⁹"Many women do noble things,
but you surpass them all."
³⁰Charm is deceptive, and beauty is
fleeting;
but a woman who fears the LORD is to
be praised.
³¹Give her the reward she has earned,
and let her works bring her praise at
the city gate.

WINE
(See Alcohol)

WISDOM
1:1-7
The proverbs of Solomon son of David,
king of Israel:

²for attaining wisdom and discipline;
for understanding words of insight;
³for acquiring a disciplined and prudent
life,
doing what is right and just and fair;
⁴for giving prudence to the simple,
knowledge and discretion to the
young—
⁵let the wise listen and add to their
learning,
and let the discerning get guidance—
⁶for understanding proverbs and
parables,
the sayings and riddles of the wise.

⁷The fear of the LORD is the beginning
of knowledge,
but fools despise wisdom and
discipline.

1:20-31

Wisdom calls aloud in the street,
    she raises her voice in the public
        squares;
²¹at the head of the noisy streets she
        cries out,
    in the gateways of the city she makes
        her speech:
²²"How long will you simple ones love
        your simple ways?
    How long will mockers delight in
        mockery
    and fools hate knowledge?
²³If you had responded to my rebuke,
    I would have poured out my heart to
        you
    and made my thoughts known to
        you.
²⁴But since you rejected me when I
        called
    and no one gave heed when I
        stretched out my hand,
²⁵since you ignored all my advice
    and would not accept my rebuke,
²⁶I in turn will laugh at your disaster;
    I will mock when calamity overtakes
        you—
²⁷when calamity overtakes you like a
        storm,
    when disaster sweeps over you like a
        whirlwind,
    when distress and trouble overwhelm
        you.

²⁸"Then they will call to me but I will
        not answer;
    they will look for me but will not
        find me.
²⁹Since they hated knowledge
    and did not choose to fear the Lord,
³⁰since they would not accept my
        advice
    and spurned my rebuke,
³¹they will eat the fruit of their ways
    and be filled with the fruit of their
        schemes."

2:1-22

My son, if you accept my words
    and store up my commands within
        you,
²turning your ear to wisdom
    and applying your heart to under-
        standing,
³and if you call out for insight
    and cry aloud for understanding,
⁴and if you look for it as for silver
    and search for it as for hidden
        treasure,
⁵then you will understand the fear of
        the Lord
    and find the knowledge of God.
⁶For the Lord gives wisdom,
    and from his mouth come knowledge
        and understanding.
⁷He holds victory in store for the
        upright,
    he is a shield to those whose walk is
        blameless,
⁸for he guards the course of the just
    and protects the way of his faithful
        ones.

⁹Then you will understand what is right
        and just
    and fair—every good path.
¹⁰For wisdom will enter your heart,
    and knowledge will be pleasant to
        your soul.
¹¹Discretion will protect you,
    and understanding will guard you.

¹²Wisdom will save you from the ways
        of wicked men,
    from men whose words are perverse,
¹³who leave the straight paths
    to walk in dark ways,
¹⁴who delight in doing wrong
    and rejoice in the perverseness of evil,
¹⁵whose paths are crooked
    and who are devious in their ways.

¹⁶It will save you also from the
        adulteress,
    from the wayward wife with her
        seductive words,
¹⁷who has left the partner of her youth
    and ignored the covenant she made
        before God.
¹⁸For her house leads down to death
    and her paths to the spirits of the
        dead.

[19]None who go to her return
   or attain the paths of life.

[20]Thus you will walk in the ways of
      good men
   and keep to the paths of the
      righteous.
[21]For the upright will live in the land,
   and the blameless will remain in it;
[22]but the wicked will be cut off from
      the land,
   and the unfaithful will be torn from
      it.

3:13-26

Blessed is the man who finds wisdom,
   the man who gains understanding,
[14]for she is more profitable than silver
   and yields better returns than gold.
[15]She is more precious than rubies;
   nothing you desire can compare with
      her.
[16]Long life is in her right hand;
   in her left hand are riches and honor.
[17]Her ways are pleasant ways,
   and all her paths are peace.
[18]She is a tree of life to those who
      embrace her;
   those who lay hold of her will be
      blessed.

[19]By wisdom the LORD laid the earth's
      foundations,
   by understanding he set the heavens
      in place;
[20]by his knowledge the deeps were
      divided,
   and the clouds let drop the dew.

[21]My son, preserve sound judgment and
      discernment,
   do not let them out of your sight;
[22]they will be life for you,
   an ornament to grace your neck.
[23]Then you will go on your way in
      safety,
   and your foot will not stumble;
[24]when you lie down, you will not be
      afraid;
   when you lie down, your sleep will
      be sweet.

[25]Have no fear of sudden disaster
   or of the ruin that overtakes the
      wicked,
[26]for the LORD will be your confidence
   and will keep your foot from being
      snared.

4:1-9

Listen, my sons, to a father's instruction;
   pay attention and gain understanding.
[2]I give you sound learning,
   so do not forsake my teaching.
[3]When I was a boy in my father's
      house,
   still tender, and an only child of my
      mother,
[4]he taught me and said,
   "Lay hold of my words with all your
      heart;
   keep my commands and you will live.
[5]Get wisdom, get understanding;
   do not forget my words or swerve
      from them.
[6]Do not forsake wisdom, and she will
      protect you;
   love her, and she will watch over
      you.
[7]Wisdom is supreme; therefore get
      wisdom.
   Though it cost all you have, get
      understanding.
[8]Esteem her, and she will exalt you;
   embrace her, and she will honor you.
[9]She will set a garland of grace on your
      head
   and present you with a crown of
      splendor."

7:4-5

Say to wisdom, "You are my sister,"
   and call understanding your kinsman;
[5]they will keep you from the adulteress,
   from the wayward wife with her
      seductive words.

8:1-9:18

Does not wisdom call out?
Does not understanding raise her voice?
[2]On the heights along the way,
   where the paths meet, she takes her
      stand;

³beside the gates leading into the city,
at the entrances, she cries aloud:
⁴"To you, O men, I call out;
I raise my voice to all mankind.
⁵You who are simple, gain prudence;
you who are foolish, gain understanding.
⁶Listen, for I have worthy things to say;
I open my lips to speak what is right.
⁷My mouth speaks what is true,
for my lips detest wickedness.
⁸All the words of my mouth are just;
none of them is crooked or perverse.
⁹To the discerning all of them are right;
they are faultless to those who have
knowledge.
¹⁰Choose my instruction instead of
silver,
knowledge rather than choice gold,
¹¹for wisdom is more precious than
rubies,
and nothing you desire can compare
with her.

¹²"I, wisdom, dwell together with
prudence;
I possess knowledge and discretion.
¹³To fear the LORD is to hate evil;
I hate pride and arrogance,
evil behavior and perverse speech.
¹⁴Counsel and sound judgment are
mine;
I have understanding and power.
¹⁵By me kings reign
and rulers make laws that are just;
¹⁶by me princes govern,
and all nobles who rule on earth.
¹⁷I love those who love me,
and those who seek me find me.
¹⁸With me are riches and honor,
enduring wealth and prosperity.
¹⁹My fruit is better than fine gold;
what I yield surpasses choice silver.
²⁰I walk in the way of righteousness,
along the paths of justice,
²¹bestowing wealth on those who love
me
and making their treasuries full.

²²"The LORD brought me forth as the first
of his works,
before his deeds of old;
²³I was appointed from eternity,
from the beginning, before the world
began.
²⁴When there were no oceans, I was
given birth,
when there were no springs
abounding with water;
²⁵before the mountains were settled in
place,
before the hills, I was given birth,
²⁶before he made the earth or its fields
or any of the dust of the world.
²⁷I was there when he set the heavens
in place,
when he marked out the horizon on
the face of the deep,
²⁸when he established the clouds above
and fixed securely the fountains of
the deep,
²⁹when he gave the sea its boundary
so the waters would not overstep his
command,
and when he marked out the foundations of the earth.
³⁰Then I was the craftsman at his side.
I was filled with delight day after day,
rejoicing always in his presence,
³¹rejoicing in his whole world
and delighting in mankind.
³²"Now then, my sons, listen to me;
blessed are those who keep my
ways.
³³Listen to my instruction and be wise;
do not ignore it.
³⁴Blessed is the man who listens to me,
watching daily at my doors,
waiting at my doorway.
³⁵For whoever finds me finds life
and receives favor from the LORD.
³⁶But whoever fails to find me harms
himself;
all who hate me love death."

9:1Wisdom has built her house;
she has hewn out its seven pillars.
²She has prepared her meat and mixed
her wine;
she has also set her table.
³She has sent out her maids, and she
calls

from the highest point of the city.
4"Let all who are simple come in here!"
    she says to those who lack judgment.
5"Come, eat my food
    and drink the wine I have mixed.
6Leave your simple ways and you will
    live;
    walk in the way of understanding.

7"Whoever corrects a mocker invites
    insult;
    whoever rebukes a wicked man
    incurs abuse.
8Do not rebuke a mocker or he will
    hate you;
    rebuke a wise man and he will love
    you.
9Instruct a wise man and he will be
    wiser still;
    teach a righteous man and he will
    add to his learning.

10"The fear of the LORD is the beginning
    of wisdom,
    and knowledge of the Holy One is
    understanding.
11For through me your days will be
    many,
    and years will be added to your life.
12If you are wise, your wisdom will
    reward you;
    if you are a mocker, you alone will
    suffer."

13The woman Folly is loud;
    she is undisciplined and without
    knowledge.
14She sits at the door of her house,
    on a seat at the highest point of the
    city,
15calling out to those who pass by,
    who go straight on their way.
16"Let all who are simple come in here!"
    she says to those who lack judgment.
17"Stolen water is sweet;
    food eaten in secret is delicious!"
18But little do they know that the dead
    are there,
    that her guests are in the depths of
    the grave.

10:31
The mouth of the righteous brings forth
    wisdom,
    but a perverse tongue will be cut out.

11:2
When pride comes, then comes disgrace,
    but with humility comes wisdom.

13:10
Pride only breeds quarrels,
    but wisdom is found in those who
    take advice.

14:6
The mocker seeks wisdom and finds
    none,
    but knowledge comes easily to the
    discerning.

14:33
Wisdom reposes in the heart of the
    discerning
    and even among fools she lets herself
    be known.

15:33
The fear of the LORD teaches a man
    wisdom,
    and humility comes before honor.

16:16
How much better to get wisdom than
    gold,
    to choose understanding rather than
    silver!

18:4
The words of a man's mouth are deep
    waters,
    but the fountain of wisdom is a
    bubbling brook.

19:8
He who gets wisdom loves his own
    soul;
    he who cherishes understanding
    prospers.

19:11
A man's wisdom gives him patience;
    it is to his glory to overlook an
        offense.

19:27
Stop listening to instruction, my son,
    and you will stray from the words of
        knowledge.

20:5
The purposes of a man's heart are deep
        waters,
    but a man of understanding draws
        them out.

20:15
Gold there is, and rubies in abundance,
    but lips that speak knowledge are a
        rare jewel.

21:16
A man who strays from the path of
        understanding
comes to rest in the company of the
        dead.

21:30
There is no wisdom, no insight, no plan
    that can succeed against the LORD.

23:23
Buy the truth and do not sell it;
    get wisdom, discipline and under-
        standing.

24:3-4
By wisdom a house is built,
    and through understanding it is
        established;
⁴through knowledge its rooms are filled
    with rare and beautiful treasures.
24:7
Wisdom is too high for a fool;
    in the assembly at the gate he has
        nothing to say.

24:13-14
Eat honey, my son, for it is good;
    honey from the comb is sweet to
        your taste.

¹⁴Know also that wisdom is sweet to
        your soul;
    if you find it, there is a future hope
        for you,
    and your hope will not be cut off.

28:2
When a country is rebellious, it has
        many rulers,
    but a man of understanding and
        knowledge maintains order.

29:3
A man who loves wisdom brings joy to
        his father,
    but a companion of prostitutes
        squanders his wealth.

29:15
The rod of correction imparts wisdom,
    but a child left to himself disgraces
        his mother.

30:1-3
The sayings of Agur son of
    Jakeh—an oracle:

This man declared to Ithiel,
    to Ithiel and to Ucal:

²"I am the most ignorant of men;
    I do not have a man's understanding.
³I have not learned wisdom,
    nor have I knowledge of the Holy
        One."

WISDOM/FOLLY
(Also see Wisdom, Folly)
3:35
The wise inherit honor,
    but fools he holds up to shame.

10:8
The wise in heart accept commands,
    but a chattering fool comes to ruin.

10:13-14
Wisdom is found on the lips of the
        discerning,
    but a rod is for the back of him who
        lacks judgment.

¹⁴Wise men store up knowledge,
but the mouth of a fool invites ruin.

10:23
A fool finds pleasure in evil conduct,
but a man of understanding delights
in wisdom.

11:29
He who brings trouble on his family
will inherit only wind,
and the fool will be servant to the
wise.

12:8
A man is praised according to his
wisdom,
but men with warped minds are
despised.

12:15-16
The way of a fool seems right to him,
but a wise man listens to advice.

¹⁶A fool shows his annoyance at once,
but a prudent man overlooks an
insult.

12:20
There is deceit in the hearts of those
who plot evil,
but joy for those who promote peace.

12:23
A prudent man keeps his knowledge to
himself,
but the heart of fools blurts out folly.

13:16
Every prudent man acts out of
knowledge,
but a fool exposes his folly.

13:20
He who walks with the wise grows wise,
but a companion of fools suffers harm.

14:1
The wise woman builds her house,
but with her own hands the foolish
one tears hers down.

14:3
A fool's talk brings a rod to his back,
but the lips of the wise protect them.

14:7-8
Stay away from a foolish man,
for you will not find knowledge on
his lips.

⁸The wisdom of the prudent is to give
thought to their ways,
but the folly of fools is deception.

14:16
A wise man fears the LORD and shuns
evil,
but a fool is hotheaded and reckless.

14:18
The simple inherit folly,
but the prudent are crowned with
knowledge.

14:24
The wealth of the wise is their crown,
but the folly of fools yields folly.

14:29
A patient man has great understanding,
but a quick-tempered man displays
folly.

14:33
Wisdom reposes in the heart of the
discerning
and even among fools she lets herself
be known.

15:2
The tongue of the wise commends
knowledge,
but the mouth of the fool gushes folly.

15:7
The lips of the wise spread knowledge;
not so the hearts of fools.

15:14
The discerning heart seeks knowledge,
but the mouth of a fool feeds on
folly.

15:21
Folly delights a man who lacks
  judgment,
  but a man of understanding keeps a
  straight course.

16:22
Understanding is a fountain of life to
  those who have it,
  but folly brings punishment to fools.

17:10
A rebuke impresses a man of discernment
  more than a hundred lashes a fool.

17:16
Of what use is money in the hand of a
  fool,
  since he has no desire to get wisdom?

17:24
A discerning man keeps wisdom in
  view,
  but a fool's eyes wander to the ends
  of the earth.

17:28
Even a fool is thought wise if he keeps
  silent,
  and discerning if he holds his tongue.

19:25
Flog a mocker, and the simple will
  learn prudence;
  rebuke a discerning man, and he will
  gain knowledge.

21:11
When a mocker is punished, the simple
  gain wisdom;
  when a wise man is instructed, he
  gets knowledge.

22:3
A prudent man sees danger and takes
  refuge,
  but the simple keep going and suffer
  for it.

23:9
Do not speak to a fool,
  for he will scorn the wisdom of your
  words.

27:12
The prudent see danger and take
  refuge,
  but the simple keep going and suffer
  for it.

28:26
He who trusts in himself is a fool,
  but he who walks in wisdom is kept
  safe.

29:9
If a wise man goes to court with a fool,
  the fool rages and scoffs, and there is
  no peace.

29:11
A fool gives full vent to his anger,
  but a wise man keeps himself under
  control.

WISE MAN
(Also see Fool, Wisdom)
3:35
The wise inherit honor,
  but fools he [the LORD] holds up to
  shame.

9:8-9
"Do not rebuke a mocker or he will
  hate you;
  rebuke a wise man and he will love
  you.
[9]Instruct a wise man and he will be
  wiser still;
  teach a righteous man and he will
  add to his learning."

10:19
When words are many, sin is not absent,
  but he who holds his tongue is wise.

12:18
Reckless words pierce like a sword,
  but the tongue of the wise brings
  healing.

13:14
The teaching of the wise is a fountain
of life,
turning a man from the snares of
death.

14:35
A king delights in a wise servant,
but a shameful servant incurs his
wrath.

15:12
A mocker resents correction;
he will not consult the wise.

15:24
The path of life leads upward for the
wise
to keep him from going down to the
grave.

15:31
He who listens to a life-giving rebuke
will be at home among the wise.

16:14
A king's wrath is a messenger of death,
but a wise man will appease it.

16:21
The wise in heart are called discerning,
and pleasant words promote
instruction.

16:23
A wise man's heart guides his mouth,
and his lips promote instruction.
18:15
The heart of the discerning acquires
knowledge;
the ears of the wise seek it out.

19:20
Listen to advice and accept instruction,
and in the end you will be wise.

20:26
A wise king winnows out the wicked;
he drives the threshing wheel over
them.

21:22
A wise man attacks the city of the
mighty
and pulls down the stronghold in
which they trust.

23:24
The father of a righteous man has great
joy;
he who has a wise son delights in him.

24:5-7
A wise man has great power,
and a man of knowledge increases
strength;
⁶for waging war you need guidance,
and for victory many advisers.

⁷Wisdom is too high for a fool;
in the assembly at the gate he has
nothing to say.

25:12
Like an earring of gold or an ornament
of fine gold
is a wise man's rebuke to a listening
ear.

27:11
Be wise, my son, and bring joy to my
heart;
then I can answer anyone who treats
me with contempt.

29:9
If a wise man goes to court with a fool,
the fool rages and scoffs, and there is
no peace.

WOMEN
2:16-19
It [wisdom] will save you also from the
adulteress,
from the wayward wife with her
seductive words,
¹⁷who has left the partner of her youth
and ignored the covenant she made
before God.
¹⁸For her house leads down to death
and her paths to the spirits of the
dead.

[19]None who go to her return
   or attain the paths of life.

5:3-6
For the lips of an adulteress drip honey,
   and her speech is smoother than oil;
[4]but in the end she is bitter as gall,
   sharp as a double-edged sword.
[5]Her feet go down to death;
   her steps lead straight to the grave.
[6]She gives no thought to the way of
      life;
   her paths are crooked, but she knows
      it not.

5:8-20
Keep to a path far from her [the
      adulteress],
   do not go near the door of her
      house,
[9]lest you give your best strength to
      others
   and your years to one who is cruel,
[10]lest strangers feast on your wealth
   and your toil enrich another man's
      house.
[11]At the end of your life you will groan,
   when your flesh and body are spent.
[12]You will say, "How I hated discipline!
   How my heart spurned correction!
[13]I would not obey my teachers
   or listen to my instructors.
[14]I have come to the brink of utter ruin
   in the midst of the whole assembly."

[15]Drink water from your own cistern,
   running water from your own well.
[16]Should your springs overflow in the
      streets,
   your streams of water in the public
      squares?
[17]Let them be yours alone,
   never to be shared with strangers.
[18]May your fountain be blessed,
   and may you rejoice in the wife of
      your youth.
[19]A loving doe, a graceful deer—
   may her breasts satisfy you always,
   may you ever be captivated by her
      love.

[20]Why be captivated, my son, by an
      adulteress?
   Why embrace the bosom of another
      man's wife?

6:23-29
For these commands are a lamp,
   this teaching is a light,
and the corrections of discipline
   are the way to life,
[24]keeping you from the immoral
      woman,
   from the smooth tongue of the
      wayward wife.
[25]Do not lust in your heart after her
      beauty
   or let her captivate you with her
      eyes,
[26]for the prostitute reduces you to a loaf
      of bread,
   and the adulteress preys upon your
      very life.
[27]Can a man scoop fire into his lap
   without his clothes being burned?
[28]Can a man walk on hot coals
   without his feet being scorched?
[29]So is he who sleeps with another
      man's wife;
   no one who touches her will go
      unpunished.

7:4-27
Say to wisdom, "You are my sister,"
   and call understanding your kinsman;
[5]they will keep you from the adulteress,
   from the wayward wife with her
      seductive words.

[6]At the window of my house
   I looked out through the lattice.
[7]I saw among the simple,
   I noticed among the young men,
   a youth who lacked judgment.
[8]He was going down the street near her
      corner,
   walking along in the direction of her
      house
[9]at twilight, as the day was fading,
   as the dark of night set in.

¹⁰Then out came a woman to meet him,
dressed like a prostitute and with
crafty intent.
¹¹(She is loud and defiant,
her feet never stay at home;
¹²now in the street, now in the squares,
at every corner she lurks.)
¹³She took hold of him and kissed him
and with a brazen face she said:

¹⁴"I have fellowship offerings at home;
today I fulfilled my vows.
¹⁵So I came out to meet you;
I looked for you and have found you!
¹⁶I have covered my bed
with colored linens from Egypt.
¹⁷I have perfumed my bed
with myrrh, aloes and cinnamon.
¹⁸Come, let's drink deep of love till
morning;
let's enjoy ourselves with love!
¹⁹My husband is not at home;
he has gone on a long journey.
²⁰He took his purse filled with money
and will not be home till full moon."

²¹With persuasive words she led him
astray;
she seduced him with her smooth
talk.
²²All at once he followed her
like an ox going to the slaughter,
like a deer stepping into a noose
²³till an arrow pierces his liver,
like a bird darting into a snare,
little knowing it will cost him his life.

²⁴Now then, my sons, listen to me;
pay attention to what I say.
²⁵Do not let your heart turn to her ways
or stray into her paths.
²⁶Many are the victims she has brought
down;
her slain are a mighty throng.
²⁷Her house is a highway to the grave,
leading down to the chambers of
death.

11:16
A kindhearted woman gains respect,
but ruthless men gain only wealth.

11:22
Like a gold ring in a pig's snout
is a beautiful woman who shows no
discretion.

12:4
A wife of noble character is her
husband's crown,
but a disgraceful wife is like decay in
his bones.

14:1
The wise woman builds her house,
but with her own hands the foolish
one tears hers down.

18:22
He who finds a wife finds what is good
and receives favor from the LORD.

19:14
Houses and wealth are inherited from
parents,
but a prudent wife is from the LORD.

21:9
Better to live on a corner of the roof
than share a house with a quarrelsome wife.

21:19
Better to live in a desert
than with a quarrelsome and ill-
tempered wife.

22:14
The mouth of an adulteress is a deep
pit;
he who is under the LORD's wrath will
fall into it.

23:26-28
My son, give me your heart
and let your eyes keep to my ways,
²⁷for a prostitute is a deep pit
and a wayward wife is a narrow well.
²⁸Like a bandit she lies in wait,
and multiplies the unfaithful among
men.

25:24
Better to live on a corner of the roof
   than share a house with a quarrel-
      some wife.

27:15-16
A quarrelsome wife is like
   a constant dripping on a rainy day;
[16]restraining her is like restraining the
      wind
   or grasping oil with the hand.

31:2-3
"O my son, O son of my womb,
   O son of my vows,
[3]do not spend your strength on women,
   your vigor on those who ruin kings."

WORD OF GOD
30:5
"Every word of God is flawless;
   he is a shield to those who take
      refuge in him."

WORRY
(See Anxiety)

WINKING
16:30
He who winks with his eye is plotting
      perversity;
   he who purses his lips is bent on
      evil.

WRATH
11:4
Wealth is worthless in the day of wrath,
   but righteousness delivers from
      death.

11:23
The desire of the righteous ends only in
      good,
   but the hope of the wicked only in
      wrath.

14:35 - 15:1
A king delights in a wise servant,
   but a shameful servant incurs his
      wrath.

[15:1]A gentle answer turns away wrath,
   but a harsh word stirs up anger.

16:14
A king's wrath is a messenger of death,
   but a wise man will appease it.

20:2
A king's wrath is like the roar of a lion;
   he who angers him forfeits his life.

21:14
A gift given in secret soothes anger,
   and a bribe concealed in the cloak
      pacifies great wrath.

22:14
The mouth of an adulteress is a deep pit;
   he who is under the LORD's wrath will
      fall into it.

24:17-18
Do not gloat when your enemy falls;
   when he stumbles, do not let your
      heart rejoice,
[18]or the LORD will see and disapprove
   and turn his wrath away from him.

YOUTH
20:29
The glory of young men is their
      strength,
   gray hair the splendor of the old.

ZEAL
(Also see Boldness)
19:2
It is not good to have zeal without
      knowledge,
   nor to be hasty and miss the way.

23:17
Do not let your heart envy sinners,
   but always be zealous for the fear of
      the LORD.

28:1
The wicked man flees though no one
      pursues,
   but the righteous are as bold as a
      lion.

LaVergne, TN USA
19 December 2009
167600LV00003B/5/A